Research Series on the Chinese Dream and China's Development Path

Drawing on a large body of empirical studies done over the last two decades, this Series provides its readers with in-depth analyses of the past and present and forecasts for the future course of China's development. It contains the latest research results made by members of the Chinese Academy of Social Sciences. This series is an invaluable companion to every researcher who is trying to gain a deeper understanding of the development model, path and experience unique to China. Thanks to the adoption of Socialism with Chinese characteristics, and the implementation of comprehensive reform and opening-up, China has made tremendous achievements in areas such as political reform, economic development, and social construction, and is making great strides towards the realization of the Chinese dream of national rejuvenation. In addition to presenting a detailed account of many of these achievements, the authors also discuss what lessons other countries can learn from China's experience.

Peiyong Gao

A Shift Toward High-Quality Development of China

SSAP

Springer

Peiyong Gao
Chinese Academy of Social Sciences
Beijing, China

Translated by Xiaoqin Zhang

Edited by Hongyan Luo

ISSN 2363-6866 ISSN 2363-6874 (electronic)
Research Series on the Chinese Dream and China's Development Path
ISBN 978-981-99-8989-8 ISBN 978-981-99-8990-4 (eBook)
https://doi.org/10.1007/978-981-99-8990-4

Jointly published with Social Sciences Academic Press
The print edition is not for sale in China Mainland. Customers from China Mainland please order the print book from: Social Sciences Academic Press.

Published with financial support of the Innovation Program of the Chinese Academy of Social Sciences

This Springer imprint is published by the registered company Springer Nature Singapore Pte Ltd.
The registered company address is: 152 Beach Road, #21-01/04 Gateway East, Singapore 189721, Singapore

Series Preface

Since China's reform and opening began in 1978, the country has come a long way on the path of Socialism with Chinese characteristics, under the leadership of the Communist Party of China. Over 30 years of reform, efforts and sustained spectacular economic growth have turned China into the world's second largest economy and wrought many profound changes in the Chinese society. These historically significant developments have been garnering increasing attention from scholars, governments, and the general public alike around the world since the 1990s, when the newest wave of China studies began to gather steam. Some of the hottest topics have included the so-called China miracle, Chinese phenomenon, Chinese experience, Chinese path, and the Chinese model. Homegrown researchers have soon followed suit. Already hugely productive, this vibrant field is putting out a large number of books each year, with Social Sciences Academic Press alone having published hundreds of titles on a wide range of subjects.

Because most of these books have been written and published in Chinese, however, readership has been limited outside China—even among many who study China—for whom English is still the lingua franca. This language barrier has been an impediment to efforts by academia, business communities, and policy-makers in other countries to form a thorough understanding of contemporary China, of what is distinct about China's past and present may mean not only for her future but also for the future of the world. The need to remove such an impediment is both real and urgent, and the *Research Series on the Chinese Dream and China's Development Path* is my answer to the call.

This series features some of the most notable achievements from the last 20 years by scholars in China in a variety of research topics related to reform and opening. They include both theoretical explorations and empirical studies and cover economy, society, politics, law, culture, and ecology, the six areas in which reform and opening policies have had the deepest impact and farthest-reaching consequences for the country. Authors for the series have also tried to articulate their visions of the "Chinese Dream" and how the country can realize it in these fields and beyond.

All of the editors and authors for the *Research Series on the Chinese Dream and China's Development Path* are both longtime students of reform and opening and recognized authorities in their respective academic fields. Their credentials and expertise lend credibility to these books, each of which having been subject to a rigorous peer review process for inclusion in the series. As part of the Reform and Development Program under the State Administration of Press, Publication, Radio, Film, and Television of the People's Republic of China, the series is published by Springer, a Germany-based academic publisher of international repute and distributed overseas. I am confident that it will help fill a lacuna in studies of China in the era of reform and opening.

Shouguang Xie

Preface

Before discussing the subject matter of this book, it is necessary to give a brief account of the following issues that may be of concern to the reader.

I. About the Title of This Book

This book is entitled *A Shift Toward High-Quality Development of China*, and the keyword of the title is "shift". In fact, "shift" is the central idea that is embodied in every aspect of this book, including its overall design and selection of topics, in addition to the title. The "shift" here refers to the change in the focus of macroeconomic analysis to high-quality development. In other words, the pursuit of high-quality development requires an all-round transformation of concepts, ideas, strategies and even positions, viewpoints, and approaches in macroeconomic analysis. It is why this book is written and also what this book is intended to highlight and demonstrate.

As a historic shift that affects the whole landscape, the Chinese economy is transitioning from a stage of high-speed growth to a stage of high-quality development, which coincides with the entry of socialism with Chinese characteristics into a new era. The introduction of the idea—"high-quality development" marks not only a change in the stage of China's economic development, but also the beginning of a new era for the Chinese economy. While each era has its defining feature, the task of development also differs from stage to stage. The environment, conditions, tasks, and requirements for China's economic development have changed, so have the ideas, thoughts, and strategies regarding economic development.

In fact, at least since the conclusion of the 18th National Congress of the Communist Party of China (CPC), as socialism with Chinese characteristics has entered a new era and China's economic development has shifted to a new stage, there have been continued discussions about how to look at the economic situation and how to carry out economic work, along with the introduction of a host of new concepts, new formulations, new assessments, new objectives, new tasks, new decisions, and new plans. While effecting corresponding adjustments in practices for growing the economy, they are also imperceptibly changing the ideas, thoughts, and strategies in macroeconomic analysis.

Looking back on the trajectory of our macroeconomic analysis, it is easy find that we have encountered various challenges in the process of the Chinese economy moving from a stage of high-speed growth to one of high-quality development. These challenges are mainly manifested in practice, but they have their roots in the fact that the long-standing paradigm of macroeconomic analysis does not harmonize with the ever-changing macroeconomic reality. Therefore, they are the result of the fierce collision between theory and practice.

Over time, more and more people have come to realize that the pursuit of high-quality development starts with making a shift to high-quality development. The "shift" should be seen not only in action, but also in ideas, thoughts, and strategies. In other words, there should be a shift to the stage of high-quality development both physically and mentally. Furthermore, on the surface, the shift should be in ideas, thoughts, and strategies; on a deeper level, it should be in positions, viewpoints, and methods. Therefore, there should be a thorough shift to the stage of high-quality development in all aspects from ideas, thoughts, and strategies to positions, viewpoints, and methods. In contrast to the shift in what is specifically done to grow the economy, which is mainly at the level of action, the shift in the paradigm of macroeconomic analysis, which is more embodied in ideas, thoughts, and strategies as well as in positions, viewpoints, and methods, is the foundation and prerequisite of crucial importance.

It is fair to say that the word "shift" aptly reveals the priority in the effort to promote high-quality development and vividly depicts the focus and challenge of macroeconomic analysis in this process. In today's China, we should accurately grasp the characteristics of and trends in the stage of high-quality development and discuss issues concerning the stage of high-quality development with the ideas, thoughts and strategies as well as positions, viewpoints, and methods that enable high-quality development. The pursuit of high-quality development should be considered not only in the determination of development ideas, the formulation of economic policies, the implementation of macroeconomic regulation, and the making of other major decisions concerning the functioning of the Chinese economy. Moreover, it should be incorporated into macroeconomic analysis centered on the above-mentioned major decisions, which also affects the functioning of the Chinese economy. It is a challenge that Chinese economists today have to face and take up.

II. About the Analytical Framework of This Book

The question is how to do it.

Understanding the shift to high-quality development is in itself a continuous process of exploration. It is certainly beneficial to develop some core concepts and relevant theories on the basis of sorting out the ideas formed so far around this issue through macroeconomic analysis and then build a logical and self-consistent analytical framework that is applicable to the theme of this book.

The idea of "high-quality development" was formally proposed at the 19th CPC National Congress, but its origin is in the deepened understanding of the current stage of China's economic development. In 2013, the CPC Central Committee reached an important conclusion that the Chinese economy was in a slowing growth phase, a painful structural adjustment phase, and a phase of absorbing the adverse effects of previous stimulus policies. In 2014, it was further summarized as the "new normal of economic development". The move was intended to reveal the characteristics of the current stage of China's economic development. There should be a shift from high to medium-high growth rate, from the focus on scale and speed to that on quality and efficiency, from increasing capacity to adjusting the stock and optimizing the increment in the effort to adjust the economic structure, and from mainly relying on the input of factors such as resources and low-cost labor to boosting innovation as the driving force of development.

All these are bound to appear when the economy reaches a certain stage of development. It is also an inevitable process for the Chinese economy to move to a more advanced stage marked by complete functions, more balanced structures, and better division of labor. Faced with such a state, the basic logic of China's economic development can only be to understand, adapt to, and guide the new normal. Based on such an understanding, the 19th CPC National Congress drew an important conclusion that the Chinese economy was shifting from a stage of high-speed growth to a stage of high-quality development.

Conclusion One: The macroeconomic analysis of the shift to high-quality development must be based on the reality that the stage of China's economic development has changed. In the final analysis, the new normal, rather than old normal, of economic development is the basic national condition that China's endeavor to grow the economy should be based on.

Fundamentally speaking, the change of the stage of economic development is determined by the change of the principal contradiction in Chinese society. The 19th CPC National Congress drew the important conclusion that the principal contradiction in Chinese society had evolved into one between the people's growing needs for a better life and unbalanced and inadequate development, for the purpose of making clear the focus of China's efforts to address major problems in the pursuit of development.

Both meeting the needs for a better life and meeting material and cultural needs are focused on ensuring that common people live a better life. However, the latter is based on the reality of material shortage and the problems to be addressed are about "availability" and "quantity", while the former is based on the primary goal of achieving moderate prosperity and the problems to be addressed are about "quality". What they represent is not a question about the stage of development. Likewise, unbalanced and inadequate development and backward social production are both major constraints on the endeavor to meet the people's needs. However, the removal of the latter focuses on the "size and speed" of the economy and seeks to build strengths in these two aspects to address the problems about "availability" and "quantity", while the removal of the former focuses on "quality and efficiency" and seeks to build strengths in these two aspects to address the problems about "quality". What they represent is not a question about the stage of development either.

More specifically, as the principal contradiction in Chinese society has changed, so has the stage of China's economic development. The change from "the contradiction between the people's ever-growing material and cultural needs and backward social production" to "that between the people's ever-growing needs for a better life and unbalanced and inadequate development" is in essence the process of the Chinese economy shifting from a stage of high-speed growth to one of high-quality development.

Conclusion Two: The macroeconomic analysis of the shift to high-quality development must be based on the reality that the principal contradiction in Chinese society has undergone a historic change. In the final analysis, high-quality development is development that can well meet the people's ever-growing needs for a better life. To meet the needs for a better life, rather than material and cultural needs, is the focus of China's endeavor to grow the economy.

Thinking should always go before action. Development practices are all guided by development thinking. The change of development stage is naturally accompanied by changes in development thinking. At the stage of high-speed growth, due to the shortage of resources, the focus of efforts would be on "availability" and "quantity", and the size and growth rate of GDP would be considered the main factors that matter. In the transition from the stage of high-speed growth to the stage of high-quality development, since moderate prosperity has been achieved on the whole, the focus of efforts should be on "quality and efficiency" in addition to the size and growth rate of GDP. We should not only consider the quality and efficiency of GDP as a core objective, but also put it before the size and growth rate of GDP and list it as a top priority.

It was based on such an important understanding that China's economic development has entered a new stage and in response to the prominent problems in China's development that the Fifth Plenary Session of the 18th CPC Central Committee held in October 2015 proposed the new development philosophy of pursuing "innovative, coordinated, green, open, and shared development". It was intended to stress the importance of the new development philosophy in the pursuit of high-quality development and the need to focus on addressing the problem of unbalanced and inadequate development. Innovation should be the primary driving force behind development, coordination an inherent feature of sustainable and healthy development, greenness a prerequisite for sustainable development and an important embodiment of people's pursuit of a better life, opening up the only way for the country to prosper, and sharing the fundamental purpose of economic development.

Conclusion Three: The macroeconomic analysis of the shift to high-quality development must be based on the reality that the development philosophy has undergone a profound change. In the final analysis, high-quality development embodies the new development philosophy. The new philosophy, rather than the old one, is the guiding principle for China's endeavor to grow the economy.

Common sense tells us that structure and size as well as supply and demand are the two basic aspects of market economy, showcasing the dialectical relationship of the unity of opposites. However, in different stages of development, different problems stand out and play different roles in the economy; the main problems and the main aspects of these problems are also different. In the stage of high-speed growth, the focus is on "availability" and "quantity" so the only way is to boost supply according to demand and thus increase the size of the economy. In the shift from the stage of high-speed growth to the stage of high-quality development, the focus on "availability" and "quantity" is replaced by that on "quality" and "efficiency"; the main problem in growing the economy is no longer a question of size, but a question of structure, and the main aspect of the problem is no longer the demand side, but the supply side.

Correspondingly, supply-side management (SSM) and demand-side management (DSM) are the two basic means of macroeconomic regulation, in the dialectical relationship of the unity of opposites. As the main problem and the major aspect of the problem in the economy have changed, the focus of macroeconomic regulation should change accordingly. The supply-side structural reform proposed by the CPC Central Committee in November 2015 is the main focus of macroeconomic regulation established on the basis of an all-round analysis of the characteristics of China's economic development in the current stage. The shift from the demand side to the supply side, from the focus on total demand to supply structure, from short-term balance to economic growth, and from mainly relying on policy adjustment to mainly relying on reform actions is the main change after supply-side structural reform replaces demand management and becomes the main focus of macroeconomic regulation.

Furthermore, the supply-side structural reform is, in essence, a radical adjustment and directional change of demand management. In this context, although it is necessary to implement demand management represented by counter-cyclical regulation, its purpose would be to facilitate the supply-side structural reform. Demand management plays a supporting role, in contrast to the supply-side structural reform that focuses on improving the structure and quality of supply.

Conclusion Four: The macroeconomic analysis of the shift to high-quality development must be based on the reality that the main focus of macroeconomic regulation has undergone a great change. In the final analysis, high-quality development means that the endeavor to pursue development is centered on the supply-side structural reform. In other words, supply-side structural reform, rather than demand management, is the main focus of China's macroeconomic regulatory system in the current stage.

There may be many more such shifts but the shift in the four aspects mentioned above is probably the most important, the profoundest, and the most fundamental. The transformation of macroeconomic analysis would not be empty words when we are deeply aware that we are in a new normal of economic development rather than the old normal, the principal contradiction in Chinese society is the contradiction between the people's needs for a better life and unbalanced and inadequate development rather than the contradiction between material and cultural needs and backward social production, it is the new development philosophy rather than the old one that guides development practices, and the main focus of macroeconomic regulation is supply-side structural reform rather than demand management, and then make corresponding adjustments in ideas, thoughts, strategies and positions, viewpoints, and methods.

If high-quality development is regarded as an edifice, the new normal of economic development, the change in the principal contradiction in Chinese society, new development philosophy, and supply-side structural reform are just like the four pillars supporting the edifice. They are integral parts of high-quality development. Based on an examination of these four core concepts and relevant theories as well as the internal logical chain that run through them, we would find a basic framework of macroeconomic analysis for the shift to high-quality development. In this way, it would not be so challenging a task to avoid impracticality in macroeconomic analysis.

III. About the Main Features of This Book

The discussion in the previous section is not only intended to sort out the issues of macroeconomic analysis for today's China, but also to examine and keep track of my own research in the field of macroeconomic analysis and my thoughts around the shift to high-quality development.

This book contains forty-one economic theory articles on high-quality development I have published since 2013, following the basic logical chain of "new normal of economic development—change in the principal contradiction in Chinese society—new development philosophy—supply-side structural reform", and based on the above-mentioned basic framework of macroeconomic analysis. These articles do share some common features, despite the differences in topic and genre and their publication over a span of seven years.

First, they are all problem-oriented. Figuring out and explaining clearly what is happening in China is conducive to solving practical problems and answering practical questions. This is the only way to conduct useful and effective research. The articles included in this book are all based on the problems in the shift to a stage of high-quality development. Their common purpose is to show how to look at the economic situation and how to do the economic work. Naturally, they have different focuses, given the different contexts and different problems in question.

Second, they are all the result of long-term research. It is the basic requirement of useful and effective research to focus on a certain field of study or subject matter for a long time and identify and examine issues over a rather long course of development. This is particularly true of macroeconomic analysis. With the deepening of our understanding of China's economic development in the current stage, we have found, screened, and studied issues regarding the trend toward high-quality economic development, and drawn a host of conclusions to help solve the problems. The articles included in this book basically cover the entire research trajectory that has formed around high-quality development and are all based on the thinking and analysis of hot and difficult issues in the process of promoting high-quality development.

Third, they all proceed from the shift to high-quality development. In my view, the biggest obstacle to the promotion of high-quality development so far is "conventional thinking", which is to grasp and deal with the shift to a stage of high-quality development with the thinking and practice of the stage of high-speed growth. Explaining how to avoid such conventional thinking is not only the theme of this book, but also a common feature of the articles chosen for this book. The articles included in this book, whenever they are written and whatever their topics are, all convey a basic message, that is, to make a shift toward high-quality development in ideas, thoughts and strategies as well as positions, viewpoints, and methods. The changed economic situation should be explained with new ideas, thoughts, and strategies. The changed work plan should be understood with new positions, viewpoints, and methods.

Fourth, they are all written for the general public. As a practical branch of knowledge, economics has always been to intended to serve the general public, close to people's everyday life. As macroeconomic analysis is even closer to people's life, it is the bounden duty of my generation of economists to tell the story of China's shift to high-quality development in a language and way that the general public find easy to understand and practical to use. The articles in this book are not academic papers for economics professionals, but theoretical articles for the general public. Thus, the language used in all these articles is straightforward, logically clear, and accessible.

IV. About the Basic Contents of This Book

This book is divided into seven chapters according to the issues discussed in the articles. These parts together form a fairly complete system.

Chapter 1 is "Facing the New Normal of Economic Development". In China, the issue of high-quality development began with the discussion about the Chinese economy entering a new normal. It was initially said that China's economic development had entered a new stage. Later on, the major change, mainly reflected in the "three overlapping phases", was summed up as a new development trend which was then described as the new normal of economic development. On this basis, a major conclusion was drawn that the Chinese economy has shifted from the stage of high-speed growth to the stage of high-quality development. There was a span of nearly five years from the beginning of discussion to the drawing of the conclusion. During this period, how to understand, adapt to, and leverage the new normal of economic development had been the focus of attention for Chinese economists. Even today, conclusions concerning high-quality development are based on the analysis of the new normal of economic development. That is why, to a large extent, high-quality development is considered synonymous with the new normal of economic development.

Chapter 2 is "Applying the New Development Philosophy". The conclusion that China's economic development has entered a new normal can be considered a current answer to the question of "how to look at" the economic situation in the midst of major change. The next task is to answer the question of "how to do" economic work in the face of the economic reality that is markedly different from that in the past. This involves at least two levels, namely thinking and action. Thinking should always go before action. The new development philosophy of pursuing "innovative, coordinated, green, open, and shared development" has emerged in the context of the formulation of the 13th Five-Year Plan. High-quality development has also been defined as a type of development that embodies the new development philosophy. Then how to guide practices in the pursuit of high-quality economic development with the new development philosophy, correct all the understandings and practices that do not suit or go against the new development philosophy has always been regarded as the core issue concerning the overall framework of high-quality economic development.

Chapter 3 is "Focusing on Supply-Side Structural Reform". Since the thinking issue has been solved, the next issue to address is action, i.e., how to do it. Supply-side structural reform has been proposed as a major adjustment to China's economic development thinking and focus of efforts in this regard. It is even argued that high-quality development is characterized by supply-side structural reform. Then, there has been many key and focal issues to be tackled not only in theory but also in practice, regarding how to promote high-quality economic development with supply-side structural reform as the priority, and how to run supply-side structural reform through the whole process of macroeconomic regulation. There have been further discussions around these issues.

Chapter 4 is "Building a Macroeconomic Regulatory System for the New Era". Focusing on supply-side structural reform means that the macroeconomic regulatory system at the stage of high-quality development needs to be restructured. In this process, it is both a priority and a challenge to well manage the relationship between supply-side structural reform and the demand management policies represented by counter-cyclical regulation. In addition, the coordination between fiscal and monetary policies and their coordination with employment, industry, investment, consumption and regional policies are among the issues to be studied and solved.

Chapter 5 is "New Interpretations of Proactive Fiscal Policy". Proactive fiscal policy introduced in the 1990s has encountered a host of challenges in many aspects, including goal setting, function determination, implementation approach, policy mix, and action route, since the Chinese economy began to make the shift to high-quality development. In response to the current-stage changes in economic development, the composition of proactive fiscal policy has been adjusted. Such gradual adjustment in practice is closely integrated with research innovation and is completed based on the mutual support of the two aspects. The use of "New Interpretations" in the title is intended to highlight the profound changes that have taken place in the composition of proactive fiscal policy. It also offers a glimpse into the effort to build a macroeconomic regulatory system for the new era.

Chapter 6 is "New Policies on Tax and Fee Cuts". Cutting taxes and fees has always been a key part of proactive fiscal policy as well as macroeconomic regulation. However, the tax and fee cuts over the past few years have been quite different compared to previous ones. The measures are mainly marked by the purpose of tax and fee cuts and the expansion from increasing demand to reducing costs with the latter as the mainstay. For example, a series of efforts involving tax and fee cuts, such as clarifying who are eligible for such cuts, what to cut, what to use to support the cuts, and in what ways the taxes and fees can be cut, are all different, so I would like to call them "new policies". Through these new ideas and new measures embodied in tax and fee cuts, we can also see the progress in relevant theoretical research behind them and the support of such research to practical operations.

Chapter 7 is "Promoting High-Quality Economic Development". The thinking about entering the new normal of economic development, the exploration focusing on the application of the new development philosophy and supply-side structural reform, and the adjustments made in proactive fiscal policy and tax and fee cuts in response to the need to rebuild the macroeconomic regulatory system have all occurred in the process of China's shift to a stage of high-quality economic development. Fundamentally, they suggest that the shift to high-quality development in ideas, thoughts, and strategies, and even in positions, viewpoints, and methods should ultimately be translated into the action to promote high-quality economic development. In particular, the top priority is to reveal the necessity of pursuing high-quality development and putting in place the systems and mechanisms for supporting high-quality development, which is also why this book has been compiled.

V. Other Matters

Here, I would like to note that it is easier said than done. The macroeconomic analysis of the shift to high-quality development is in no way an easy task, be it the shift in ideas, thoughts and strategies, or that in positions, viewpoints, and methods.

In fact, China's course of development since the 18th CPC National Congress has reminded us time and again that the current performance of the economy is different from what we have known. The current landscape of macroeconomic regulation is also different from the theoretical framework we have learned from textbooks. Facing the changes in the performance of the economy and macroeconomic regulation, we have been adjusting our ideas, thoughts, and strategies as well as positions, viewpoints, and methods. However, perhaps due to conventional thinking or the force of habit, we may embrace new thinking on high-quality development when there is smooth progress but fall back to old thinking and even the old model of high-speed growth when resistance is met. It can be an extremely painful and long process to change from being aware of to being subconscious about driving high-quality development and to abandon conventional thinking at both theoretical and practical levels. However, we have no choice but to strive forward despite all the challenges.

In view of that, it is absolutely necessary to repeatedly remind ourselves that we are in a stage of high-quality development rather than a stage of high-speed growth, and that the former is very different from the latter.

In this regard, the views presented in this book are mine alone, and I hope they are of some value to the readers.

Beijing, China
February 2020

Peiyong Gao

Contents

About the Author

Peiyong Gao is Member and Vice President of the Chinese Academy of Social Sciences, Delegate to the Chinese People's Political Consultative Conference, Member of the State Council Academic Degrees Committee, and Vice Chair of the Sun Yefang Economic Science Foundation. Gao's previous positions include Assistant to the President of the Renmin University of China, President of the Institute of Finance and Trade Economics of the Chinese Academy of Social Sciences, President of the National Academy of Economic Strategy of the Chinese Academy of Social Sciences, and Director of the Institute of Economics of the Chinese Academy of Social Sciences. Gao's areas of specialty are finance economics, finance and taxation theories, and tax policy analysis.

Chapter 1
Facing the New Normal of Economic Development

1 Introduction

As a starting point for the macroeconomic analysis of the shift to high-quality development, this chapter, comprising seven articles, is entitled "Facing the New Normal of Economic Development".

The Chinese economy's shift to high-quality development begins with thinking about the new normal of economic development. Its origin can be traced back to the Central Economic Work Conference held in December 2012, the first national conference held after the 18th CPC National Congress. In the face of the major change in China's economic development, the conference adjusted macroeconomic policies in four aspects, while drawing an important conclusion that "the Chinese economy has entered the stage of single-digit growth". This opened a prologue to the discussion about how to look at the economic situation and how to do economic work. It was in such a context that "Four Changes in the Macroeconomic Policy Landscape" was written.

One of the most striking changes brought about by the economic slowdown in 2013 was the sharp decline in the growth rate of fiscal revenue. In China, fiscal revenue has always been considered as a real measure of financial strength. For a time, people in all sectors expressed differing views about how to look at the decline and what to do, so it was necessary to provide the general public with a more accurate analysis from a professional. I was therefore invited to write two articles, "Unfazed by the Slowdown in Fiscal Revenue Growth" and "Understanding the Current Fiscal Situation Correctly".

Unlike in other countries, local government debt in China has been vied for and criticized at the same time. Lack of transparency and potential risks are the main accusations against it, which have been further amplified in the context of "three overlapping phases". Then where is the future of local government debt? To answer the question, I wrote "Realizing Local Government Debt New Normal by Deepening Reform" in August 2014. At that time, the idea of "new normal" had been put forward,

P. Gao, *A Shift Toward High-Quality Development of China*,
Research Series on the Chinese Dream and China's Development Path,
https://doi.org/10.1007/978-981-99-8990-4_1

along with related ideas such as not blindly pursuing GDP and deepening reform to solve the deep-seated problems. The main point raised in this article is to achieve a smooth transition of local government debt's development to the new normal in the process of comprehensively deepening reform.

Economic situation has always been closely linked with fiscal situation. As the new normal of economic development was widely used to describe the changes in economic situation, "the new normal of fiscal affairs" was also used to describe the changes in fiscal situation. Later on, such saying was no longer used for various considerations, but the idea of understanding the changes in fiscal situation as a trend and a reality to break new ground in managing fiscal affairs has been undoubtedly embraced. The article "Thoroughly Understanding the Fiscal New Normal" was written at the invitation of the Chinese Ministry of Finance. Its core idea is that the serious imbalances between government revenue and expenditure following the slowdown in fiscal revenue are caused by the laws underlying economic development. Therefore, we must adjust our ideas, mindset, strategies and policies across the board.

That the principal contradiction in Chinese society has changed is a political message put across at the 19th CPC National Congress. Since the economy and politics are inseparable, connecting this political message to economic development, we can find that the change of the principal contradiction and that of the economic development stage actually come down in the same vein. The change of the principal contradiction in Chinese society marks not only the entry of socialism with Chinese characteristics into a new era, but also the beginning of China's shift to the new stage of high-quality economic development. Therefore, it is necessary to include the change of the principal contradiction in the framework of economic analysis and give it an economic interpretation. "Fully Grasping the Economic Significance of the Change in the Principal Contradiction in Chinese Society" is an article written based on my study of the guiding principles of the 19th CPC National Congress.

The economic situation is becoming increasingly complex and challenging as we move into the new normal, which poses a challenge to macroeconomic analysis on a daily basis. All the problems need to be addressed as a whole. All the policy choices need to be prioritized. It is also necessary to address the problems and implement macroeconomic policies in the context of the stage of high-quality development, and to ensure that macroeconomic analysis is accurate and effective. "Proper Macroeconomic Analysis Amid a Complex and Challenging Situation" is an article I wrote as the editor-in-chief's message for *Economic Research Journal*.

2 Four Changes in the Macroeconomic Policy Landscape[1]

With the conclusion of the Central Economic Work Conference in December 2012, China's macroeconomic policy landscape has undergone important changes in four aspects. These changes will, to a large extent, determine the direction of the Chinese economy in 2013 and the years to come, exerting a significant impact on China's economic and social development.

I. **Positioning of macroeconomic policies: to help achieve sustained and healthy economic development as well as social harmony and stability**

In the past, the positioning of macroeconomic policies would be considered, in most cases, from the perspective of economic development, and priority or focus would always be given to rapid economic growth. A review of the formulations put forward at Central Economic Work Conferences shows that we used the saying "sustained, rapid and healthy growth" in the 1990s. Since the beginning of the twenty-first century, we have used other sayings such as "sustained, rapid, balanced and healthy growth", "stable and fast growth", "fast and sound growth", "sound and fast growth", and once again "stable and fast growth". In other words, the function of macroeconomic policies is always defined by the requirement for "fast" economic growth.

The Central Economic Work Conference of December 2012, however, defined the functional positioning of macroeconomic policies as "to help achieve sustained and healthy economic development as well as social harmony and stability". The word "fast" is absent for the first time and the scope of macroeconomic policies has been extended to the field of social development, which is apparently a very important change.

The use of adjectives "sustained and healthy" instead of "stable and fast" for economic development and the listing of "social harmony and stability" together with "sustained and healthy economic development" in defining the function of macroeconomic policies are sending us at least four messages.

First, as China enters the middle and late stages of industrialization, its economy is shifting from high-speed growth to medium-speed growth, entering a stage of single-digit growth. People have gradually reached a consensus on this point.

Second, as the international financial crisis evolves, there is a growing consensus on the long duration and depth of the crisis. For example, we have already concluded that the low-speed growth of the world economy will continue and it is hard to predict when the world economy will emerge from the crisis. We realize that the important period of strategic opportunity for China's development has seen great changes in the implications and circumstances of the international environment. It would be no longer a traditional opportunity of simply being integrated into the global division of labor system, expanding exports and accelerating investment. Rather, it is a new opportunity for us to stimulate domestic demand, increase innovation capacity, and

[1] The article is a slightly revised edition of "Four Major Changes in Macroeconomic Policies" that was first published in *Economic Daily* on February 8, 2013.

change the growth model. It is also recognized that the imbalance between economic downturn and overcapacity has intensified so we must have a sense of urgency.

Third, as the economic growth rate slows down, the focus of economic development must shift to improving quality and efficiency and pursuing a speed that is based on quality, efficiency and sustainability. There is a growing consensus on this point. On the basis of that, five specific criteria have been introduced, namely growth in a real sense, growth accompanied by the increase of employment, growth featuring the combination of economic growth and the increase of residents' income, growth accompanied by the increase of efficiency, and growth that can be sustained by resources available and the environment.

Fourth, as social problems in China have increased in both quantity and severity, people have agreed more than ever on the relationship between China's economic growth and overall social stability and the relationship between development, stability and reform. Including both "social harmony and stability" and "sustained and healthy economic development" in the function of macroeconomic policies means that we need to connect economic development with social development. Linking the sustained and healthy development of the economy with the harmony and stability of society therefore becomes a very important item on the agenda of macroeconomic policies.

II. Role of macroeconomic policies: to apply both counter-cyclical regulation and structural adjustment

Conventionally macroeconomic policies are used as tools against the economic cycle. Introducing expansionary measures during a recession and tightening ones during inflation is an appropriate description of what macroeconomic regulation is. In the case of China, at least since the Asian financial crisis in 1998, macroeconomic policies have all been devised to achieve counter-cyclical regulation, from the mix of "proactive fiscal policy and appropriate monetary policy" in the beginning to that of "proactive fiscal policy and prudent monetary policy" and "prudent fiscal and monetary policies" later on as well as the combination of "proactive fiscal policy and moderately easy monetary policy" and "proactive fiscal policy and prudent monetary policy" in recent years.

Compared to the conventional focus of leveraging counter-cyclical regulation, the Central Economic Work Conference used a different formulation this time, namely "giving full play to the role of both counter-cyclical regulation and structural adjustment". In other words, the macroeconomic policies for 2013 must highlight both counter-cyclical regulation and structural adjustment. Such a change is surely made based on a thorough consideration.

First, as the global economy continues to fluctuate and the problems of imbalances, lack of coordination and unsustainable development become increasingly prominent, more and more facts have shown that the international financial crisis this time is the result of intertwined cyclical and structural factors, mainly caused by the imbalance in economic structure. A real recovery cannot be achieved on the basis of the existing economic structure. To keep the economy on the track of sustained and healthy development, we must intensify efforts in the strategic adjustment of the economic structure and embrace a completely different growth model.

Second, the Chinese economy is currently confronted with both "downward economic pressure and overcapacity". If macroeconomic regulation targeted at one of the two problems fails to address the other at the same time, neither of the problems will be solved. Only by combining counter-cyclical regulation and structural adjustment can the design of macroeconomic policies be in line with China's economic reality.

Third, the response to the crisis should avoid damaging the economic structure. In other words, the crisis should not be tackled at the cost of damaging the economic structure. At present, the only choice for us is to proceed from the adjustment of the industrial structure and strive to alleviate overcapacity and downturn economic pressure. In doing so, we will eventually manage to boost economic growth through structural adjustment or achieve economic growth and structural adjustment at the same time.

III. Objectives of macroeconomic policies: steady growth, structural adjustment, price control and risk mitigation

In the response to the crisis this time, the objective of macroeconomic policies was initially set to be "maintaining growth". When maintaining growth was considered the overriding task, we could naturally concentrate our efforts on this one objective and go all out. Later on, as the economic fluctuation slowed down and the situation changed, "maintaining growth" was replaced by "stabilizing growth" and more objectives of macroeconomic policies were gradually introduced. Following the objective of stabilizing growth, "controlling prices" was added in response to the price hike driven by excess liquidity and "adjusting structure" was added in response to increasingly prominent structural problems in the economy. As a result, the three objectives of stabilizing growth, adjusting structure and controlling prices were set.

In 2013, as various debts incurred in crisis response operations needed to be cleared, potential risks in the financial field gradually emerged and preventing systemic and regional financial risks became an important task for increased macroeconomic regulation. Therefore, in addition to the above-mentioned three objectives, the Central Economic Work Conference added "preventing risks" to the list of macroeconomic policy objectives. Now, the four objectives are steady growth, structural adjustment, price control, and risk mitigation.

The problem is that when there are three, four or even more objectives, we would have to carefully use macroeconomic regulation resources, focus on multiple fronts at the same time. This actually sends us three messages.

First, due to limited resources, the macroeconomic regulation operations of 2013 should and have to strike a balance between steady growth, structural adjustment, price control, and risk mitigation. This means that much room is left for macroeconomic regulation now.

Second, even though the need to stabilize growth has become urgent, we should not go all out or devote major efforts to stabilize growth, as we did in the past. Instead, we must consider multiple objectives.

Third, given the multiple objectives, the use of macroeconomic regulation resources would be like a tug-of-war—more resources will be allocated to whichever aspect comes under great pressure (severity of the situation). Therefore, the priority of macroeconomic regulation is subject to change.

IV. Mix of macroeconomic policies: towards prudence with a combination of "proactive fiscal policy and prudent monetary policy"

The Central Economic Work Conference decided to continue implementing a proactive fiscal policy and a prudent monetary policy, bringing such a combination to the third year. However, the same combination or the unchanged policy names may have different implications. A careful review of the plans made at the Central Economic Work Conference shows that the combination of proactive fiscal policy and prudent monetary policy for 2013 is a macroeconomic regulation arrangement that tends to be prudent.

First, developed economies such as European countries, the United States, and Japan are launching a new round of quantitative easing policies, which is bound to drive the devaluation of major currencies around the world. The pressure of potential inflation and asset bubbles would be once again intensified. The spillover effect will surely affect China. The potential risks in China's financial sector are accumulating and emerging. With the change of government, there may be a new round of activities by local financing platforms. The inflation pressure caused by excess liquidity in the past has never been alleviated while new inflation pressure from both external and internal sources is emerging. All these will leave very limited room for the monetary policy to function, so that the focus will be placed on controlling prices and preventing risks.

Second, the fiscal deficit will increase in 2013, considering the three pillars of a proactive fiscal policy—deficit increase, tax reduction and spending increase. However, the deficit must be controlled below the 3% international security line, due to the European sovereign debt crisis, the U.S. fiscal cliff and China's potential risks in the financial sector. Tax reduction is apparently a main feature of the positive fiscal policy in 2013, but common sense tells us that the expansionary effects of tax cuts are relatively small and indirect compared with spending increase. Spending-boosting measures are acceptable, but there must be constraints in 2013. Governments at all levels should not only practice frugality and strictly control general expenditures, but also spend money on important matters that must be addressed. All these will, to some extent, weaken the expansionary effects of proactive fiscal policy operations.

Third, due to diminishing marginal effect, the "efficacy" of expansionary operations has declined. This means that even if large-scale economic expansion measures, such as those of 2008 and 2009, were used again, their expansionary effect would not be as large as that in those 2 years. It also means that in order to achieve economic growth marked by quality, efficiency and sustainability and pursue sustained and healthy economic development by changing growth model and improving the economic structure, we must take into account multiple objectives such as stabilizing growth, adjusting structure, controlling prices and preventing risks, and find a way to strike a proper balance between counter-cyclical regulation and structural adjustment.

3 Unfazed by the Slowdown in Fiscal Revenue Growth[2]

I. **Staying alert to the decline in fiscal revenue growth**

The most noticeable part of the economic data for the first quarter of 2013 released by the National Bureau of Statistics of China is probably the slowdown in fiscal revenue. The country's fiscal revenue in Q1 registered 3203.4 billion yuan, up 6.9%, 7.8 percentage points lower than that in the same period of last year. Specifically, the central government's revenue increased by 1460.6 billion yuan, down 0.2% year on year. Tax revenue totaled 2739.9 billion yuan, up 6%, 4.3 percentage points lower than that in the same period of last year.

These are just numbers on the surface. There are even more to look if we look further. First, the growth rate of fiscal revenue was not only lower than the 7.7% GDP growth rate over the same period, but also lower than the 8% growth rate of annual budgeted revenue. Second, in previous years, the growth rate of fiscal revenue was always at a higher level before going down. Third, the growth rate of fiscal revenue has stayed above 20 or even 30% for many years. Fourth, China does not have a mechanism like that in European countries and the United States, through which fiscal expenditure is automatically cut as fiscal revenue falls. In fact, in contrast to the decline in fiscal revenue growth, fiscal expenditure grew by 12.1% in the first quarter of 2013, 5.2 percentage points higher than the growth rate of fiscal revenue. Fifth, in the previous years, the growth rate of fiscal expenditure was always at a lower level before going up. Sixth, the amount of the Central Budget Stabilization Fund is less than one hundred billion yuan. Seventh, there are precedents where the expected level of tax reduction is lower than the actual level due to the program of replacing BT with VAT. Take Shanghai as an example. In 2012, the expected tax reduction at the beginning of the year and the actual amount were twelve billion yuan and twenty-five billion yuan respectively.

Considering all these, we need to stay alert to the slowdown in fiscal revenue and the possible imbalance between fiscal revenue and expenditure caused thereof.

II. **Accepting it as a hard reality and an inevitable outcome**

However, we should not be and need not to be alarmed, looking beyond fiscal revenue and expenditure and to the overall macroeconomic landscape.

The economy determines public finance, which is a basic rule well known to people. After more than 30 years of reform and opening up, the Chinese economy has entered the middle and late stage of industrialization. As labor cost rises, the demographic dividend is decreasing. The adjustment to vigorously develop the service

[2] This article is a slightly revised edition of a piece that was first published in *Guangming Daily* on April 26, 2013.

sector inevitably causes the growth of labor productivity and a slowdown in economic growth. In other words, as the Chinese economy shifts from high-speed to medium-speed growth and enters the stage of single-digit growth, the growth of fiscal revenue will naturally slow down. This is the first aspect.

The current international financial crisis is not simply a cyclical crisis in the traditional sense, but a crisis in which structural and cyclical factors are interwoven, or even more one caused by structural factors. Given that it is mainly caused by the global economic restructuring and that the Chinese economy has become deeply integrated with the global economy, we will have to go through a very painful and long process of transformation and adjustment on deeper levels. In this process, as the economy continues to fluctuate and its growth rate goes down, fiscal revenue will also enter a period of continuous fluctuation and slowdown. This is the second aspect.

The high-speed or even ultra-high-speed growth of China's fiscal revenue that has lasted for many years started in 1994. Before that, we also experienced years of slowdown in fiscal revenue. The trajectory of fiscal revenue growth over the past 30-plus years shows us at least two points. One is that the continuous high-speed growth of fiscal revenue after 1994 is to a large extent a correction of the previous continuous decline in the growth rate of fiscal revenue, which is remedial in nature. The remedy will not last forever and fiscal revenue growth is bound to get back on track when it reaches a certain point. The other is that the continuous high-speed growth of fiscal revenue after 1994 can be considered, to a large extent, the outcome of the fiscal and tax reforms in 1994 so it is like a dividend brought by the reforms. Such a dividend will not increase forever, either. It will surely enter into a state of decline after a period of time. This means that the continuous high-speed growth of fiscal revenue, especially that higher or even much higher than the economic growth rate, is a special phenomenon that occurs at a certain stage of development. It is normal only when the growth of fiscal revenue is in line with economic growth. This is the third aspect.

Under China's current tax system, more than 70% of the government's tax revenue comes from indirect taxes such as VAT, BT and excise tax. It means that most of China's tax revenue are a component of prices. It is tied to the prices of goods and services, rising and falling with prices, and fluctuates violently due to slight changes in prices. When the economy is growing at a high speed, tax revenue is likely to grow faster than the economy. When economic growth slows down, tax revenue is likely to grow at a lower speed than the economy. Therefore, as long as China's current tax system and the composition of tax revenue sources determined by such a system remain unchanged, it is expected that China's economic slowdown will bring about an even greater decline in the growth rate of tax revenue and fiscal revenue. This is the fourth aspect.

In view of the above, we can conclude that the current slowdown in fiscal revenue is not only a hard reality we have to accept, but also an inevitable outcome of economic development. In a sense, it is bound to occur in fiscal revenue as the Chinese economy is in a period of transformation and adjustment on deeper levels. Given that, we should face it calmly and embrace the idea of "practicing frugality" in pursuing fiscal and economic development in the future.

III. Laying a good institutional foundation for "practicing fiscal frugality"

It will not be easy for China to bid farewell to the high-speed growth of fiscal revenue of yesteryear and shift to the normal track of "practicing fiscal frugality". This is because, after all, the government has had considerable revenue for so long a time. Many officials have been used to spending money lavishly and quite a few would often spend money for the sake of political achievement. Some have even created a model of collecting extra revenue and improving welfare every year. In the context of falling fiscal revenue growth, especially continuous decline, the following problems are likely to come up if no substantive measures are taken.

For example, as fiscal revenue decreases and spending pressure increases, tax authorities may be assigned impractical tasks and have to impose higher taxes on businesses and residents in order to ease the imbalance between revenue and expenditure and rank higher in fiscal revenue.

Another example is that as revenue in the general budget decreases, unconventional means may be used to earn revenue and unauthorized charges may thus be increased to maintain the spending momentum and even to satisfy the officials' need to improve their own welfare and continue their achievements.

Moreover, when the reduction of fiscal revenue endangers the balance between government revenue and expenditure, or one expenditure or some special expenditures, the pace of structural tax reduction may be slowed down to maintain the government's plans on financial resources and determined expenditures.

When the reduction of fiscal revenue impedes the achievement of economic targets or the government's investment introduction plans, local debt financing vehicles may be used again to escape risk control regarding debt scale, which may incur systemic and regional financial risks.

There may be many more such problems. All these listed and unlisted problems are by no means alarmist, but chronic institutional problems that exist in the process of China's economic and social development. Therefore, the plan on practicing frugality in response to the slowdown in fiscal revenue must not be just a slogan or for the short term. Instead, it should be adopted as a long-term strategy and integrated into the efforts to promote fiscal and economic development. Moreover, a series of substantive reforms should be carried out to lay the institutional foundation for the sustainable and healthy development of public finance and the economy.

4 Understanding the Current Fiscal Situation Correctly[3]

As the Chinese economy enters a new stage of development, the growth of China's fiscal revenue has shown a downward trend. This has drawn much attention from all sectors of society. In a sense, it is a hotspot issue that has arisen amid the change of economic situation in the country. The heated discussion and strong response at least suggest that it is something unfamiliar to most people. Many young people may have never experienced this, and many older people may have not seen such a situation for a long time. It is therefore necessary for us to examine and explain such a not-well-known economic reality using new ideas and new perspectives.

I. **How to assess the fiscal situation is directly related to the frame of reference used**

The assessment of fiscal situation is often directly related to the frame of reference used. The conclusions often differ according to the frame of reference, and sometimes entirely different results may even be obtained.

For example, China's fiscal revenue was 8902.7 billion yuan from January to August 2013. The analysis of this figure is often based on the "past" growth trajectory of fiscal revenue. However, "the past" can be a long or short period of time, so there must be a range. The difference in range selection will lead to that in the result of analysis.

If the past is defined as the same period of last year, we will find that fiscal revenue growth in 2013 was 8.1%, 2.7 percentage points lower than the 10.8% in the first 8 months of 2012.

If the past is defined as previous 10 years, we will find that fiscal revenue growth in 2013 dropped by 14.29 percentage points compared with the average annual growth of 22.39% between 2003 and 2012.

If the past is defined as the previous 19 years, we will find that fiscal revenue growth in 2013 dropped by 12.1 percentage points compared with the average annual growth of 20.2% between 1994 and 2012.

If the past is defined as the previous 34 years, we will find that fiscal revenue growth in 2013 fell by 7.1 percentage points compared with the average annual growth of 15.2% between 1979 and 2012.

If the past is defined as the 15 years from 1979 to 1993, fiscal revenue growth in 2013 fell by only 0.84% point compared with the average annual growth of 8.94% between 1979 and 1993.

The growth trajectory of China's fiscal revenue shows that the decline in fiscal revenue growth since 2013 changes considerably as the defined range of the past changes. Taking the decade (2003–2012) of super-fast fiscal revenue growth as the frame of reference, it is natural to draw the conclusion that the current decline in fiscal revenue growth is sharp and the situation is rather serious. Taking the 19 years (1994–2012) of rapid fiscal revenue growth as the frame of reference, the current

[3] This is a slightly revised version of an article first published in the *People's Daily* on November 12, 2013.

decline in fiscal revenue growth seems to be not that serious. Taking the 34 years (1979–2012) of both low-speed and high-speed fiscal revenue growth as the frame of reference, the current decline in fiscal revenue growth becomes a single digit which is acceptable. Furthermore, if we take the 15 years (1979–1993) of continued decline in fiscal revenue growth as the frame of reference, the current decline in fiscal revenue growth becomes so slight that it is almost negligible.

This in fact tells us that it is unnecessary to worry about the current fiscal situation in China. We should stay calm and optimistic.

II. The current slowdown in fiscal revenue growth rate is consistent with the normal pattern of economic development

Some facts must be considered if we examine the slowdown in fiscal revenue in a historical context, especially against the special background of the international financial crisis.

First, the economy determines public finance, which is a basic rule well known to people. After more than 30 years of reform and opening up, the Chinese economy has entered a new stage of development. As labor cost rises, the demographic dividend is decreasing. The adjustment to vigorously develop the service sector inevitably causes the growth of labor productivity and a slowdown in economic growth. In other words, as the Chinese economy shifts from high-speed to medium-speed growth and enters the stage of single-digit growth, the growth of fiscal revenue will naturally slow down.

Second, the current international financial crisis is not simply a cyclical crisis in the traditional sense, but a crisis in which structural and cyclical factors are interwoven, or even more one caused by structural factors. Given that it is mainly caused by the global economic restructuring and that the Chinese economy has become deeply integrated with the global economy, we will have to go through a very painful and long process of transformation and adjustment on deeper levels, facing the heavy task of adjusting China's economic structure. In this process, as the economy continues to fluctuate and its growth rate goes down, fiscal revenue will also enter a period of continuous fluctuation and slowdown.

Third, the high-speed or even ultra-high-speed growth of China's fiscal revenue that has lasted for many years started in 1994. Before that, we had also experienced years of slowdown in fiscal revenue growth rate. The trajectory of fiscal revenue growth over the past 30-plus years shows us that the continuous high-speed growth of fiscal revenue after 1994 is to a large extent a correction of the previous continuous decline in the growth rate of fiscal revenue, which is remedial in nature. The remedy will not last forever and fiscal revenue growth is bound to get back on track when it reaches a certain point.

Fourth, the continuous high-speed growth of fiscal revenue after 1994 can be considered, to a large extent, the outcome of the fiscal and tax reforms in 1994 so it is like a dividend brought by the reforms. Such a dividend will not increase forever, either. It will surely enter into a state of decline after a period of time. This means that the continuous high-speed growth of fiscal revenue, especially that higher or even much higher than the economic growth rate, is a special phenomenon that occurs at a certain stage of development. It is normal only when the growth of fiscal revenue is in line with economic growth.

Fifth, fiscal revenue in China is mainly tax revenue. Under the current tax system, more than 70% of the government's tax revenue comes from indirect taxes such as VAT, BT and excise tax. It means that most of China's tax revenue are a component of prices. It is tied to the prices of goods and services, rising and falling with prices, and fluctuates violently due to slight changes in prices. When the economy is growing at a high speed, tax revenue is likely to grow faster than the economy. When economic growth slows down, tax revenue is likely to grow at a lower speed than the economy. Therefore, as long as China's current tax system and the composition of tax revenue sources determined by such a system remain unchanged, it is expected that China's economic slowdown will bring about an even greater decline in the growth rate of tax revenue and fiscal revenue.

The current slowdown in fiscal revenue is not only a hard reality we have to accept, but also an inevitable outcome of economic development. In a sense, it is bound to occur in fiscal revenue as the Chinese economy is in a period of transformation and adjustment on deeper levels. Therefore, we should face it calmly.

III. **The current fiscal situation is hardly serious in the macroeconomic context**

The above analysis is made based on the data for public revenue in general budget. What makes it more complicated is that in today's China public revenue, or revenue in general budget, is not all the revenue of the government. In addition to public revenue, the Chinese government also has the following sources of income, namely budgets of government-managed funds, budgets of social security funds, and budgets of state capital operations.

Based on the budget figures for 2013, the share of public revenue in the government's total revenue is only about 65%. The proportion of the remaining three types of budgeted revenue is about 35%. This means that the analysis of the impact of the slowdown in fiscal revenue should not be confined to the scope of public revenue, but should cover all the four types of revenue.

Once the revenue in budgets of government-managed funds, budgets of social security funds, and budgets of state capital operations is brought into focus, we will come to a completely different conclusion.

Take, for example, the revenue in budgets of government-managed funds and budgets of social security funds for which the data are currently available. According to the data released by the Ministry of Finance, in the first 6 months of 2013, revenue of China's government-funded funds amounted to 2106.1 billion yuan, an increase of 587 billion yuan or 38.6% over the same period of last year. Revenue of China's social security funds was 1527.6 billion yuan, up 15.6% over the same period of last year. The growths in these two types of government revenue were respectively 27.8 and 4.8 percentage points higher than the growth of public revenue (10.8%) in the same period. The special phenomenon that both decrease and increase exist across all types of government revenue is characteristic of the period of institutional transformation. It tells us that we just consider public revenue in general budget, we may conclude that the fiscal situation has become severe. However, if we examine

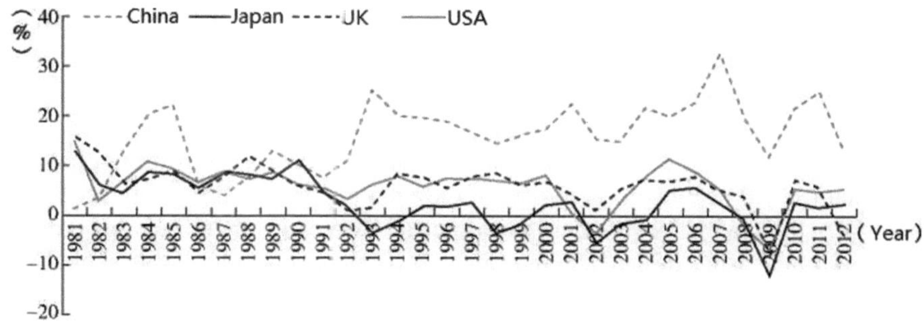

Fig. 1 Fiscal revenue growth in China and some developed countries, 1981–2012

all types of government revenue and look at the whole picture, we may find that the current fiscal situation in China is hardly serious.

From another point of view, we can further deepen our understanding by going beyond vertical comparisons and making horizontal comparisons with a global vision.

Take the data for representative countries and regions in 2012 for example. The growth rates of their fiscal revenue are as follows: OECD countries such as Australia (8.54%), Austria (4.27%), Canada (3.54%), France (5.85%), Germany (5.59%), Japan (2.1%), the UK (0.54%), the United States (5.21%), Belgium (4.52%), Denmark (− 1.29%), Finland (1.55%), Greece (− 5.6%), the Netherlands (1.71%), Iceland (8.05%), Ireland (1.44%), Norway (6.57%), Portugal (− 12.54%), Spain (0.6%), Sweden (2.1%), Switzerland (− 0.4%) and Italy (2.47%); emerging market economies and China's neighboring countries, such as India (0.04%), Russia (0.03%), and Singapore (− 2.16%); Taiwan of China (2.65%).

Compared with the growth rates of fiscal revenue of OECD countries (see Fig. 1), emerging market economies, or China's neighboring countries, the current growth rate of China's fiscal revenue is higher or even far higher than the average international level.

This also tells us that globally speaking the current 8.1% growth in China's fiscal revenue can be considered a good indicator under normal conditions.

IV. **Practicing fiscal frugality means "to get back on track"**

After a discussion about the current slowdown in China's fiscal revenue, we can immediately draw a basic conclusion that after nearly 20 years of high-speed or even ultra-high-speed growth, China's fiscal revenue is making a shift as its economic growth enters a new stage. In other words, against the background of the Chinese economy entering a new stage of development, China's fiscal revenue has gone out of the special development period and returned to the right track. In this sense, a decline in growth rate is inevitable. At present, to practice fiscal frugality is actually to get back on track.

Recognizing that the growth rate of China's fiscal revenue has dropped to a new level and that this trend is irreversible, we have to and must consider it normal and stay calm and cautious. Embracing the idea of getting back on track, we should bear the pressure of slowdown in fiscal revenue and make proper plans for fiscal revenue and expenditure and relevant fiscal policy adjustments.

First, since China's macroeconomic situation has undergone important changes and excessive government spending is not conducive to economic restructuring and the sustained and healthy development of the economy, it is undoubtedly necessary to stabilize the scale of government spending and its proportion in GDP and prevent them from increasing further. This means that governments at all levels should not only practice frugality, strictly control general expenditures, and spend money on important matters that must be done. Moreover, even for public investment that must be increased, while encouraging investment by the private sector, we should focus on the field of infrastructure that will benefit the people in the long term.

Second, since improving the economic structure is important for both the present and future of China's economic development and the key to resolving overcapacity and economic restructuring is to thoroughly transform government functions, it is absolutely necessary to further adjust and improve the structure of government spending while stabilizing its scale and proportion in GDP. This means that we must abandon the traditional thinking of increasing government investment and spending on construction for economic growth and make the right choice of spending more on areas important to people's livelihoods.

Third, since China's current pressure in fiscal revenue and expenditure is closely related to the improper approach to government budget management, and "promoting open, transparent, and standard operations" has become an important goal of the government's budget system reform, it is even more necessary to comprehensively deepen fiscal and tax reforms and regulate the government's practices and mechanisms for collecting revenue and spending the money. This means that in the next stage of fiscal and tax reforms we must face up to and break through the obstacles from vested interests within the government, and truly practice full-scope government budget management. The considerable dividends created by the fiscal and tax reforms can be used to ease the current pressure in fiscal revenue and expenditure.

Fourth, since China has made important adjustments to the framework of its macroeconomic policies, and the current focus of the policies is to ensure stability, it is surely necessary to maintain policy continuity and thus to stabilize market expectations and show the determination to promote economic restructuring. This means that facing the slowdown in both economic growth and fiscal revenue growth, we must remain calm and adhere to proactive fiscal policy and prudent monetary policy. As long as the macroeconomic change is within a reasonable range and within the scope of active regulation, we should make no major adjustments to macroeconomic policies due to the pressure in fiscal revenue and expenditure and changes in the fiscal situation. With the stability of fiscal policy and monetary policy, we will leave enough room for the self-regulation of the market and create a market environment of fair competition, laying a solid foundation for the market to play a decisive role in resource allocation.

5 Realizing Local Government Debt New Normal by Deepening Reform[4]

I. Local government debt risks: presenting a complex situation quite different from previous ones

At present, the local government debt in China remains below the internationally recognized safety line in terms of the economic and financial strength of the whole country. Although the overall scale is not worrying, if we look closer at the local level, we will find that while the overall risks are under control, there are wide local differences in economic development, government debt management, and control on government debt. Some regions have already encountered difficulties in repaying debt, so in fact there are local risks. If we look beyond the short-term perspective and focus on the long term, we can also find that, while short-term risks are under control, various institutional factors behind local government debt risks are still playing their roles. The severity of the situation in some parts of the country is likely to spread nationwide. Therefore, there are in fact long-term risks.

It is worth noting that the local and long-term risks surrounding local government debt have emerged in the process of the Chinese economy making a shift to a new normal. There are three basic characteristics to consider. Firstly, after more than 30 years of high-speed growth, the industrial structure and factor input structure supporting China's economic growth have changed, and the Chinese economy has shifted from high-speed to medium–high-speed growth. Secondly, in the process of economic restructuring, mainly through addressing overcapacity, the price that has to be paid is the merger and reorganization of enterprises and even their withdrawal from the market. Thirdly, the spillover effects of stimulus policies since 2008 have continued, thus narrowing the room for macroeconomic policy selection and regulation.

The Chinese economy is now in a slowing growth phase, a painful structural adjustment phase, and a phase of absorbing the adverse effects of previous stimulus policies. In such a new context, local government debt risks are interwoven with a series of new problems that are quite different from previous ones. In the meantime, the prevention and defusing of local government debt risks are also faced with a series of new challenges that are quite different from previous ones. All these are making the situation very complex. Not only does the growth rate of fiscal revenue decline as economic growth slows down, but the pressure on fiscal expenditure rises with the pain of structural adjustment. Given the increasing challenge in fiscal revenue and expenditure, less room is left for incremental adjustment. The selection of macroeconomic policies is constrained due to the need to absorb the adverse effects of previous stimulus policies. Traditional macroeconomic regulation mechanisms and approaches are also facing many challenges as the economic downturn pressure intensifies. In a relatively tense macroeconomic situation, it is

[4] This is a slightly revised version of an article first published in *Guangming Daily* on September 10, 2014.

increasingly difficult to change the vested interests. How the economic system would function when the economy is making a shift is yet to be fully understood. In addition, the economic, political, cultural, social, and ecological advancement systems as well as Party building system are also undergoing changes in the process of deepening reform across the board. The difficulty in coping with risks is increasing given the considerable uncertainty in the institutional environment.

II. **Special perspectives: identifying the sources of local government debt risks**

In fact, local government borrowing is neither a bad thing nor something unique to China. In China and many other countries, there have been successful cases of developing the economy in debt. However, once we look at the current local government debt in China from special perspectives, we can see the fundamental reason for the risks or problems in local government debt is the very special institutional background of its formation and evolution.

Special Perspective One: The strong demand for borrowing stems from the strong impulse to attract investment.

One of the basic facts that can be observed is that in today's China local governments have a strong need to borrow. Nearly all local governments would grab every chance to borrow money and even consider it better to be highly indebted.

The strong demand for borrowing stems from the strong demand for investment which results from the pursuit of GDP growth. In this chain of relations with a special institutional background, the fierce competition between local governments in attracting investment is in fact the main driving force behind China's rapid economic growth for more than 30 years.

The introduction of investment always comes with a price. Then what exactly are local governments offering to attract investment?

Prior to 1994, local governments mainly relied on indiscriminate tax incentives to attract investment. Therefore, the competition between local governments in attracting investment at the time was mainly manifested in how much tax incentives they would offer.

The fiscal and tax reforms of 1994 made it impossible to offer indiscriminate tax incentives. As a result, arbitrary charges began to replace tax incentives. Arbitrary charges were levied on enterprises and residents to obtain funds that were used as incentives for investors. It became a new way for local governments to attract investment.

In the late 1990s, arbitrary charges were made impossible because of the tax-for-fee reform. Local governments had to find another way to attract investment. As a result, land-use rights were sold to obtain extra funds and infrastructure and various public facilities were provided for investors.

In 2008, the situation took a new turn. On the one hand, the practice of bidding, auctioning and listing made the sale of land-use rights increasingly well-managed. On the other hand, the international financial crisis affected China, and expansionary economic measures were needed to counter the crisis and maintain growth. Local governments' demand for investment attraction was coupled with the introduction of anti-crisis policies. In response to the slogan of scaling up government investment, local financing platforms began to be widely used. In the context of crisis response, local financing platforms were not subject to the budget constraints on local governments and could attract investment in the name of boosting government investment, thus driving GDP growth. As a result, the scale of local government debt grew exponentially.

A review of history shows us that local government debt today is closely connected to the indiscriminate tax incentives, arbitrary charges, and improper sale of land-use rights in the past. From pursuing development and political achievements to launching projects, increasing investment and borrowing money, this logical chain of local government debt reminds us that the root cause of the problem is in the unlimited and blind pursuit of investment attraction caused by the only criterion of GDP growth. As long as this root cause is not addressed, the debt demand of local governments is bound to grow. As long as this special institutional factor is not eliminated, local government debt will certainly lead to risks, or even risks that may jeopardize the country's long-term stability.

Special Perspective Two: The flawed debtor personality originates from the flawed fiscal management system.

A borrower should repay money as agreed, which is a basic principle in the debt business. However, this principle is not followed in local government borrowing in China. The results of different studies show that a large number of local governments do not intend to repay debt in the beginning, and many are insolvent at the time of debt repayment. In other words, local governments are not debtors with sound personality.

What exactly is the problem? Fundamentally speaking, the formation of flawed debtor personality is directly related to the flawed fiscal management system. Although China seeks to adopt a revenue-sharing fiscal system, many facts are showing a deviation from the track of revenue-sharing system.

The revenue-sharing fiscal system involves at least three components, namely division of responsibility, classification of taxes, and tiered management. The division of responsibility means that the responsibilities of governments at all levels should be clearly defined along with the scope of fiscal expenditure. The classification of taxes is to divide taxes into central taxes, local taxes and shared taxes so as to clarify the sources of revenue for central and local governments. Tiered management means that governments on different levels exercise budget management independently and take care of their own revenue and expenditure.

Looking at the current fiscal management system, however, we can easily find that China has been far from being qualified on the three fronts in the past two decades. Moreover, the gap is actually widening after a series of so-called adjustments. A typical example is that 70% of the central government's fiscal expenditure should be allocated to local governments as tax rebates and transfer payments, and about 50% of local governments' revenue depend on the central government's appropriations. What's more, the majority of such appropriations are directly-granted special transfer payments and general transfer payments are obtained by local governments pulling strings with the central government.

Such heavy reliance on the central government and the considerable uncertainty in the institutional environment will not only make the local fiscal revenue and expenditure system flawed, but also make it difficult for the local governments to make long-term plans. Local governments cannot fully control their revenue and expenditure and are thus not capable of taking full responsibility for related activities. Over time, the foundation for implementing tiered fiscal management is weakened and local governments' sound personality as the primary fiscal management body is inevitably damaged. At this point, once the control over local governments' borrowing is slightly relaxed, they are very likely to resort to blind borrowing just like a naughty child who has been under the strict control of parents for a long time.

From the deviation from the revenue-sharing fiscal system to the flawed fiscal revenue and expenditure system, irresponsible actors, flawed debtor personality, and blind borrowing, this logical chain of local government debt tells us that the root cause of the problem is in the structure of the fiscal management system deviating from the track of revenue-sharing fiscal system. As long as the local fiscal revenue and expenditure system is flawed, it is difficult for the local governments to be responsible actors and then debtors with sound personality. As long as the institutional environment is not thoroughly changed, local government debt will always be linked to risks which may not exist today but will emerge sooner or later.

III. Solutions: addressing both the symptoms and root causes of local government debt in the process of deepening reform

Considering the extreme complexity of local government debt in response to the new normal of the economy and that the institutional flaws behind local government debt are the sources of real and potential risks, it is imperative to change the thinking for preventing and defusing local government debt risks and solving related problems. The only way is to deepen reform and adopt reform measures that address both local and overall needs as well as immediate and long-term interests.

One strategic choice is to start with the pilot program on local government bonds and then advance the reform to the level of local government performance assessment and fiscal revenue and expenditure system. In the process of deepening reform across the board, the management of local government debt will make a smooth transition to the new normal.

First, focusing on institutional reform and promoting the pilot program on local government bonds. Local governments, as primary-level fiscal management bodies, should have the right to borrow money. In any case, local government borrowing is a necessary measure to speed up economic development. Therefore, efforts should be made to facilitate local government borrowing. However, it is necessary to strengthen the management of local government debt at the same time. In fact, only through reform initiatives such as the pilot program on local government bonds can we identify and address various problems with local government debt, including local and long-term risks. Then it is possible for us to find an approach to managing local government debt that suits China's realities in the process of seeking solutions to the problems.

However, the pilot program on local government bonds is just a technical adjustment to address the current problem, rather than a fundamental reform. In other words, what it addresses is the external manifestation, rather than the core, of the local government debt problem. Therefore, the ultimate purpose of the pilot program is to address the institutional root cause of the local government debt problem.

Second, building a local government performance evaluation system in line with China's efforts to promote the modernization of governance. It is only natural that local governments pursue political achievements. However, the pursuit of achievements should not be limited to GDP and should not simply be unlimited and blind pursuit of investment. Since there is already a GDP-based assessment system that people are used to and a new one is yet to be put in place, it is necessary to abolish the GDP-based assessment system and incorporate the assessment of local governments and officials' performance in the endeavor to promote economic, political, cultural, social, and ecological progress and the reform of Party building system, from the overall perspective of advancing the modernization of governance. The ultimate purpose is to establish a system for comprehensively assessing the needs of local governments to make political achievements.

In this way, local governments will no longer focus on GDP- and investment-oriented competition, and then embark on pursuing political achievements.

Third, improving the local fiscal system and restructuring the revenue-sharing fiscal system. Different from public organizations covered by government budgets, local governments have two types of financial power, namely independently managing revenue and expenditure and balancing revenue and expenditure. Such financial power should be based on a sound fiscal revenue and expenditure system. In other words, with the support of a sound revenue and expenditure system, local governments cannot independently exercise the power of managing and balancing revenue and expenditure. It is certainly not the local public finance under a revenue-sharing fiscal system. Apparently, improving the local fiscal revenue and expenditure system by rebuilding the revenue-sharing fiscal system is the prerequisite for local governments to develop a sound debtor personality.

Faced with the arduous task of improving the local fiscal revenue and expenditure system and rebuilding the revenue-sharing fiscal system, it is obviously necessary to establish the following basic understandings.

Firstly, the revenue-sharing system is not a money-sharing system. Just as the rural reform of the year was to change grain rationing to farmland distribution, the introduction of revenue-sharing fiscal system in 1994 was about sharing money, be it the sharing of total revenue or the sharing of revenue by category, or fiscal contracting. Therefore, on the basis of dividing central taxes, local taxes and shared taxes, the central and local governments should have their sound revenue and expenditure systems respectively and manage their own affairs in a relatively stable environment. It is one of the basic characteristics of a revenue-sharing fiscal system.

Secondly, tiered fiscal management is not to manage money as needed. Just as the finance of public organizations covered by government budgets is not the same as that of primary-level governments, in a big country like China, tiered fiscal management should not be based on the principle of allocating funds according to the size of assigned task. In that case, tiered fiscal management is likely to be reduced to financial management of public organizations covered by government budgets, or single-level fiscal management. Therefore, sound fiscal revenue and expenditure systems at both central and local levels should be established in accordance with the principle of tiered fiscal management, so that central and local governments manage affairs separately under a tiered management system. It is one of the basic prerequisites for the implementation of tiered fiscal management.

Thirdly, the power to tax is not equal to financial power. In a country of unitary system like China, it is necessary to emphasize that the legislative power for taxation is in the central government. However, it does not mean that the fiscal management power cannot be delegated to local governments. On the basis of centralizing the legislative power, local governments should be given the power to organize and balance revenue and expenditure independently. It is one of the necessary conditions not only for tiered fiscal management, but also for the adoption of a revenue-sharing fiscal system.

6 Thoroughly Understanding the Fiscal New Normal[5]

The assessment of China's current economic situation inevitably involves an examination of the fiscal situation which is an important aspect for observation as one of the most comprehensive economic indicators.

According to the general public budget, national fiscal revenue in 2014 was 14,034.974 billion yuan, an increase of 8.6% over 2013. It seems to be an acceptable figure compared with the 7.4% GDP growth over the same period. If we look deeper, however, some facts behind this figure are extremely alarming.

Firstly, the 8.6% growth in fiscal revenue was achieved when a series of special measures had been taken, including increasing the profits contributed by some financial institutions. If the decline in fiscal revenue growth had been ignored and no special measures had been taken, it would be impossible to achieve such a growth rate and China would most likely fail to meet the budgetary target of 8% growth in fiscal revenue for 2014.

Secondly, in the 11th Five-Year Plan period, national fiscal revenue grew by 21.3% annually on average, nearly ten percentage points higher than the GDP growth rate in the same period. Even in 2011, the first year of the 12th Five-Year Plan period, the growth rate of national fiscal revenue once reached 25%. In 2014, however, the figure became 8.6%. Such a sharp decline in just 3 years is absolutely rare in the world history of public finance.

Thirdly, the decline has further accelerated since the beginning of 2015. In January, the growth rate of national fiscal revenue was only 3.4%, lower than the GDP growth

[5] This is a slightly revised version of an article first published in *Economic Daily* on March 13, 2015.

rate of the same period. Moreover, considering the feature of fiscal revenue growth—"staying at a higher level before going down", the replacement of BT with VAT in 2015 at the cost of cutting taxes of about four hundred billion yuan, and a further reduction of taxes on small and micro enterprises, it would be very difficult to achieve the budgetary target of 7.3% growth in national fiscal revenue for 2015.

Fourthly, the growth of China's fiscal revenue has been 20% or even more than 30% for many years, so people are used to the model of collecting extra revenue and improving welfare every year. Over the years, due to a host of institutional factors, China has failed to create a mechanism for cutting fiscal expenditure automatically with the decrease of fiscal revenue like that in Europe and the United States. In fact, in contrast to the slowdown in fiscal revenue, the growth rate of fiscal expenditure has not been substantially reduced since 2014. The huge pressure brought by the imbalance between fiscal revenue and expenditure cannot be underestimated.

Fifthly, since the beginning of reform and opening up, China has always followed a basic principle in the choice of fiscal policy, namely keeping in mind the overall interests and pursuing stable economic and social development despite the imbalance between fiscal revenue and expenditure when necessary. In 2014, a series of expansionary actions of reducing revenue and increasing expenditure were taken to meet the need for maintaining growth. In 2015, in the face of increasing economic downward pressure and risk of deflation, it is imperative to strengthen proactive fiscal policy and improve its effectiveness. Undoubtedly, this will further increase the pressure of revenue decline and expenditure growth, making fiscal management in 2015 even more challenging.

All the facts mentioned above suggest that the current fiscal situation is getting grave. We should not take it lightly, but try to draw new conclusions using new ideas and new perspectives. If fiscal revenue and expenditure is examined in the context of the new normal of economic development, we may come to the following understandings or conclusions:

First, the economy determines public finance, which is a basic rule well known to people. After more than 30 years of reform and opening up, the Chinese economy has entered a new normal of development. As labor cost rises, the demographic dividend is decreasing. The adjustment to vigorously develop the service sector inevitably causes the growth of labor productivity and a slowdown in economic growth. In other words, as the Chinese economy shifts from high-speed to medium-speed growth and enters the stage of single-digit growth, the growth of fiscal revenue will naturally slow down.

Second, the high-speed or even ultra-high-speed growth of China's fiscal revenue that has lasted for many years started in 1994. Before that, we also experienced years of slowdown in fiscal revenue. The trajectory of fiscal revenue growth over the past 30-plus years shows us at least two points. One is that the continuous high-speed growth of fiscal revenue after 1994 is to a large extent a correction of the previous continuous decline in the growth rate of fiscal revenue, which is remedial in nature. The remedy will not last forever and fiscal revenue growth is bound to get back on track when it reaches a certain point. The other is that the continuous high-speed growth of fiscal revenue after 1994 can be considered, to a large extent, the outcome of the fiscal and tax reforms in 1994 so it is like a dividend brought by the reforms. Such a dividend will not increase forever, either. It will surely enter into a state of decline after a period of time. This means that the continuous high-speed growth of fiscal revenue, especially that higher or even much higher than the economic growth rate, is a special phenomenon that occurs at a certain stage of development. It is normal only when the growth of fiscal revenue is in line with economic growth.

Third, fiscal revenue in China is mainly tax revenue. Under the current tax system, more than 70% of the government's tax revenue comes from indirect taxes such as VAT, BT and excise tax. It means that most of China's tax revenue are a component of prices. It is tied to the prices of goods and services, rising and falling with prices, and fluctuates violently due to slight changes in prices. When the economy is growing at a high speed, tax revenue is likely to grow faster than the economy. When economic growth slows down, tax revenue is likely to grow at a lower speed than the economy. Therefore, as long as China's current tax system and the composition of tax revenue sources determined by such a system remain unchanged, it is expected that China's economic slowdown will bring about an even greater decline in the growth rate of tax revenue and fiscal revenue.

Fourth, public finance does have a role to play to serve the overall interests of economic and social development, but this does not mean that we can be mindless of the pressure and difficulties we may face in order to achieve our macroeconomic goals. Instead, based on a comprehensive and detailed analysis of the various factors affecting fiscal revenue and expenditure, contingency plans should be made for handling various possible risks and proactive actions should be taken to prevent them. This will help to make relevant decisions and measures more reliable. In other words, proactive fiscal policy this time is an expansionary action aimed at driving the economy in the context of the new normal of economic development and radical change in the fiscal situation. Therefore, a very different approach should be adopted for proactive fiscal policy.

It can be concluded that the current slowdown in fiscal revenue and the resulting grim situation of fiscal revenue and expenditure are not only the reality we have to accept, but also an inevitable outcome of economic development. In fact, practicing fiscal frugality is to get back on track. In other words, compared with fiscal easing in the past, practicing frugality is the new normal of China's public finance.

In the face of all these changes, we must adjust our ideas, mindset, strategies and policies across the board and learn to live with the new normal. With a series of new actions that adapt to and lead the new normal, we should place the focus of day-to-day fiscal activities and fiscal policy operations on following the track of the new normal of public finance.

7 Fully Grasping the Economic Significance of the Change in the Principal Contradiction in Chinese Society[6]

The principal contradiction in Chinese society has changed from "the contradiction between the people's ever-growing material and cultural needs and backward social production" to "that between the people's ever-growing needs for a better life and unbalanced and inadequate development". This is undoubtedly a major conclusion drawn by the 19th CPC National Congress from an overall perspective. The rich implications of this historic shift that affects the whole landscape should be understood from multiple angles, and the economy is definitely an important one. Therefore, in the process of developing socialist economy, it is of both theoretical and practical significance to think about and explain the change of principal contradiction from the perspective of economics.

From the perspective of economics, the change of principal contradiction can be summed up as the change of demand and supply and their relationship. On this basis, it can be incorporated into the framework of economic analysis.

I. The change of principal contradiction from the perspective of demand

The people's material and cultural needs and their needs for a better life can both be explained from the perspective of demand.

Demand is both abstract and concrete. It is even clearly embodied. In the new era, people's growing needs for a better life can be seen at least on two different levels.

First, material and cultural needs which are undoubtedly needs in the traditional sense. In the past, limited by economic conditions and horizons, the people expressed or could express either material or cultural needs. In the new era, the main change in the needs on this level is an "upgrade", namely new and higher requirements are put forward. Specifically, it is embodied in material and cultural products. Such upgraded needs can also be expressed as the needs for higher-level and higher-quality material and cultural products.

Second, the needs for democracy, rule of law, fairness, justice, security, the environment, etc. They are apparently growing needs that have emerged on the basis of the needs in the traditional sense, along with economic development and social progress. The concrete manifestation of needs on this level in reality is people's increasing awareness of democracy, fairness, rule of law, participation, supervision and rights protection. People's needs have gone beyond material and cultural realms. Therefore, the main change in the needs on this level in the new era is the expansion of scope, from material and cultural needs to diverse, multi-level and multi-faceted needs. It is mainly embodied in institutional arrangement and policy design, and such expanded needs can also be expressed as the growing needs for institutional and policy products.

Furthermore, people's needs for a better life include both personal needs expressed by individuals or families, and public needs expressed by communities. Both

---

[6] This is a slightly revised version of an article first published in *Economic Research Journal*, No. 12, 2017.

upgraded needs for material and cultural products and expanded needs for institutional and policy products involve private goods and services that meet personal needs and public goods and services that meet public needs. Common sense tells us that the supply system of private goods and services is mainly the market, while that of public goods and services is mainly the government. Therefore, people' needs for a better life can be further expressed as the needs for private goods and services provided mainly by the market and the needs for public goods and services provided mainly by the government.

A series of changes in demand have occurred with the change of principal contradiction in Chinese society, including the upgrade from material and cultural needs to the needs for democracy, the rule of law, fairness, justice, security and the environment, and the expansion from material and cultural products to institutional and policy products, from personal needs to public needs, and from the market system that provides private goods and services to the government system that provides public goods and services. This is a main angle from which we can interpret the economic significance of the change in principal contradiction in Chinese society.

II. **The change of principal contradiction from the perspective of supply**

The so-called unbalanced and inadequate development is in fact an unbalanced and inadequate supply that affects the satisfaction of the people's needs for a better life.

The supply can be abstract and concrete, and there are even clearly defined actors. In the new era and considering the people's needs for a better life, unbalanced and inadequate development can be seen at least on two different levels.

First, the development in material and cultural fields is unbalanced and inadequate. It is mainly reflected in the unbalanced industrial structure coupled with overcapacity, coexistence of advanced productive forces and traditional, relatively backward and even primitive productive forces, and very uneven distribution of productive forces.

Second, the development in institutional and policy fields is unbalanced and inadequate. It is mainly reflected in the low level of the rule of law, weaknesses in social development, slow progress in cultural development, many problems in ecological development, and the wide gaps in development and income between different regions and between urban and rural areas.

Furthermore, the unbalanced and inadequate development in the material and cultural fields and in the institutional and policy fields can be seen in the development of both private and public goods and services. In addition, it should be noted that that development of private goods and service mainly corresponds to the market, while that of public goods and services mainly corresponds to the government. Therefore, it can also be expressed as the imbalance and inadequacy of private goods and services provided by the market system and the imbalance and inadequacy of public goods and services provided by the government system. It can be concluded that the market system is the main constraint on the unbalanced and inadequate development of private goods and services while the government system is the main constraint on the unbalanced and inadequate development of public goods and services. In this sense, the unbalanced and inadequate development can also be attributed to the imbalance and inadequacy in market and government supply.

In other words, in the face of the people's ever-growing needs for a better life, both the market system and the government system have the responsibility to solve or correct the problem of unbalanced and inadequate development. Not only should the market play a decisive role in resource allocation, but also the government should play a better role.

A series of changes in supply have occurred with the change of principal contradiction in Chinese society, including unbalanced and inadequate development in the material and cultural fields and the institutional and policy fields, unbalanced and inadequate development of private and public goods and services, the imbalance and inadequacy of private goods and services provided by the market system and public goods and services provided by the government system, and the imbalance and inadequacy in market and government supply. This is a main angle from which we can interpret the economic significance of the change in the principal contradiction in Chinese society.

III. The change of principal contradiction from the perspective of supply–demand relationship

The change of principal contradiction in Chinese society in the new era is, of course, the result of the change of supply–demand relationship, the two main aspects involved in the principal contradiction.

The shift from "material and cultural needs" to "the needs for a better life" and that from solving the problem of "backward social production" to solving the problem of "unbalanced and inadequate development" reflect the requirements in China's current stage of development and the priorities of the country's development initiatives.

In the past, faced with "the contradiction between the people's growing material and cultural needs and backward social production" and the reality that the main aspect of the contradiction is backward social production, the focus of efforts to grow the economy was naturally on the size of the economy, especially on economic shortage, and thus the size of GDP and its growth speed. GDP growth was basically regarded as the only yardstick for judging whether the economic situation was good or bad. A fast growth rate means a good situation; a slow growth rate means a bad situation. A faster growth suggests a good situation and effectiveness of efforts while a slower growth suggests a bad one and ineffectiveness of efforts. The pursuit of high-speed growth and the only focus on GDP were seen everywhere across the country.

In the new era, facing the "contradiction between the people's ever-growing needs for a better life and unbalanced and inadequate development" and the reality that the main aspect of the contradiction is unbalanced and inadequate development, the focus of the efforts to grow the economy should naturally be shifted to quality and efficiency. Moreover, the focus on material and cultural products should be expanded to all areas and aspects concerning all-round human development and social progress, including material and cultural products as well as institutional and policy products. In the meantime, considering that the people's ever-growing needs for a better life are more expressed in their needs for institutional and policy products and the main constraint on such growing needs is the unbalanced and inadequate supply of the government system, the top priority should be giving equal importance to the supply of material and cultural products and that of institutional and policy products to accelerate the modernization of governance and establish a modern governance system that better meets the people's ever-growing needs in economic, political, cultural, social and ecological areas.

In other words, the top priority of the efforts to grow the economy in the new era is to pursue more equitable and sustainable development featuring higher quality and better efficiency and better achieve all-round development of all social programs and better develop socialism with Chinese characteristics while continuing to advance economic development.

IV. **Conclusion**

Interpretating the economic significance of the change in the principal contradiction in Chinese society is not just for the sake of academic research but has greater importance in five aspects. First, it helps to identify the main factors that affect the satisfaction of the people's aspirations, expectations and needs for a better life. Second, it helps to clarify the responsibilities of the market and government systems in meeting the people's needs for a better life and create a new model in which the market plays a decisive role, and the government plays a better role. Third, it helps to find ways to effectively set up the system and mechanism for solving the problem of unbalanced and inadequate development. Fourth, it helps to reveal the shift of attention from material and cultural needs to the needs for a better life and from backward social production to unbalanced and inadequate development, and guide practices for developing the economy in the new era. Fifth, it helps to understand the necessity of continuing to focus on economic development and giving priority to improving the quality of development and all-round development, so as to meet the people's ever-growing needs for a better life with more balanced and adequate supply.

8 Proper Macroeconomic Analysis Amid a Complex and Challenging Situation[7]

China's economic situation since the beginning of 2019, if summed up in one sentence, is marked by the interplay of both short-term and long-term, external and internal, and cyclical and structural problems. This undoubtedly poses a challenge to the current macroeconomic analysis.

If we were only facing short-term, external and cyclical problems, we could gain theoretical and methodological support from conventional macroeconomic theories

[7] This is a slightly revised version of an article first published in *Economic Research Journal*, No. 1, 2019.

represented by demand management as well as inspiration from domestic and international crisis response practices. If we were facing only long-term, internal and structural problems, the macroeconomic regulatory system of the new era that has taken shape since the 18th CPC National Congress and meets the needs for high-quality development as well as relevant explorations that have continued for years can also provide us with a whole set of conclusions and action plans.

However, when problems of the two aspects come together and affect each other, macroeconomic analysis becomes not so simple and the support on theoretical and practical levels becomes not so effective.

Apparently, we need to address problems in both aspects. We should not adopt strong stimulus policies that will harm long-term development for the purpose of achieving short-term balance and offsetting economic downward pressure. Nor should we only focus on long-term development and structural adjustment but respond slowly to short-term fluctuations and economic downward pressure, thus driving economic growth out of an appropriate range. Therefore, the focus and challenge of conducting macroeconomic analysis in the current stage is to properly deal with the relationships between size and structure, immediate and long-term interests, and domestic and international markets, and strengthen policy coordination.

Considering objectives in both aspects does not mean giving equal importance to them. Problems can be divided into primary and secondary ones, so can policy clues. To maintain the good momentum of economic development, it is of course necessary to strengthen counter-cyclical regulation against short-term shocks, but compared to structural and supply-side problems, total output and demand-side problems are ultimately secondary ones. Demand management policy is not parallel to supply-side structural reform. We should not change course because of local and immediate problems or jump back to the demand side from the supply side when we encounter difficulties. Therefore, a focus of current macroeconomic analysis is to integrate measures for stabilizing total demand into supply-side structural reform and skillfully align them with structural adjustment.

Both the total output control on the demand side and the structural adjustment on the supply side must be based on the basic reality that the Chinese economy has shifted to a stage of high-quality development. High-quality development is not a label or a slogan but has a set of real implications. Every era has its defining theme and there is a particular mission for each stage of development. We should not look at today's economic situation from the perspective of high-speed growth or copy the practices in the stage of high-speed growth when introducing macroeconomic regulation today. The new development philosophy, supply-side structural reform, change of growth model and other major strategies in response to the characteristics of the high-quality development stage are the fundamental prerequisite for defining development ideas, formulating economic policies and implementing macroeconomic regulation at present and in the period ahead. Therefore, under the guidance of Xi Jinping Thought on Socialist Economy with Chinese Characteristics for a New Era, it is the core element and soul of current macroeconomic analysis to blaze a path of macroeconomic regulation that is consistent with the stage of high-quality development.

The graver the situation becomes and the more complex and volatile the environment is, the more accurate and effective macroeconomic analysis should be. The basic premise of being accurate is being expert. Only when we stay focused on a particular field of expertise and keep following developments in this field can we do research that really helps solve problems. The basic premise of being effective is being down-to-earth. Only when we are down-to-earth, focus on a certain field or a certain aspect of the problem, and conduct comprehensive and systematic research as well as strict and full investigation, can we possibly produce useful, reliable and effective results. Therefore, being expert and down-to-earth, instead of being reckless and superficial, should be considered a fundamental principle for carrying out macroeconomic analysis in the current stage.

Chapter 2
Applying the New Development Philosophy

1 Introduction

High-quality development embodies the new development philosophy. The part, comprising five articles, is entitled "Applying the New Development Philosophy".

"Innovative, coordinated, green, open and shared development" was formally proposed at the Fifth Plenary Session of the 18th CPC Central Committee. It was originally called the Five-pronged Development Philosophy and later changed to the New Development Philosophy. Before that, there were similar formulations such as new ideas, thoughts and strategies on economic development. In this regard, the new development philosophy is based on such new ideas, thoughts and strategies and is actually an epitome of them. The guidelines, objectives, tasks and major measures for China's economic and social development during the 13th Five-Year Plan period should clearly reflect a series of requirements ranging from the new ideas, thoughts and strategies to the new development philosophy. The article "An Epitome of New Ideas, Thoughts and Strategies on Economic Development" was written based on a study of the guiding principles of the Fifth Plenary Session of the 18th CPC Central Committee.

As socialism with Chinese characteristics enters a new era, what should Chinese economists do and what are the issues of the time they face? The question must be answered. I wrote the article "Major Issues Facing Chinese Economic Research in the New Era" at the invitation of the Theory Department of *People's Daily*, In the article, I listed all the issues and explained them briefly.

Xi Jinping Thought on Socialist Economy with Chinese Characteristics for a New Era, which focuses on the new development philosophy, is derived from a series of new ideas, thoughts and strategies for economic development since the 18th CPC National Congress. To understand and implement the new development philosophy in macroeconomic regulation, it is undoubtedly necessary to look back on the formation of China's new ideas, thoughts and strategies on macroeconomic regulation since the 18th CPC National Congress and then sort out the basic framework of

P. Gao, *A Shift Toward High-Quality Development of China*,
Research Series on the Chinese Dream and China's Development Path,
https://doi.org/10.1007/978-981-99-8990-4_2

profound changes in the theories and practices of China's macroeconomic regulation. To that end, I wrote the article "Profound Changes in the Theory and Practice of Macroeconomic Regulation: A Basic Framework".

In the second half of 2018, the trade frictions between China and the United States posed serious threat to the Chinese economy, which was already facing severe challenges. What should we do about the major uncertainties related to China's development, and how should we respond to the economic situation marked by worrying changes amid stability? As it concerns economic development in 2019 and beyond, we must give answer the questions prudently. I wrote the article "Sustaining Effective Macroeconomic Regulation Under Steady Economic Performance in a Constantly Changing Environment" at the invitation of *Qiushi* magazine. The basic idea of the article is that in the face of changes amid economic stability, we must maintain the focus of macroeconomic regulation, adhere to the new development philosophy, continue with the supply-side structural reform as the main task, and stabilize expectations with a stable macroeconomic environment.

The pursuit of high-quality development is the fundamental requirement for defining development ideas, formulating economic policies and implementing macroeconomic regulation at present and in the period ahead. It has been considered the general guideline for the new stage of China's economic development. Since the biggest obstacle to the promotion of high-quality economic development is conventional thinking, the key is naturally to give up conventional thinking. The theme of the article "Pursuing High-quality Development Calls for 'Thinking Outside the Box'" is how to identify and give up conventional thinking to avoid some specious decisions in the process of promoting high-quality development and thus ensure steady progress in the pursuit of high-quality economic development.

2 An Epitome of New Ideas, Thoughts and Strategies on Economic Development[1]

Since the 18th CPC National Congress, academics and decision makers have been thinking deeply about the profound and complicated changes in the domestic and international economic landscape. More importantly, on the basis of constantly deepen its understanding of the laws underlying governance by a communist party, the building of socialism, and the development of human society, the CPC Central Committee has gradually produced a series of new ideas, thoughts and strategies concerning economic development. The Proposal of the CPC Central Committee on Formulating the 13th Five-Year Plan for National Economic and Social Development adopted at the Fifth Plenary Session of the 18th CPC Central Committee is an epitome of such new ideas, thoughts and strategies.

---

[1] This is a slightly revised edition of "An Epitome of the Party's New Ideas, Thoughts and Strategies in Leading Economic Development", first published in *Finance and Trade Economics*, No. 12, 2015.

It is undoubtedly necessary to review how these new ideas, thoughts and strategies on economic development have formed.

The Central Economic Work Conference held from December 15 to 16, 2012 was the first important national conference held after the 18th CPC National Congress. On the basis of comprehensively assessing the economic and social situations at home and abroad, the conference did not place emphasis on "fast" economic growth for the first time. Such formulations as "sustained, rapid, coordinated and healthy growth", "stable and relatively fast growth", "fast and healthy growth" and "healthy and fast growth" were no longer used. Instead, the goal of economic work was defined as "achieving sustained and healthy economic development and social harmony and stability", and the focus of leading economic work was put on improving the quality and efficiency of development and accelerating the creation of a new growth model. In addition, to strengthen and improve macroeconomic regulation, the composition of macroeconomic policies as a tool of counter-cyclical regulation was changed for the first time. The role of macroeconomic policies was no longer limited to ironing out cyclical fluctuations but was defined as "enabling counter-cyclical regulation and promoting structural adjustment", so their functions became two-folded.

The Third Plenary Session of the 18th CPC Central Committee was held in November 2013. In the Decision of the CPC Central Committee on Several Major Issues Concerning Deepening Reform Across the Board adopted by the Plenary Session, systematic arrangements were made for deepening reform across the board based on the conclusion that China has entered a new stage of development and a critical period of reform In such a context, reform was introduced into the scope of macroeconomic policies. Under the heading of "Improving the Macroeconomic Regulatory System", the main tasks of macroeconomic regulation were clearly defined as maintaining the balance of economic output, promoting the coordination of major economic structures and improving the distribution of productive forces, mitigating the impact of cyclical fluctuations, preventing regional and systemic risks, stabilizing market expectations, and achieving sustained and healthy economic development.

At the Central Economic Work Conference held in December 10–13 of the same year, "pursuing progress while maintaining stability" was added to "reform and innovation". It was stressed that while following the general principle of pursuing progress while maintaining stability, reform and innovation should be carried out in all areas of economic and social development, reform should be leveraged to promote development, change of growth model, structural adjustment and the improvement of people's lives, and reform ideas and approaches should be used to improve macroeconomic regulation. On this basis, a new topic was brought up, namely comprehensively understanding the relationship between sustained and healthy development and GDP growth. It was put forward that the pursuit of development should not be simply considered the same as increasing GDP. Opportunities should be seized to maintain GDP growth in an appropriate range and promote economic restructuring so that the quality and efficiency of economic development can be improved without producing any adverse impact. China should do its job well in a calm and down-to-earth manner and make great efforts to promote reform and innovation to tap the powerful impetus of development and the huge potential of domestic demand.

At the Central Economic Work Conference held from December 9–11, 2014, the conclusion that China has entered a new stage of development and a critical period of reform was further described as the "new normal of economic development". Besides, focusing on the new normal of economic development, the new trends in China's economic development were comprehensively analyzed from nine aspects, including consumption demand, investment demand, export and balance of payments, production capacity and industrial organization mode, comparative advantages in production factors, characteristics of market competition, resource and environmental constraints, accumulation and resolution of economic risks, resource allocation model and ways of macroeconomic regulation. The conclusion drawn from the analysis is that the Chinese economy is moving to a more advanced stage marked by complete functions, more balanced structures, and better division of labor, and is shifting from high-speed to medium–high-speed growth, from the model of extensive growth based on scale and speed to the model of intensive growth based on quality and efficiency, from a structural adjustment focusing on incremental capacity expansion to one that combines stock adjustment and increment improvement, and from traditional growth engines to new ones. Understanding the new normal, adapting to it and guiding its development constitute the major theme of China's economic development both at present and in the period ahead.

The Fifth Plenary Session of the 18th CPC Central Committee held in October 26–29, 2015 reviewed and adopted the Proposal of the CPC Central Committee on Formulating the 13th Five-Year Plan for National Economic and Social Development. On the basis of a deep understanding of the new normal of economic development and a series of new ideas, thoughts and strategies on governance created thereof, China mapped out a blueprint for its development in the next 5 years and a longer period. Since the international financial crisis has damaged the engine of world economic growth, a new one is yet to take shape, and the impetus of China's economic growth from world economic growth has weakened, we must rely more on domestic drivers of development. Given the slow growth in global demand and trade, the rise of protectionism, and the scarcity of market resources, we must rely more on stimulating domestic demand to drive economic growth. Since the world is poised for a new round of scientific and technological revolution and industrial transformation, developed countries are promoting re-industrialization, developing countries are accelerating industrialization, and the cost of production factors in China is rising rapidly, we must accelerate the shift from factor-driven to innovation-driven development. In this process, we should stay committed to the pursuit of innovative, coordinated, green, open and shared development. In addition, we should focus on improving the quality and efficiency of development, accelerate the creation of systems, mechanisms and growth model advancing the new normal of economic development, maintain strategic focus, and pursue progress while maintaining stability. We should advance economic, political, cultural, social, and ecological progress and Party building in a coordinated way and ensure the building of a moderately prosperous society in all respects on schedule.

Apparently over the past 3 years major changes have taken place in the ideas, thoughts and strategies of the CPC for leading economic work, including defining the goal of economic work as "achieving sustained and healthy economic development and social harmony and stability" for the first time, bringing up the brand-new topic of fully understanding the relationship between sustained and healthy development and GDP growth, giving macroeconomic policies the dual functions of countercyclical regulation and structural adjustment for the first time, introducing a series of ideas such as pursuing innovative, coordinated, green, open, and shared development and focusing on improving the quality and efficiency of development, reaching the conclusion that China has entered a new stage of development and a critical period of reform, making systematic arrangements for deepening reform across the board, comprehensively analyzing the trends in China's economic development and further describing it as the "new normal of economic development", understanding the new normal, adapting to it and guiding its development, accelerating the creation of systems, mechanisms and growth model advancing the new normal of economic development, making it clear that sustainable and healthy economic development must be based on the stimulation of domestic demand, and drawing up for blueprint China's development in the next 5 years and beyond. These changes are the result of the CPC's deepening understanding of the laws underlying economic performance under the new normal of economic development. It also suggests that the CPC has reached a new height in its understanding of accelerating the creation of systems, mechanisms and growth model advancing the new normal of economic development.

In other words, in the 13th Five-Year Plan period, we are in a very different environment and stand at a new historical starting point. Therefore, all the economic research efforts centering on the development objectives of the 13th Five-Year Plan should be based on the new development environment and new development stage, and advanced based on the brand-new development ideas, thoughts and strategies. At present, it is particularly important to align macroeconomic policies with the goal of building a moderately prosperous society in all respects on schedule and integrate them into the Four-Pronged Comprehensive Strategy and the Five-Sphere Integrated Plan to promote the sustained and healthy development of the economy and society in an all-round way.

First, it is an indispensable task to maintain a medium–high economic growth rate and ensure that by 2020 China's GDP and per capita income of urban and rural residents are double what they were in 2010. Macroeconomic policies should and must be devised based on such a premise. Given the sluggish global economic and trade growth and the increasingly severe downward economic pressure at home, the expansion of domestic demand is in fact the focus of macroeconomic policies at least in the next 5 years. To reach the goal of doubling GDP and per capita income, China's annual economic growth must be at least above 6.5%. To that end, we must unlock the potential of domestic demand and ensure such demand stays at a sufficient level.

This means that we should not only continue to expand macroeconomic policies, but also increase their robustness and efficiency, to lock in the goal of achieving medium–high economic growth with sufficient domestic demand.

Second, since China's shift to a medium–high-speed economic growth is the result of the interplay between cyclical and structural factors and the effect of using counter-cyclical expansionary policies to stimulate demand and drive growth is wearing off, the policy of expanding domestic demand should be carried out together with the effort to combine demand management with supply-side structural adjustment. While moderately expanding domestic demand, efforts should be made to improve the quality and efficiency of the supply system, gain impetus for sustained economic growth, and promote the improvement of China's overall productive forces. This means that the macroeconomic policies aimed at boosting domestic demand are naturally focused on the demand side, but they cannot and should not be limited to demand. Working on both the demand and supply sides and maintaining a balance between stabilizing growth and making structural adjustment will become a standard part of the macroeconomic policies for expanding domestic demand in line with the new normal of economic development.

Third, in the context of the new normal of economic development, counter-cyclical expansionary operations and structural adjustment should not be limited to the level of policy arrangements. There should also be institutional reform. In fact, to achieve medium–high economic growth with a roughly fixed potential growth rate, we must rely on the potential growth rate and reform dividends, both of which are indispensable. The production of reform dividends is therefore an even more important factor to rely on. Some of the reform dividends are immediate, while others will take time. As long as the reform in relevant fields is substantially advanced and no less than 0.3 percentage point is added to the potential growth rate of 6.2% through reform, the target of achieving medium–high-speed economic growth can be achieved. This means that the macroeconomic policies aimed at boosting domestic demand are naturally devised on the policy level, but we cannot and should not be limited to policy design. We should go beyond policy design and consider institutional reform. The efforts to expand domestic demand should be synergized with the deepening of reform across the board. It should and must be an important focus of our efforts during the 13th Five-Year Plan period to introduce new systems and mechanisms for the implementation of macroeconomic policies for expanding domestic demand in conjunction with reforms in economic, political, cultural, social, ecological and other fields.

Fourth, since we are starting from a new historical starting point and conducting a series of policy operations based on the conclusion that China's economic development has entered a new normal, it is very important to make comprehensive and timely adjustments to the ideas, thoughts and practices that we have been accustomed to and devise macroeconomic policies that embody the new ideas, thoughts and strategies of the new central leadership on economic work. For example, the market should play a decisive role in resource allocation. Whatever businesses can decide themselves should be left to the market. The government should take the initiative to do a good job in fulfilling its due responsibilities and knows well what to do and what not to do. What we want is quality, efficient and sustainable development as well as development supported by sufficient employment and the improvement of labor productivity, return on investment, and efficiency in resource allocation. Keeping economic growth rate at a certain level is mainly to ensure employment. Macroeconomic policies should stay focused and send out a positive message of promoting economic restructuring. As long as economic performance stays within an appropriate range, macroeconomic policies should remain basically stable. The side effects of strong stimulus policies on economic development should be avoided. All these mean that macroeconomic policies should and must be based on the reality that the Chinese economy is moving to a more advanced stage marked by complete functions, more balanced structures and better division of labor, and must be aligned with the new normal of economic development. This offers an opportunity to create a new mix of macroeconomic policies under the new normal of economic development.

Fifth, the landscape of China's macroeconomic regulation is evolving along with the changes in the situation, the assessment of the situation and the thinking about national governance. The functions of macroeconomic policy have been defined to cover both counter-cyclical regulation and structural adjustment. Moreover, the objectives of macroeconomic policies have been set to include many aspects, such as stabilizing growth, ensuring employment, preventing risks, adjusting the structure, stabilizing prices, improving people's lives, and promoting reform. This means that we have to allocate the limited resources of macroeconomic regulation to perform the dual functions and reach multiple objectives at the same time. This also means that the room left for macroeconomic regulation is reduced so frequent adjustment of objectives or focus will be inevitable. Therefore, macroeconomic policies must be implemented and advanced with the dual functions and multiple objectives on mind. To give play to the fundamental role of consumption or the key role of investment in driving economic growth, we should put ourselves in such a complex and volatile context. In the process of coordination and integration, we should seize the opportunity of expanding domestic demand, and explore the ways of and mechanisms for doing so.

In short, an important conclusion can be drawn. The guiding principle, objectives, tasks and major measures for China's economic and social development during the 13th Five-Year Plan period, as set out at the Fifth Plenary Session of the 18th CPC Central Committee, embody a series of new ideas, thoughts and strategies on the CPC's governance since the 18th CPC National Congress and provide theoretical guidance for growing the economy in the context of the new normal of economic development.

3 Major Issues Facing Chinese Economic Research in the New Era[2]

Socialism with Chinese characteristics has entered a new era, posing a host of major economic questions to us. Answering these questions on both theoretical and practical levels not only concerns the cause of the CPC and that of the country, but also directly affects the development of socialist economy and that of philosophy and social sciences with Chinese characteristics. Therefore, it is of great significance to think about the questions from economic perspectives and give answers to them in the new historical context of the country's development.

I. Thoroughly reviewing China's economic development practices and telling a good story about the Chinese economy

The entry of socialism with Chinese characteristics into a new era is the result of long-term efforts. Such efforts certainly involve multiple aspects and angles, including the effort to development the economy. While we are proud of the remarkable achievements that we have made in the endeavor to develop socialist economy, from the founding of the People's Republic of China to the introduction of the reform and opening-up policy and then the entry into a new era, one question that cannot be avoided and must be answered is how the Chinese economy has got to where it is today.

Economics is a highly practical science and one of its fundamental roles is to review practices. Chinese economists should certainly look at China's practices in developing the economy, analyze them and summarize the laws underlying such practices, grasping the overall process of China's economic development.

China's success in economic development is by no means accidental. It must be because we have done something right. We may have crossed the river by feeling the stones, but they must be the right stones. What we have done right cannot be found in Western economics textbooks, nor can they be borrowed from classic Marxist writers. It can only come from China's exploratory efforts and be rooted in China's national conditions. To sum up what has been done right in practice and clearly explain the course of China's economic development is a theoretical innovation and a theoretical contribution to economics.

It is fair to say that we have not done enough or performed well enough so far on the front of reviewing China's practices in developing a socialist economy. Because of that, not only do the stories about the Chinese economy spread across the world not match China's economic success, but also the discourse power of Chinese economists on the world stage does not match the status of the Chinese economy in the world. It might not affect the bigger picture in the past. In the new era, however, telling a good story about the Chinese economy and giving voice to Chinese economists in the world is no longer a matter of choice but something we what must do and must do well. The question is how to do it.

---

[2] This is a slightly revised version of an article first published in *People's Daily* on January 8, 2018.

Firstly, we should sort out the basic trajectory of China's economic development. This apparently requires a historical analysis. Based on an extensive review of historical materials about China's reform and opening up for nearly 40 years and economic development for nearly 70 years, we should look at history in an objective and all-round way, summarize the essential factors, and clearly explain how the Chinese economy has evolved.

Secondly, we should summarize China's basic experience in pursuing economic development. All the practices China has adopted in the past 40 years of reform and opening up and 70 years of economic development should be examined thoroughly and objectively. Based on historical analysis, we can draw conclusions about China's basic experience and lessons in the pursuit of economic development.

Lastly, we should define the basic laws underlying China's economic development. Economics is a science which is about identifying the laws of development and creating a theoretical system. Therefore, on the basis of reviewing the basic trajectory China's economic development and summarizing its experience in this regard, it is necessary to upgrade it to the level of laws and make innovative theoretical generalizations. Otherwise, the Chinese miracle will remain at the level of experience, instead of reaching the theoretical height.

The basic trajectory, experience and laws constitute a trilogy in which we sum up China's practices in developing the economy and tell a good story about the Chinese economy.

II. **Adequately understanding the change of principal contradiction in Chinese society and doing a good job in explaining its economic significance**

As socialism with Chinese characteristics enters a new era, the principal contradiction in Chinese society has changed from "the contradiction between the people's ever-growing material and cultural needs and backward social production" to "the contradiction between the people's ever-growing needs for a better life and unbalanced and inadequate development". Such a historical change that concerns the overall landscape can certainly be explained from various aspects and perspectives. In particular, from the standpoint of socialist economic development, giving an explanation in an economic sense is not only a clear theme, but also a job that must be done well.

From the perspective of economics, the change of principal contradiction can be attributed to the change in the relationship between demand and supply.

From the perspective of demand, the people's needs for a better life are in fact their demand for a better life. The demand is both abstract and concrete. It is even clearly embodied. In the new era, the people's growing needs for a better life can be seen at least on two different levels.

First, material and cultural needs which are undoubtedly needs in the traditional sense. In the new era, the main change in the needs on this level is an "upgrade", namely new and higher requirements are put forward. Specifically, it is embodied in material and cultural products. Such upgraded needs can also be expressed as the needs for higher-level and higher-quality material and cultural products.

Second, the needs for democracy, rule of law, fairness, justice, security, the environment, etc. The concrete manifestation of needs on this level in reality is people's increasing awareness of democracy, fairness, rule of law, participation, supervision and rights protection. Undoubtedly, they are growing needs that have emerged on the basis of the needs in the traditional sense. The people's needs have gone beyond material and cultural realms. The main change in the needs on this level in the new era is the expansion of scope. It is mainly embodied in institutional arrangement and policy design, and such expanded needs can also be expressed as the growing needs for institutional and policy products.

Furthermore, both upgraded needs for material and cultural products and expanded needs for institutional and policy products involve private and public goods and services. Common sense tells us that the supply system of private goods and services is mainly the market, while that of public goods and services is mainly the government. Therefore, the people' needs for a better life can be further expressed as the needs for private goods and services provided mainly by the market and the needs for public goods and services provided mainly by the government.

A series of changes in demand have occurred with the change of principal contradiction in Chinese society, including the upgrade from material and cultural needs to the needs for democracy, the rule of law, fairness, justice, security and the environment, and the expansion from material and cultural products to institutional and policy products and from the market system that provides private goods and services to the government system that provides public goods and services. This is a main angle from which we can interpret the economic significance of the change in principal contradiction in Chinese society.

From the perspective of supply, unbalanced and inadequate development is in fact an unbalanced and inadequate supply. The supply can be abstract and concrete, and there are even clearly defined actors. In the new era and considering the people's needs for a better life, unbalanced and inadequate development can be seen at least on two different levels.

First, the development in material and cultural fields is unbalanced and inadequate. It is mainly reflected in the unbalanced industrial structure coupled with overcapacity, coexistence of advanced productive forces and traditional, relatively backward and even primitive productive forces, and very uneven distribution of productive forces.

Second, the development in institutional and policy fields is unbalanced and inadequate. It is mainly reflected in the low level of the rule of law, weaknesses in social development, slow progress in cultural development, many problems in ecological development, and the wide gaps in development and income between different regions and between urban and rural areas.

Furthermore, the unbalanced and inadequate development in the material and cultural fields and in the institutional and policy fields can be seen in the development of both private and public goods and services. In addition, it should be noted that that development of private goods and service mainly corresponds to the market, while that of public goods and services mainly corresponds to the government. Therefore, it can also be expressed as the imbalance and inadequacy of private goods and services provided by the market system and the imbalance and inadequacy of public goods and services provided by the government system. It can be concluded that the market system is the main constraint on the unbalanced and inadequate development of private goods and services while the government system is the main constraint on the unbalanced and inadequate development of public goods and services.

In other words, in the face of the people's ever-growing needs for a better life, both the market system and the government system have the responsibility to solve or correct the problem of unbalanced and inadequate development. Not only should the market play a decisive role in resource allocation, but also the government should play a better role.

A series of changes in supply have occurred with the change of principal contradiction in Chinese society, including unbalanced and inadequate development in the material and cultural fields and the institutional and policy fields, unbalanced and inadequate development of private and public goods and services, and the imbalance and inadequacy of private goods and services provided by the market system and public goods and services provided by the government system. This is a main angle from which we can interpret the economic significance of the change in the principal contradiction in Chinese society.

Interpretating the economic significance of the change in the principal contradiction in Chinese society is not just for the sake of academic research but has greater importance in five aspects. First, it helps to identify the main factors that affect the satisfaction of the people's aspirations, expectations and needs for a better life. Second, it helps to clarify the responsibilities of the market and government systems in meeting the people's needs for a better life. Third, it helps to find ways to effectively set up the system and mechanism for solving the problem of unbalanced and inadequate development. Fourth, it helps to reveal the shift of attention from material and cultural needs to the needs for a better life and from backward social production to unbalanced and inadequate development. Fifth, it helps to understand the necessity of continuing to focus on economic development and giving priority to improving the quality of development and all-round development.

III. Starting with adjustment of the macroeconomic system and exploring the laws underlying the modernization of economic system

The major change in the principal contradiction in Chinese society has posed many new challenges for the work of the CPC and the country. Its main manifestation in the economic field is the urgent need to build a modern economic system that effectively meets the people's needs for a better life.

Modernizing the economic system is a complex, systematic project involving a wide range of fields and exerting wide influences. Focusing on the main task of supply-side structural reform, the report delivered by President Xi Jinping at the 19th CPC National Congress made strategic arrangements in terms of innovation-driven development, rural revitalization, coordinated regional development, economic reforms, and opening up. Considering the modernization of the economic system an urgent requirement for getting us smoothly through this critical transition or a strategic goal for China's development means that the CPC and the Chinese government need to make major adjustments to the ideas, thoughts and strategies for guiding economic work. In particular, the adjustment of the macroeconomic regulatory system has a fundamental role to play. The focus and direction of the adjustment of the macroeconomic regulatory system is certainly to support the supply-side structural reform that puts quality and efficiency first.

As for supply-side structural reform, President Xi Jinping once said, "The CPC Central Committee has proposed to promote supply-side structural reform which is a major adjustment made to the thinking and focus of China's economic development on the basis of comprehensively analyzing the long cycle of the world economy and the new normal of China's economic development… We should consider supply-side structural reform as the overriding theme of economic development and economic work at present and in the coming period."[3] Since this is a major adjustment that involves the thinking and focus of China's economic development, it is not only profound but also fundamental. Since this is a decision made based on a comprehensive analysis of the long cycle of the world economy and the new normal of China's economic development, rather than a short-term or partial analysis, the adjustment is not short-term but would affect a fairly long period. What it concerns is not only the composition of macroeconomic policies, but also macroeconomic theories. Therefore, compared with the macroeconomic theories and the macroeconomic regulatory system that we are quite familiar with, the macroeconomic regulatory system focusing on supply-side structural reform and the modernization of the economic system is an unprecedented challenge.

To sum up, the challenges facing Chinese economists in this field involve at least four aspects.

First, changed perspective of analysis. In the past, the basic perspective of economic situation analysis was around cyclical factors and factors concerning total economic output. A situation would be either attributed to the influence of cyclical factors or regarded as the result of factors concerning total economic output. The economy would move forward amid cyclical downturns and overheating, caused by the imbalance between total demand and supply.

However, as economic development enters a new normal, the outstanding problems facing the Chinese economy are partly caused by cyclical and total output factors, but the root cause is the unsmooth flow of economic activities brought by major structural imbalances. The outstanding problems have changed, so the analysis based on cyclical and total output factors appears to be inadequate and limited. Since the root cause is the unsmooth flow of economic activities brought by major structural imbalances, the focus of economic situation analysis should naturally turn to the major structural imbalances represented by the imbalances in industrial structure and regional development.

Second, changed development thinking. In the past, the growth rate of GDP was often considered the only yardstick for assessing the economic situation. A fast growth rate would mean a good situation while a slow one would mean a bad situation. A faster growth would suggest the effectiveness of our efforts while a slower one

[3] Xi (2017).

would suggest ineffectiveness. The pursuit of high-speed growth and the only focus on GDP were seen everywhere.

However, in the face of the historical change that the Chinese economy has shifted from a stage of high-speed growth to a stage of high-quality development, the economic development philosophy we uphold today is marked by innovation, coordination, greenness, openness and sharing and the goal is to achieve more equitable and sustainable development featuring higher quality and efficiency. Since the economic development thinking has changed, GDP growth rate is not the only gauge for the assessment of economic situation and economic work. In addition, quality and efficiency indicators should be introduced and used as the central yardstick. Now that the objectives of economic development have changed, implementing stimulus policies for short-term economic growth is no longer an option we focus on. Instead, we should pursue sustained and healthy development of the economy and focus on improving the quality and efficiency of economic development.

Third, changed policy focus. In the past, the focus of macroeconomic policies was demand management. Keeping a close eye on demand, we would introduce counter-cyclical regulation in response to the cyclical fluctuations of the economy and the increase or decrease in total demand to ensure short-term stability.

However, the current focus of macroeconomic policies is supply-side structural reform. Since the focus of macroeconomic policies has shifted from the demand side to the supply side, efforts should be concentrated on the supply side. We should proceed from stimulating the vitality of economic growth and striving to achieve a new dynamic balance between supply and demand. Since the focus of macroeconomic policies is to solve structural problems instead of total output problems, the main approach which may not exclude total demand regulation would be structural adjustment and short-term counter-cyclical operations are no longer the main option. Since the main objective of macroeconomic policies is to improve the quality of supply and improve the supply structure, cyclical fluctuations and supply–demand imbalances should still be included in the scope of regulation. However, a series of major structural imbalances, represented by the imbalances in industrial structure and regional development, have become the focus of regulation. The top priority is to promote reforms for improving the quality, efficiency and impetus of economic development.

Fourth, changed approach to policy implementation. In the past, macroeconomic regulation was mainly achieved through policy operations. Various policy arrangements were made to fulfill the objectives of macroeconomic regulation and related systems and mechanisms were barely affected.

However, macroeconomic regulation in the current stage must break away from the limitation of policy operations and be extended to the level of systems and mechanisms. The main approach is to introduce reform initiatives to skillfully combine policy adjustments with institutional arrangements. Now that the prominent problems have changed from total output imbalances to structural imbalances and short-term counter-cyclical operations are no longer as effective as they were, we can only shift the focus of efforts to structural adjustment. Since the fundamental cause of supply-side structural problems is in systems and mechanisms, policy operations are definitely not enough, and the reform of systems and mechanisms has to be carried out. The fundamental way is to break through the obstacles in systems and mechanisms through reform, and to pave the way for supply-side structural reform by promoting various basic reforms.

In light of the changes that have taken place and we are going through, the report delivered at the 19th CPC National Congress put forward the task of "developing new ways to improve macroeconomic regulation". Recognizing that the precondition for accomplishing the task is to improve macroeconomic theories, we should also note that some seemingly new approaches are emerging in the efforts to develop the macroeconomic regulatory system and modernize the economic system. The main reason is that theoretical explanation is not clear, or not clear enough to make the majority understand the situation. A conclusion that can be drawn immediately is that the task facing Chinese economists is rather tough when it comes to exploring the laws underlying the efforts to develop the macroeconomic regulatory system and modernize the economic system with supply-side structural reform as the theme.

IV. **Developing Socialist political economy with Chinese characteristics for a new era**

Socialism with Chinese characteristics has entered a new era, which is manifested in both practical and theoretical achievements. The path, theory, system, and culture of socialism with Chinese characteristics should be developed in an all-round way at the same time. In this sense, a more important and urgent task for Chinese economic researchers in the new era is to focus on the major issues facing China's and the world's economic development and build a socialist political economy with Chinese characteristics that fully embodies Chinese characteristics, Chinese style and Chinese vision in guiding principles, discipline system, academic system, and discourse system. As President Xi Jinping once said, "We should introduce to the world not only Chinese food, but also Chinese academics, Chinese theories, and Chinese philosophy and social sciences. We should present the world a developing and opening China that is contributing to human civilization.[4]"

To build a theoretical system requires the preparation of a well-balanced framework and sufficient components. Although it is not easy to do that for China in a new era of socialism with Chinese characteristics, the basic conditions are already in place.

As far as the former is concerned, the most fundamental task of socialist political economy with Chinese characteristics is to help solve China's problems under the guidance of Marxism and based on China's practices. Therefore, we should focus on what we are doing when seeking to build socialist political economy with Chinese characteristics at a new historical starting point. This means to identify major issues concerning the overall development of the CPC and the country in China's practices of promoting economic reform and development so that the research of socialist political economy with Chinese characteristics is in line with our practical

[4] Xi (2016).

concerns. Producing useful research results on that basis to achieve positive interactions between economic theories and practices should and must be the focus of efforts to create a theoretical framework of socialist political economy with Chinese characteristics.

As far as the latter is concerned, there is nothing to worry about. The practices of reform and opening up for nearly 40 years and those of economic development for nearly 70 years, as well as the views, propositions, ideas and thoughts that have actually played a role in supporting those practices are the basic components of socialist political economy with Chinese characteristics. In other words, although China has followed a path of economic development different from that in Western countries and Chinese economists have made theoretical contributions using a research paradigm that is different from those of mainstream Western economists and Marxist classic writers, they have been proved to be the right thing to do. However, we need to make a comprehensive review of these components to produce a new theory with scientific rationality and devise new practices.

For Chinese economists, this is the only way to build socialist political economy with Chinese characteristics and to make their due contributions to global economics.

4 Profound Changes in the Theory and Practice of Macroeconomic Regulation: A Basic Framework[5]

Xi Jinping Thought on Socialist Economy with Chinese Characteristics for a New Era is derived from a series of new ideas, thoughts and strategies for economic development since the 18th CPC National Congress. One of the important areas is macroeconomic regulation. It is undoubtedly necessary to look back on the guiding principles of the annual Central Economic Work Conferences and the formation of China's new ideas, thoughts and strategies on macroeconomic regulation since the 18th CPC National Congress and then sort out the basic framework of profound changes in the theories and practices of China's macroeconomic regulation.

The Central Economic Work Conference held in December 2012 was the first important national conference held by the CPC Central Committee after the 18th CPC National Congress. Facing the fundamental change in China's economic development, how should we look at the economic situation? The CPC Central Committee, with Xi Jinping at its core, put forward an important view that "the world economy has moved from a period of rapid development before the crisis to a period of deep transformation and adjustment", and "the Chinese economy has entered a period of single-digit growth". It was based on such a conclusion that the conference made two major policy adjustments. First, the emphasis was not placed on "fast" economic growth for the first time. Such formulations as "sustained, rapid, coordinated and

[5] This is a slightly revised version of an article first published in the column on Xi Jinping's Economic Thoughts on Socialism with Chinese Characteristics for a New Era in *Social Sciences in China*, No. 9, 2018.

healthy growth", "stable and relatively fast growth", "fast and healthy growth" and "healthy and fast growth" were no longer used. Instead, the goal of economic work was defined as "achieving sustained and healthy economic development and social harmony and stability". Second, the role of macroeconomic policies as a tool of counter-cyclical regulation was changed for the first time. It was no longer limited to ironing out cyclical fluctuations but was defined as "enabling counter-cyclical regulation and promoting structural adjustment", so their functions became two-folded. Therefore, the practice of simply focusing on attracting and making investment, launching projects, and beefing up production needed to be corrected and the focus of leading economic work was put on improving the quality and efficiency of development and accelerating the creation of a new growth model.[6]

The Central Economic Work Conference held in December 2013 reached an important conclusion about "three overlapping phases" that the Chinese economy was in a slowing growth phase, a painful structural adjustment phase, and a phase of absorbing the adverse effects of previous stimulus policies. On this basis, a new topic was brought up, namely comprehensively understanding of the relationship between sustained and healthy development and GDP growth. It was put forward that the pursuit of development should not be simply considered the same as increasing GDP. Opportunities should be seized to maintain GDP growth in an appropriate range and promote economic restructuring so that the quality and efficiency of economic development can be improved without producing any adverse impact. China should do its job well in a calm and down-to-earth manner and make great efforts to promote reform and innovation to tap the powerful impetus of development and the huge potential of domestic demand.[7]

At the Central Economic Work Conference held in December 2014, the conclusion about "three overlapping phases" was further described as the "new normal of economic development". Focusing on the new normal of economic development, the new trends in China's economic development were comprehensively analyzed from nine aspects, including consumption demand, investment demand, export and balance of payments, production capacity and industrial organization mode, comparative advantages in production factors, characteristics of market competition, resource and environmental constraints, accumulation and resolution of economic risks, resource allocation model and ways of macroeconomic regulation. The conclusion drawn from the analysis is that the Chinese economy is moving to a more advanced stage marked by more balanced structures and more complex division of labor, and is shifting from high-speed to medium–high-speed growth, from the model of extensive growth based on scale and speed to the model of intensive growth based on quality and efficiency, from a structural adjustment focusing on incremental capacity expansion to one that combines stock adjustment and increment improvement, and from traditional growth engines to new ones.[8]

---

[6] Xi (2017, p. 315).

[7] Xi (2017, p. 73).

[8] Xi (2017, pp. 74–79).

After answering the question of how to look at it, the question of how to do it naturally follows.

In October 2015, the Fifth Plenary Session of the 18th CPC Central Committee reviewed and adopted the Proposal of the CPC Central Committee on Formulating the 13th Five-Year Plan for National Economic and Social Development. On the basis of a deep understanding of the new normal of economic development and a series of new ideas, thoughts and strategies on governance created thereof, China introduced the philosophy of pursuing innovative, coordinated, green, open and shared development. It was also stressed that "innovative development focuses on addressing the issue of growth drivers", "coordinated development focuses on redressing imbalances", "green development focuses on creating harmony between man and nature", "open development focuses on coordinating internal and external development", and "shared development focuses on ensuring social equity and justice".[9] President Xi Jinping regarded it as "a solution in response to the new normal of China's economic development and the sluggish recovery of the world economy".[10]

The Central Economic Work Conference held in December 2015, guided by the new development philosophy, made a major decision to advance supply-side structural reform and further clarified the priorities of economic development. Moreover, focusing on advancing supply-side structural reform, the conference specified five structural reform tasks of "cutting overcapacity, reducing excess inventory, deleveraging, reducing costs, and strengthening areas of weakness".[11] As a major innovation in the endeavor to adapt to and advance the new normal of economic development and practice the new development philosophy, President Xi Jinping pointed out, "The CPC Central Committee has proposed to promote the supply-side structural reform which is a major adjustment made to the thinking and focus of China's economic development on the basis of comprehensively analyzing the long cycle of the world economy and the new normal of China's economic development, a major measure to resolve the difficulties and problems in China's economic development, and an inevitable requirement and choice for cultivating new growth drivers, forming new first-mover advantages, and achieving innovation-driven development."[12]

The Central Economic Work Conference held in December 2016 gave a systematic summary of the important progress made in the macroeconomic field since the 18th CPC National Congress, including "drawing the conclusion on economic development entering the new normal", "developing a policy system guided by the new development philosophy and centered on supply-side structural reform", and "following the general principle of seeking progress while ensuring stability".[13] The basic features of supply-side structural reform were further defined as "the ultimate purpose of satisfying demand, the main focus of improving the quality of supply,

---

[9] Xi (2016, pp. 38–42).

[10] Xi (2017, p. 33).

[11] Xi (2017, pp. 98–101).

[12] Xi (2017, p. 107).

[13] Xi (2017, pp. 111–113).

and the fundamental way of deepening reform".[14] In the meantime, its key tasks were extended from cutting overcapacity, reducing excess inventory, deleveraging, lowering costs, and strengthening areas of weakness to agriculture, the real economy and the real estate sector. A macroeconomic policy framework adapting to the new normal of economic development had taken shape in China, addressing a host of issues from how to look at the changed economic situation, how to work under the new normal of economic development, and the methodology for doing economic work well.

In October 2017, the report delivered to the 19th CPC National Congress took stock of China's economic development since the 18th CPC National Congress and concluded that the principal contradiction in Chinese society had changed to the contradiction between the people's ever-growing needs for a better life and unbalanced and inadequate development and that the Chinese economy had shifted from a stage of high-speed growth to a stage of high-quality development. Promoting high-quality development was not only defined as an inevitable requirement for maintaining sustained and healthy economic development, but also considered a fundamental prerequisite for defining development ideas, formulating economic policies and implementing macroeconomic regulation at present and in the period ahead. On the basis of defining the nature of China's economic development at present and in the near future, the modernization of the economic system was recognized as both an urgent requirement for getting us smoothly through this critical transition and a strategic goal for China's development. Then, strategic arrangements were made from such aspects as innovation-driven development, rural revitalization, coordinated regional development, economic system reform and opening to the outside world.

The Central Economic Work Conference held in December 2017 was the first national conference convened by the CPC Central Committee after the 19th CPC National Congress. At the conference, a series of new ideas, thoughts and strategies on economic work put forward since the 18th CPC National Congress were described as Xi Jinping Thought on Socialist Economy with Chinese Characteristics for a New Era. Moreover, it was clearly pointed out that China's economic development had entered a new era, marked by the shift of the Chinese economy from a stage of high-speed growth to a stage of high-quality development. Promoting high-quality development has become a fundamental requirement for defining development ideas, formulating economic policies, and implementing macroeconomic regulation at present and in the period ahead.

A series of new ideas, thoughts and strategies on macroeconomic regulation constitute China's macroeconomic regulation thinking, an important part of Xi Jinping Thought on Socialist Economy with Chinese Characteristics for a New Era. They include setting the goal of economic work as "to achieve sustained and healthy economic development and social harmony and stability, defining the role of macroeconomic policies as "counter-cyclical regulation and structural adjustment", reaching the important conclusion that the Chinese economy was in a slowing growth phase, a painful structural adjustment phase, and a phase of absorbing the adverse effects of

---

[14] Xi (2017, p. 115).

previous stimulus policies, comprehensively analyzing the major changes in China's economic development and further describing them as the "new normal of economic development", understanding the new normal, adapting to it, and guiding its development, shifting the focus to improving the quality and efficiency of economic development and taking decisive measures to change growth model, adjust the structure and alleviate overcapacity, proposing the new development philosophy of pursuing innovative, coordinated, green, open and shared development, making the major decision on supply-side structural reform, leading the economy towards more equitable and sustainable development featuring higher quality and efficiency, following the general principle of seeking progress while maintaining stability and mastering the scientific methods for doing economic work well, developing a policy system guided by the new development philosophy and centered on supply-side structural reform and an economic policy system that adapts to the new normal of economic development, putting forward that the Chinese economy has shifted from a stage of high-speed growth to a stage of high-quality development, clearly pointing out that China's economic development has entered a new era, and planning for the modernization of the economic system with high-quality development as the fundamental purpose.

Clearly, Xi Jinping Thought on Socialist Economy with Chinese Characteristics for a New Era was formed on the basis of taking stock of China's practices in reform, opening up and socialist economic development. A series of profound changes have taken place in China's macroeconomic regulation theories and practices, which are useful and have been proved to be right. They are not only the theoretical crystallization of China's 5-year endeavor of promoting economic development, but also the latest achievements of socialist political economy with Chinese characteristics and intellectual treasures of the CPC and the country. We must uphold them over the long term and continue to enrich and develop them.

5 Sustaining Effective Macroeconomic Regulation Under Steady Economic Performance in a Constantly Changing Environment[15]

Since the beginning of the second half of 2018, short-term and long-term, external and internal, cyclical and structural problems have compounded one another, posing new challenges to the Chinese economy and to the economic policy framework for achieving high-quality development in the new era that is taking shape.

Profound changes in the external environment would apparently increase domestic economic downward pressure. Will such changes and the increasing economic downward pressure affect our conclusions on the stage of high-quality development? Will the principal problem in economic performance and the main aspects of the problem change as a result?

[15] This is a slightly revised version of an article first published in *Qiushi*, No. 2, 2019.

To keep the economy operating within a proper range, the impact of external demand should be offset by counter-cyclical regulation to expand domestic demand. Does the implementation or intensification of a series of actions based on the demand side and oriented to expanding domestic demand mean that the main focus of macroeconomic policies will change as a result?

In the face of China-U.S. trade frictions, the most uncertain factor in China's development, it is natural to adjust policies in a timely manner in line with the changing situation and do a good job in macroeconomic regulation. Do the adjustments on the policy level, especially those in proactive fiscal policy and prudent monetary policy, mean that the focus of the economic work will change accordingly?

Under the guidance of Xi Jinping Thought on Socialism with Chinese Characteristics for a New Era, the recently concluded Central Economic Work Conference offered clear and unambiguous answers to these and other similar questions on the basis of deepening the understanding of the laws underlying economic work under the new circumstances and making arrangements for economic work in 2019.

I. The main problems in the Chinese economy's functioning remain supply-side structural ones

For a long period of time, according to the principles of traditional macroeconomics, we would analyze the economic situation from two perspectives, namely cyclical factors and total output factors. From the former perspective, the economy always moves forward in cyclical fluctuations, either cyclical downturn or cyclical overheating. Therefore, economic downturn and overheating are both considered cyclical or short-term. From the latter perspective, both economic downturn and overheating are caused by the imbalance between total demand and supply. Economic downturn is caused by total demand being less than total supply, and economic overheating is caused by total demand being greater than total supply. Therefore, no matter total demand is less or greater than total supply, the main problem lies in total supply and demand, and the main aspect of the problem is on the demand side.

However, as the Chinese economy is shifting from a stage of high-speed growth to a stage of high-quality development, the basic economic situation, the main problems in it and the main aspects of such problems are all changing. The changes in the economic situation are increasingly characterized by the compounding of cyclical changes and new development trends and of short-term and long-term changes. "Despite cyclical and total output factors, the root cause of prominent problems in the functioning of the economy is the major structural imbalance."[16] Total supply and demand is not or no longer the main problem, and the demand side is not or no longer the main aspect of the problem. "Structural problem is the most prominent, and the main aspect of the problem is on the supply side."[17]

This indicates that the traditional way of analyzing the economic situation is divorced from China's economic reality, and its limitations are becoming increasingly prominent. It is therefore imperative to expand the perspective. Attention should be

[16] Xi (2017, p. 113).

[17] Xi (2017, p. 105).

paid not only to the short-term economic fluctuations, but also to long-term structural factors. The effort to iron out short-term fluctuations on the demand side should be skillfully combined with the solution to long-term structural problems on the supply side. We should not only pay attention to the balance between supply and demand, but also improve the supply structure. The effort to address "acute diseases" manifested in supply–demand imbalance should be closely linked with efforts to address "chronic diseases" represented by a series of major structural imbalances such as those in industrial structure and regional development.

Looking at the new problems and challenges facing the Chinese economy from such a perspective, we can find that all these new problems and challenges have emerged in the process of shifting from a stage of high-speed growth to a stage of high-quality development. They are a manifestation of painful structural adjustment and a reflection of the deep-seated problems accumulated over the years. They are ultimately problems and challenges in the process of advancement which are to some extent inevitable. In the face of the complex and severe external environment and the economic downturn pressure, it is of course necessary to make adjustments on the demand side and take corresponding measures to stabilize total demand. In the end, however, there are main and secondary problems. Compared with structural and supply-side problems, the total output and demand-side problems are secondary. The adjustments on the demand side are ultimately minor and anticipatory. Profound changes in the external environment and possible shocks to external demand will not change the basic situation of China's economic development in the stage of high-quality development. This should not change our basic conclusions about the main problems in the functioning of the economy and the main aspects of such problems.

This means that, fundamentally speaking, the main problems in the functioning of the Chinese economy currently are still structural ones and the main aspect of the problems remains on the supply side. Therefore, based on the understanding that "we must look at the current situation from the long-term perspective and recognize China's bright development prospects in the long run", the Central Economic Work Conference reached an important conclusion that "the main problems in the functioning of the Chinese economy are still supply-side structural ones".

This tells us that we should focus on the main problems in the stage of high-quality development and the main aspects of such problems and address the problems and challenges that the supply system does not adapt to changes in the demand structure and that it is difficult for the economy to achieve a benign cycle. It is the fundamental way to maintain the sustained and healthy development of the Chinese economy and overall social stability.

II. **Pursuing supply-side structural reform as the main task**

Overall, the focus of China's macroeconomic policies used to be demand management. Its basic feature was to focus on the demand side and practice counter-cyclical regulation for short-term stability amid cyclical economic fluctuations. Whenever the economy went down and total demand was insufficient, actions would be taken to increase total demand. Whenever the economy was overheating and total demand was excess, actions would be taken to reduce total demand. Such a way of managing total demand was frequently adopted in the country's stage of high-speed growth.

However, as the brand-new idea of supply-side structural reform was put forward to replace demand management as focus of macroeconomic policies, profound changes have taken place in the landscape of China's macroeconomic policies. Since the focus of supply-side structural reform is on the supply side rather than the demand side, efforts are concentrated on the supply side. Supply-side structural reform is to solve structural problems rather than total output problems, so the approach which may not exclude demand management is structural adjustment. The core objective of supply-side structural reform is to improve the quality and structure of supply, so short-term counter-cyclical operations may still be adopted but are no longer the main option.

This shows that supply-side structural reform is in essence a radical adjustment to demand management. The way of managing total demand that has been used for many years is no longer the fundamental solution to all the problems. It is replaced by supply-side structural reform that is aimed at improving the structure and the quality of supply. While continuing to use the good elements of demand management thinking, adopting supply-side structural reform as the focus of macroeconomic policies at present and in the period ahead[18] has become an irreplaceable new approach to China's macroeconomic regulation.

Looking at the new problems and challenges facing the Chinese economy from such a perspective, we can find that these new problems and challenges are mainly structural ones from the supply side. In the face of complex and severe external environment and economic downward pressure, it is of course necessary to boost domestic demand in response to fluctuations in external demand and strengthen counter-cyclical regulation in response to short-term shocks. In the end, however, there are primary and secondary policy clues. To improve the structure and quality of supply, the stimulation of domestic demand is not a parallel objective, and counter-cyclical regulation should be carried out accurately at a proper pace.

This means that the focus of China's macroeconomic policies is still supply-side structural reform rather than demand management. The main purpose of strengthening counter-cyclical regulation and stabilizing total demand is to enable supply-side structural reform instead of returning to the old path of demand management. Therefore, based on the understanding that "we must accurately control the extent of macroeconomic regulation, make proactive and fine adjustments, and strengthen policy coordination", the Central Economic Work Conference not only reaffirmed the commitment to the central task of supply-side structural reform, but also put forward the policy of consolidating the gains in the five priority tasks, strengthening the dynamism of micro entities, upgrading industrial chains, and ensuring unimpeded flows in the economy, to further deepen supply-side structural reform.

This tells us that we must continue to follow the path of supply-side structural reform, strengthen the dynamism of micro entities, upgrade industrial chains, and

---

[18] Xi (2017, pp. 107–108).

ensure unimpeded flows in the economy on the basis of consolidating the achievements in "cutting overcapacity, reducing excess inventory, deleveraging, lowering costs, and strengthening areas of weakness", and consider it a general requirement for furthering supply-side structural reform and spurring high-quality economic development both at present and in the period ahead. Only in this way can we fundamentally address the problems and challenge facing the Chinese economy.

III. **Further advancing reform and introducing measures in accordance with market principles and the rule of law**

In the past, the implementation of macroeconomic regulation in China was mainly based on or reflected in policy operations. Various policy variables and arrangements were used to achieve the objectives of macroeconomic regulation. One item on the agenda of the annual Central Economic Work Conference was to plan for macroeconomic policies for the next year. This was obviously in line with the analysis of the economic situation based mainly on cyclical and total output factors, and for the pursuit of short-term stability. The main approach was to cope with cyclical fluctuations and supply–demand imbalances using various short-term counter-cyclical operations. Such operations were always on the policy level without affecting related systems and mechanisms.

However, as the economic situation has undergone profound changes and in particular supply-side structural reform has become the focus of macroeconomic policies, the implementation of macroeconomic regulation must not be limited to policy operations and be extended to the level of systems and mechanisms, mainly relying on reform actions. "Supply-side structural problems are caused by distorted allocation of factors, which is an obstacle in systems and mechanisms."[19] To overcome the obstacles in systems and mechanisms, policy operations are no longer enough and there is a need for the reform of systems and mechanisms. The core and key of supply-side structural reform is to identify imbalances in the supply structure and carry out reform to improve the supply structure, capacity and quality. The fundamental approach of supply-side structural reform is to deepen reform.[20] Reform should be used to remove obstacles in systems and mechanisms and pave the way for supply-side structural reform by pushing forward various basic reforms.

This indicates that, as the focus of macroeconomic policies in line with the stage of high-quality development, supply-side structural reform is still within the scope of policy, but not limited to policy operations. It also involves institutional changes, even mainly driven by reforms. In other words, it is necessary to skillfully combine policy adjustments with reform actions, and closely match the medium- and long-term effects of reform with the short-term effects of macroeconomic policies, so as to gather stable and sustainable impetus for economic growth.

Looking at the new problems and challenges facing the Chinese economy with such a perspective, we can find out that these new problems and challenges are increasingly embodied in the deep-seated structural problems under external impact.

[19] Xi (2017, p. 106).

[20] Xi (2017, p. 115).

In the face of the complex and severe external environment and economic downturn pressure, it is of course necessary to adjust policies, pay attention to short-term supply–demand balance, and strengthen counter-cyclical regulation. However, compared with the "acute diseases" such as economic downturn and insufficient demand, what we need to focus on addressing remain "chronic diseases" represented by structural imbalances. While carrying out various policy operations, we should extend our vision to the level of systems and mechanisms, step up reform efforts in key areas, and launch a number of effective major reform measures to ensure that reform plays a leading role. Only in this way can accomplish the real purpose of macroeconomic regulation.

This means that China's macroeconomic regulation in the current stage should rely on policy arrangements and more on reform actions, and the fundamental way is to deepen reform. Therefore, based on a series of understandings, such as "upholding the centralized, unified leadership of the CPC Central Committee and giving full play to its leading role", and "fully using the initiative of all parties to form a strong synergy for the bigger picture", the Central Economic Working Conference made a strategic plan of "further advancing reform and introducing measures in accordance with market principles and the rule of law" for macroeconomic regulation.

This tells us that only under the centralized, unified leadership of the CPC Central Committee can we deepen reform, focus on strengthening the dynamism of micro entities, push forward reform in relevant fields, and gather impetus for development through reform. Only in this way can we win the hard battle of supply-side structural reform.

IV. Maintaining the focus of macroeconomic regulation and stabilizing expectations with a stable macro-environment

Since the main problems in the functioning of the Chinese economy and the main aspects of such problems remain unchanged, the macroeconomic policy landscape featuring supply-side structural reform remains unchanged, the mechanism for implementing macroeconomic regulation with deepening reform as the fundamental approach remains unchanged, and the Chinese economy has shifted from a stage of high-speed growth to a stage of high-quality development, based on the Central Economic Work Conference's understanding that it is necessary to respond to public concerns in a timely manner and actively guide market expectations in a targeted manner, we can draw a very important conclusion that in the face of a generally stable economic performance some of which caused concern, we must maintain the focus of macroeconomic regulation and stabilize expectations with a stable macroeconomic environment.

The focus of macroeconomic regulation here at least has significance on the three levels.

First, in terms of guiding principles, we should fully implement Xi Jinping Thought on Socialist Economy with Chinese Characteristics for a New Era. Since the 18th CPC National Congress, the CPC Central Committee with Xi Jinping at its core has put forward and formed a series of new ideas, thoughts and strategies on economic work in response to the radical changes in China's economic development. A series of profound changes have taken place in China's theories and practices of macroeconomic regulation. These new ideas, thoughts and strategies have been developed in response to the characteristics of China's current development stage, and are fundamental to defining development ideas, formulating economic policies and implementing macroeconomic regulation at present and in the period ahead. We should embrace them in the long term. It is not right to panic and return to the old road whenever we run into difficulties. Even if we have paid a price for the time being, it is not right to ignore the changes that have taken place in the theories and practices of macroeconomic regulation behind and slip back into conventional thinking.

Second, in terms of overall composition, we should maintain the continuity and stability of macroeconomic policies. We should not be shaken by external shocks in our basic conclusions about the stage of economic development and economic situation, or in our determination to further deepen supply-side structural reform. We should not replace the pursuit of quality with speed targets in the face of economic downturn, jump back from the supply side to the demand side, leave behind structural problems, and focus on total output problems. Nor should we change course in the face of economic downturn, introduce fiscal stimulus, and ask the central bank to relax regulation.

Third, in terms of operation, we should introduce regulation in time and make proactive and minor adjustments to address new problems and challenges, which is essential for improving macroeconomic regulation and maintaining economic performance within an appropriate range. The adjustments should not be significant. Slow response does no good but excessive regulation is also harmful. We should neither cause massive impact on the existing economic policy framework and macroeconomic regulatory system, nor follow the old path we took in responding to the international financial crisis 10 years ago. The adjustments should be included in the main task of supply-side structural reform and skillfully combined with structural adjustments.

An important purpose of maintaining the focus of macroeconomic regulation is to stabilize expectations by maintaining a stable macroeconomic environment, and to prevent frequent and excessive policy adjustments from causing panic and producing a negative impact on the economy. We must understand that it takes a price to act on major strategic decisions such as supply-side structural reform and change of growth model and the tasks will not be accomplished easily. As long as the direction is correct, we should be focused and resilient, and we should not give up halfway because of local and immediate problems.

In fact, from the second half of 2018 to the convening of the Central Economic Work Conference, in response to the economic downturn pressure brought by China-U.S. trade frictions and their escalation, China launched a series of new targeted measures and policies which should be properly grasped and implemented on the premise of identifying the profound changes in them.

For example, although the "proactive fiscal policy" remained unchanged and it was noted that the policy should be implemented more effectively, the "proactive" here was no longer simply equivalent to "expansionary". In addition to increasing domestic demand, the policy was also intended to promote structural adjustment so that the fiscal policy could "play a bigger role in boosting domestic demand and structural adjustment".

Another example is that although the policy of tax and fee cuts remained unchanged and would be implemented on a larger scale, the main objective was not only to stimulate demand but also but to reduce cost and the latter was more important. Tax and fee reduction was no longer based on listing additional deficit and issuing more treasury bonds but was combined with the reduction of government expenditure.

Besides, although the measure of increasing the scale of investment continued, it was no longer purely targeted at quantity, but focused on stimulating effective investment and linking it with supply-side structural reform and the tough battle of financial risk mitigation. The purpose of expanding investment was to "gather pace in strengthening the areas of weakness in important fields of economic and social development" through "structural adjustment".

Moreover, listing additional deficit was also involved but the consideration was based on a thorough assessment of the financial risks facing China and the occurrence, evolution and consequences of the debt crisis in Europe and the U.S. so as to always stay alert to fiscal deficit and financial risks and ensure success in the prevention and mitigation of major risks.

There are many such examples. Apparently, while maintaining the overall continuity and stability of macroeconomic policies, we should make proper and minor adjustments, work towards our own objectives, keep the pace of development, and strive to do a good job in performing every task, translating pressure into a driving force for accelerating high-quality economic development. This is a strong signal sent out by the Central Economic Work Conference as well as a strategic choice we should make in the face of China-U.S. trade frictions and a series of new problems and challenges, such as changes in a general stable economic performance some of which caused concern.

Now at the stage of high-quality development, we must have full resolve and confidence strategically.

6 Pursuing High-Quality Development Calls for "Thinking Outside the Box"[21]

It is self-evident that high-quality development is of great significance to the Chinese economy as a fundamental requirement for defining development ideas, formulating economic policies, and implementing macroeconomic regulation at present and in the period ahead. It is imperative to take stock of the efforts to promote high-quality economic development, identify the main obstacles and remove them with practical and effective measures.

---

[21] This is a slightly revised edition of an article first published in *Economic Daily* on July 12, 2019.

In doing so, we would immediately find that the biggest obstacle to high-quality economic development, both in theory and in practice, is nothing less than conventional thinking. The key move is to say goodbye to conventional thinking.

First, theoretical thinking. In the face of new circumstances and problems presented by the pursuit of high-quality development, people are aware of the necessity to introduce theoretical innovation and change their way of thinking as well as the need to keep pace with the times in academic research and policy consulting. However, the training they have received in economics and the methods of economic analysis they have used are largely derived from traditional economic theories represented by Keynesianism. They are so used to the traditional theoretical and methodological support for the pursuit of fast growth. The new theoretical and methodological support for the pursuit of good quality is still being developed so it is relatively new to people. As a result, when there is smooth progress, they would take the initiative to discuss high-quality development, analyze the economic situation and propose economic policies based on new ideas, thoughts and strategies. When resistance is met, however, they would panic and easily fall back into the old ideas, thoughts and strategies, and into the trap of conventional thinking.

It is natural that people would shift between the two situations. They may be shouting the slogan of promoting high-quality development, but the idea of pursuing high-speed growth is deep-rooted. As they vacillate between old and new theories and drift away from the track of high-quality development, they would misjudge the situation, give the wrong prescription, and even repeat the mistake of pursuing high-speed growth and using old methods to address new situations and problems. Therefore, to promote high-quality economic development, we must go through a process of making the shift from conscious to subconscious theoretical transformation through deep reflection and careful consideration.

Second, practical operations. In the face of the new requirements and tasks for promoting high-quality development, people are aware that it is imperative to introduce innovation in practices and change their thinking and to correct the ways of doing things that are not suitable for the achievement of high-quality development. However, the course of economic development they have witnessed, and the model of economic development are largely rooted in an environment of high-speed economic growth. People are well accustomed to the traditional practices for achieving fast growth. New methods and practices are still being explored for achieving good quality. As a result, when there is smooth progress, people may stress the importance of high-quality development and seek to guide economic development practices using new ideas, overcoming path dependence. Once resistance is met, however, it is possible that people fall back into old ideas and conventional thinking.

Both smooth progress and resistance are normal. A lot of work may have been done, but perhaps in a wrong way. Vacillating between old and new practices and drifting away from the track of high-quality development have led to frequent missteps and even the mistake of pursuing high-speed growth again, leading to some unwanted results. Therefore, to promote high-quality economic development, we must go through a process of making the shift from conscious to subconscious practical transformation through constant learning and repeated attempts.

It can be an extremely painful and long process of transformation from being conscious to subconscious in the promotion of high-quality development and giving up conventional thinking on both theoretical and practical levels. We have no other choice but press ahead. Only in this way can we avoid some specious decisions, and steadily pursue the path of high-quality economic development.

Therefore, it is necessary that we stay alert and repeatedly tell ourselves that we are in a stage of high-quality development rather than a stage of high-speed growth and that the former is very different from the latter.

In the stage of high-quality development, the purpose of development is to meet the people's ever-growing needs for a better life rather than material and cultural needs. The focus is to pursue innovated, coordinated, green, open and shared development rather than the size and growth rate of GDP. The main problems in the functioning of the economy are structural problems rather than total output problems and the main aspects of such problems are on the supply side rather than the demand side. The focus of macroeconomic policies is supply-side structural reform rather than demand management. The main approach to macroeconomic regulation is deepening reform rather than adjusting policies. In a word, we must use the ideas, thoughts, strategies, and discourse system that match the requirements of high-quality development and discuss issues concerning the stage of high-quality development, avoiding impracticality in this process.

Furthermore, since promoting high-quality development is a path that conforms to the laws underlying economic development and a necessity for socialism with Chinese characteristics to enter a new era and for China's economic development to enter a new stage. It is worth enduring the short-term pain and the temporary price. It is highly undesirable to be hesitant or even change course because of local and immediate problems. Therefore, the only way to promote high-quality development is to look beyond the short-term changes and difficulties and at the long-term prospects of the Chinese economy to build confidence in the pursuit of high-quality development.

To sum up, we must say goodbye to conventional thinking for promoting high-quality economic development. It is not desirable that our thinking still stays at the stage of high-speed growth when we are already in the stage of high-quality development.

Chapter 3
Focusing on Supply-Side Structural Reform

1 Introduction

To pursue high-quality development means to focus on supply-side structural reform. This chapter, comprising five articles, is entitled "Focusing on Supply-side Structural Reform".

In December 2015, the CPC Central Committee proposed to promote supply-side structural reform and defined five key tasks of cutting overcapacity, deleveraging, reducing excess inventory, lowering costs, and strengthening areas of weakness. Therefore, taxation was associated with cost reduction, and reducing overall tax burdens was then regarded as an important way to lower costs. Since this was positioning tax reduction in the context of supply-side structural reform and examining China's overall tax burdens from the perspective of supply-side structural reform, the operations concerning tax and fee cuts and this would work out would be very different from those in the past. How to tread a new path of tax reduction would naturally draw attention from all sectors of society. It was against such a background that I wrote the article "Deliberating Tax Reduction in the Context of Supply-side Structural Reform".

By the end of 2016, the practice of cutting overcapacity, deleveraging, reducing excess inventory, lowering costs, and strengthening areas of weakness had been adopted for one year. Information collected from all sources indicates that cost cutting is the most important task that involve the largest amount of money, meet the least objection and are most effective in producing practical results. It is clearly attributable to the natural link between cost reduction and supply-side structural reform. I find that cost cutting is not a natural supply-side action, a natural action of structural adjustment, and even a natural reform action. With supply-side structural reform, there will be cost reduction operations and such operations will be carried out only when supply-side structural reform is pushed forward. Therefore, we should seek to find out how cost reduction would work out and base cost reduction operations on accurate analysis. "Cost Cutting: A Natural Supply-side Structural Reform Action"

P. Gao, *A Shift Toward High-Quality Development of China*,
Research Series on the Chinese Dream and China's Development Path,
https://doi.org/10.1007/978-981-99-8990-4_3

was a talk I gave at the 2016 Annual Meeting of the Cost Research Society of China, which was published in the first issue of *International Taxation in China* in 2017.

The Central Economic Work Conference held in December 2016 made it clear that we had developed a policy system guided by the new development philosophy and centered on supply-side structural reform. Thus, supply-side structural reform was positioned as a main policy. It was then defined as the focus of economic development and economic work at present and in the period ahead. In such a context, the significance of supply-side structural reform in macroeconomic regulation and overall economic work was rapidly enhanced. Therefore, major problems emerged one after another, such as how to further understand supply-side structural reform, how to further deepen supply-side structural reform, and how to link supply-side structural reform with the endeavor to build a modern economic system that can effectively meet the people's ever-growing needs for a better life. The two articles "Winning the Tough Battle of Supply-side Structural Reform" and "Improving the Quality of Supply System as the Main Task" were written in such a context.

The economic situation has become more complex and graver since the beginning of 2020. While the external environment is changing, the internal downward pressure is also increasing. How should we look at the goal of ensuring the economy operates within a proper range set by the Central Economic Work Conference and what should we do? I attempted to make a systematic analysis of the issue in the article "Ensuring Economic Operation Within Proper Range: How to Look at it and What to Do?". The main idea is that the proper range should be grasped from two dimensions: quantity and quality. Macroeconomic regulation should include both counter-cyclical regulation and supply-side structural reform, and the latter shall prevail. The causes of economic downturn should be assessed from short-term, external, and cyclical as well as long-term, internal, structural and institutional perspectives. Short-term and long-term objectives should be focused on addressing both the symptoms and root causes. Supply–demand balance and structural improvement should be properly balanced. In addition, the intensity and pace of counter-cyclical regulation should be well managed. The macroeconomic regulation operations that focus on ensuring the economy operates within a proper range pose a test to our capacity for deepening supply-side structural reform.

2 Deliberating Tax Reduction in the Context of Supply-Side Structural Reform[1]

At the meeting on July 26, 2016, the Political Bureau of the CPC Central Committee included "reducing overall tax burdens" in the list of priorities for lowering costs, provoking a strong response from all sectors. While no further official information

[1] * This is a slightly revised version of an article first published in *Guangming Daily* on September 7, 2016.

has been released so far, there has been much discussion about tax cuts, and eager anticipation.

It was the first time that the idea of reducing overall tax burdens was introduced in China in recent years. Until then, most of the related formulation published in the press and online had been at most about stabilizing tax burdens. In particular, the decision makers recognized it as the right strategy and effective way to the fulfillment of the five major tasks of cutting overcapacity, deleveraging, reducing excess inventory, lowering costs, and strengthening areas of weakness. We should not be surprised by the attention drawn to tax reduction but should instead take it seriously. We should actively and steadily put it into action on the basis of in-depth analysis and accurate assessment.

One question must be answered in this process. Compared with previous tax cuts, what makes tax reduction against the background of supply-side structural reform different?

I. **From structural tax reduction to reduction on total tax revenue**

This round of tax reform proposed at the Third Plenary Session of the 18th CPC Central Committee is carried out on the basis of stabilizing tax burdens. However, involving no changes in overall tax burdens does not mean that there is no tax reduction involved. The focus of this round of tax reform is to gradually increase the proportion of direct taxes. This tells us four things. First, for the purpose of stabilizing tax burdens, the gradual increase in the proportion of direct taxes would be naturally accompanied by the gradual decrease in the proportion of indirect taxes. A smaller proportion of indirect taxes actually means tax reduction. Second, it is clear that what are to be reduced are indirect taxes rather than all taxes. Third, since the increase in some taxes comes with the decrease in other taxes, tax reduction would not affect the level of tax burdens. Fourth, since the total tax revenue does not decrease, the original balance between fiscal revenue and expenditure would not be upset. Therefore, tax reduction does not involve direct cost, namely the cost of cutting government spending or increasing fiscal deficit. Tax cuts in such a context are usually called structural tax reduction.

The proposal of reducing overall tax burdens made at the meeting of the Political Bureau of the CPC Central Committee goes beyond stabilizing tax burdens and the changes caused thereof cannot be underestimated. First, since the focus is on reducing overall tax burdens, what is needed to be done is to make a substantial reduction in the scale of tax revenue. Second, to reduce the level of tax burdens, the target of reduction can be specifically defined as indirect taxes, or either indirect or direct taxes. Third, since there is no structural adjustment, as the total tax revenue changes, the original balance between fiscal revenue and expenditure would be upset. Therefore, tax reduction has a direct cost—either a reduction in government spending or an increase in fiscal deficit. Fourth, if tax reduction is combined with the current round of tax reform, there is a choice that can produce a win–win outcome—the combination of total quantity and structural factors. While ensuring the level of tax burdens is lowered, special efforts should also be made to reduce indirect taxes. Tax cuts in such a context can be called reduction on total tax revenue.

II. From cutting taxes on the demand side to that on the supply side

Tax cuts are nothing new in China, but those in the past were mostly on the demand side. We are familiar with both the mechanism and the practices of tax reduction directed at the demand side and aimed at increasing total demand. Firstly, the target of tax reduction is on the demand side, namely the reduction in tax burdens is intended to cause an increase in the disposable income of businesses and individuals, thereby stimulating investment and consumption. Secondly, since the purpose is to reduce total tax revenue, there is basically no need to identify specific types of taxes. Reducing taxes for businesses or individuals and direct or indirect taxes can all help to stimulate investment and consumption. Thirdly, considering the need to increase total demand, tax cuts are usually not made in tandem with cuts in government spending to avoid the offsetting of effects. Fourthly, as long as government spending is not cut at the same time, the original balance between fiscal revenue and expenditure will be upset. Therefore, it is the inevitable logic of tax reduction for the purpose of increasing total demand to achieve tax reduction by increasing fiscal deficit.

Tax cuts on the supply side aimed at promoting structural reform are absolutely new in China. Since the background and goal of tax reduction are different, the mechanism and related practices have their unique features. First, for lowering costs, tax reduction should be implemented to reduce burdens on businesses and individuals. As long as it is substantial but not nominal reduction of burden, resource allocation power should be transferred which means that the fiscal deficit after tax reduction should be coped with by cutting government spending. Second, if fiscal deficit is still increased for tax reduction, it would be the same as previous tax reduction practices for stimulating demand, which is against the original purpose of lowering costs. In other words, only when tax cuts go along with cuts in government spending can they be defined as tax reduction promoting supply-side structural reform. Third, given the complementarity between moderately increasing total demand and advancing supply-side structural reform, the practices of cutting government spending and increasing fiscal deficit can both be adopted but the former should prevail. Fourth, the policy objective of cost reduction should be linked with the objective of improving the structure of tax system, and targeted tax reduction measures can be implemented. While ensuring the objective of cost cutting for businesses is achieved, the focus of tax reduction should be on indirect taxes.

III. Major adjustment in the composition of macroeconomic policies

Shifting from structural tax reduction to reduction on total tax revenue and from tax reduction on the demand side to that on the supply side marks a major adjustment in the composition of China's macroeconomic policies.

From the Asian financial crisis to the global financial crisis, at least in the past 30 years, China's macroeconomic policies have always involved tax reduction but it has been introduced without affecting overall tax burdens and the scale of government spending. To make tax cuts without reducing overall tax burdens, the only option is structural tax reduction. To do that without reducing the scale of government spending, the only option is to increase fiscal deficit. Although such operations can help increase total demand and improve the tax structure, strictly speaking, they are not tax cuts in the full sense since the substantial burden on businesses and individuals will not be reduced. They are not tax cuts that work on both the demand and supply sides and mainly on the supply side either since the final allocation of resources will not be changed.

The most profound change brought about by putting reduction on total tax revenue on the agenda and integrating it with the structural reform to lower costs is that overall tax burdens are no longer untouchable but can and should be reduced along with the change of macroeconomic situation in the context of advancing supply-side structural reform. The scale of government spending is no longer untouchable, but can and should be reduced along with the adjustment in macroeconomic policies. Therefore, the traditional practice of not reducing overall tax burdens or cutting government spending is abandoned. A new composition of China's macroeconomic policies has emerged, marked by the shift to the key tasks of structural reform including cutting overcapacity, deleveraging, reducing excess inventory, lowering costs, and strengthening areas of weakness through the reduction of overall tax burdens, and increasing fiscal deficit and reducing government spending at the same time.

It is very important to reach such an understanding. It reminds us that in the face of the new developments in the endeavor to advance supply-side structural reform, we must comprehensively adjust the ideas, thoughts and strategies that we used to take for granted, adapt to the new composition of macroeconomic policies, and leverage it towards the goal of supply-side structural reform. This means that in light of the changes in the macroeconomic situation and policies, overall tax burdens and the scale of government spending should be adjusted in a timely and appropriate manner. It is the major theme of China's macroeconomic regulation at present and in the period ahead.

IV. **Dispelling the notion that tax cuts must lead to growing deficits**

It should be admitted that before the Political Bureau's meeting proposed reducing overall tax burdens tax-cutting operations had been, with a few exceptions, associated with growing deficit. No matter what the purpose or the form of a tax cut may be, reduction in total tax revenue was almost always thought to lead to growing deficits.

One typical example is current policy of tax and fee cuts represented by the replacement of BT with VAT. As a source of funding for a series of policies and measures such as comprehensively implementing the replacement of BT with VAT, abolishing or suspending a number of government-managed funds and consolidating some of these funds, and expanding the coverage of exemption from administrative charges, the fiscal deficit in 2016 increased by 560 billion yuan over the previous year, with the deficit-to-GDP ratio rising to three percent.

This is undoubtedly necessary for moderately increasing total demand and creating a stable macroeconomic environment for supply-side structural reform. The problem now is that as the urgency and importance of supply-side structural reform grows, the focus of tax reduction should and must be shifted to the cost-reducing supply-side structural reform in due course. To that end, we should seize the rare opportunity presented by the adjustment in the composition of macroeconomic policies and go beyond the conventional thinking that tax cuts must be linked to fiscal deficit. Government spending should be cut so as to mitigate the impact of tax cuts on the deficit. In any case, it would be the right strategy and effective way to push forward supply-side structural reform.

In fact, from the perspective of cost-effectiveness, we can find that simply increasing fiscal deficit for tax reduction is not only unsustainable but also involves some financial risks.

In 2016 alone, the fiscal deficit of 2.18 trillion yuan and the deficit-to-GDP ratio of 3%, which are included in the budget and publicly disclosed, are calculated only according to the general public budget. China has enforced the new budget law since 2015. The biggest change in the new law compared with the old one is that in addition to the general public budget it also covers three other types of budgets, namely budgets of government-managed funds, budgets of social security funds, and budgets of state capital operations.

If the fiscal deficit in 2016 is calculated with all types of budgets included, at least four factors should be taken into account. First, the special local bonds included in the budgets of government-managed funds are in fact a form of local government debt. Second, the funds for specific projects with a ninety-percent interest subsidy from the government are, in a sense, quasi-government bonds. Third, the local government bonds for debt swap that are permitted to be issued in the amount of several trillion yuan are generally not included in the deficit of the current year according to international practices. However, in China, such local debts had never been recognized as deficit and since they were given legitimacy, they have been recognized as deferred deficit. Fourth, in the current process of promoting PPP, in fact, many local government debts are incurred. All these apparently deserve our special attention when tax cuts are being made.

Common sense tells us that financial, debt, corporate, or any other risk will eventually lead to fiscal risks. The fiscal risks associated with tax reduction in the current circumstances should not be ignored. Only by addressing tax reduction and fiscal risks holistically and forestalling fiscal risks can supply-side structural reform be pushed forward in a comprehensive way.

V. **Cutting government spending is feasible**

Furthermore, today's China still needs to maintain the stability of its macro policies and stabilize growth and increase domestic demand by properly increasing necessary fiscal expenditure and government investment. This in no way means that there is no room for cutting government spending.

In the spirit of practicing fiscal frugality, we can see that there are at least four possibilities. First, the fiscal deposits amounting to trillions of yuan can be partly attributed to the mismatch between actual expenditure progress and budget. However, we should not rule out the possibility that the expenditure in budget is too high and the actual expenditure is much lower. Second, a larger quantity of deposits from government agencies and organizations may not directly under the control of financial authority we should not rule out the possibility that there is a portion that can be put to better use or written off by cutting the next year's budget. Third, since the CPC Central Committee adopted the eight-point decision on improving Party conduct, the scale of official spending has been greatly reduced. The reduced spending can and should be embodied in the reduction in the expenditures of relevant government agencies and organizations. Fourth, there is no denying that government agencies and organizations sometimes spend money lavishly or use money for the sake of spending money. Based on a careful examination of all cases, we may find that a considerable part of such expenditures can be cut.

There are many other factors like this. It is not impossible to cut taxes and government spending at the same time as long as we make up our minds and consider issues from the standpoint of the cause of the CPC and the country.

The above discussion can be boiled down to one point, namely tax reduction in the context of supply-side structural reform should and must follow a new path different from the past one.

3 Cost Cutting: A Natural Supply-Side Structural Reform Action[2]

I. The changing meaning of cost cutting

Cost cutting is undoubtedly one of the prevailing trends in China's economic development today. Since the Central Economic Work Conference in 2016 proposed the supply-side structural reform and made plans for the five major tasks of cutting overcapacity, deleveraging, reducing excess inventory, lowering costs, and strengthening areas of weakness, the idea of cost cutting has been frequently discussed on different occasions. Moreover, with the passage of time, we have gained an increasingly deeper understanding of its significance.

The significance of cost, an economic concept, should be self-evident. It is just that for a not-so-short period of time in the past, we focused too much on growth rate and too little on the costs of achieving or sustaining growth. As a result, the concept of cost which should never be forgotten imperceptibly faded out of the vision of many people. Even for economists who specialize in economic analysis, talking about cost and considering cost as a dimension of analysis is often a novelty.

In today's China, the significance of cost cutting is so strongly stressed because first of all we have reached an important conclusion that economic development has entered a new normal. Since the current economic environment is the new normal, the only option is to bear in mind the major changes in the economic situation and recognize that understanding the new normal and guiding its development constitutes the major theme for China's economic development at present and in the period ahead so as to tread a new path of growing the economy. Cost cutting is apparently such

[2] * This is a slightly revised version of an article first published in *International Taxation in China* No. 1, 2017.

a new path that is innovative. In other words, only in the context of the new normal of economic development and the shift to a track centered on improving the quality and efficiency of development can people realize the importance of cost once again and be driven to pursue the lowering of costs as an important economic measure.

The significance of cost cutting is also closely related to our policy system guided by the new development philosophy and centered on supply-side structural reform. Since the major problems in China's economic performance are caused not by cyclical and total output factors, but by structural factors or the interrupted flow of economic activities caused by major structural imbalances, the new focus of macroeconomic policies should naturally be on the prominent problems that are quite different from past ones and on finding a way out from the supply side and structural adjustment. Furthermore, since the fundamental cause of these major structural imbalances lies in institutional obstacles, in the failure of the market to play a decisive role in resource allocation, and in the failure of the government to better play its due role, to achieve a new dynamic balance between supply and demand by means of reform is undoubtedly the new focus of macroeconomic policies. Cost cutting is apparently a new focus on both the supply side and structural adjustment, as well as a new focus on achieving a new balance between supply and demand through reform. In other words, only in the context of shifting the focus of macroeconomic policies from the demand side to the supply side and from total output adjustment to structural adjustment, and only when reform plays an important role in helping achieving the purpose of macroeconomic policies, is it possible to ensure that cost, an important economic concept, plays its due role and cost cutting is part, or even a focus, of supply-side structural reform.

II. **Cost cutting is closely connected with supply-side structural reform**

Operations for fulfilling the five tasks in the last year show that compared with the other four tasks cost cutting is probably the most important task that involve the largest amount of money, meet the least objection and are most effective in producing practical results.

First, cost cutting is a natural supply-side action. As is well known to all, in the balance between total supply and demand, all the factors counting as costs, such as consumption, savings and taxation, are always placed on the side of total supply. Since the factors counting as costs are surely on the supply side, the actions related to cost cutting must also take place on the supply side. The corresponding changes in the factors counting as costs are often involved.

Second, cost cutting is a natural action for structural adjustment. Common sense tells us that costs never occur alone. There are always other factors associated with costs. Costs are what they are relative to particular factors, or what are incurred in order to achieve benefits or profits. Since costs are always tied to other related factors and serve as a component of a whole system that has a trade-off relationship with other related factors, the actions related to cost cutting must come down to structural adjustment. The corresponding changes in other related factors in the system are also involved.

Third, cost cutting is a natural reform action. The rationale is very simple. No matter it involves household consumption and savings or the government's tax revenue, cost cutting is a major adjustment in the distribution of interests. It cannot be achieved solely through policy-level arrangements or design but must be accompanied by reform actions. Since reform is the prerequisite for lowering costs, cost reduction-related actions must be accompanied by reform planning and implementation. What are needed are not general policy arrangements but major reform actions.

All these tell us a very important fact that cost cutting is a natural supply-side structural reform action. Supply-side structural reform is bound to be accompanied by cost-reduction operations. Such operations will be carried out only when supply-side structural reform is pushed forward. The two are closely associated with each other.

III. Special attention to cost cutting in the context of supply-side structural reform

Cost cutting is so important that it must be done with great caution. However, this is not an easy task.

It is fair to say that we are familiar to and have the expertise on macroeconomic regulation in the old normal of economic development. For example, over the decades of reform and opening up, the practice of adopting austerity policies when the economy is overheating and expansionary policies when it is cooling down has taken root in the depths of our minds. However, we are not familiar with macroeconomic regulation in the context of the new normal of economic development, and it is even difficult to give clear explanations based on our previous knowledge and research experience. The main problems have changed, and what we have to address them are also different from those in the past. This naturally requires different ideas, thoughts and strategies of macroeconomic regulation.

In terms of lowering costs, especially cost reduction operations in line with the policy system focusing on supply-side structural reform, we should pay special attention and be cautious to avoid falling into the stereotypes and causing specious results.

Take reducing taxes and fees for businesses for example. In today's China, taxes and fees are undoubtedly the costs most urgently needed to be reduced for businesses but reducing the tax and fee burden of businesses is not a new concept. We made policy arrangements for tax and fee cuts from the financial crisis in Southeast Asia to the international financial crisis. However, in the past, the main purpose of reducing the tax and fee burden was to increase the disposable income of businesses and increase total demand, so it was the adjustment of total output, and the focus was on the demand side. In contrast, the main purpose of reducing the tax and fee burden of businesses today is to reduce their costs and improve the quality of supply. It is structural adjustment, and the focus is on the supply side. Moreover, the driving force of the former is mainly policy arrangement, while the latter, though inseparable from policy arrangement, is mainly based on reform actions. This is a huge change. When it comes to tax and fee cuts, we must think clearly and plan carefully before taking any action.

Apparently, tax and fee cuts under the condition of increasing fiscal deficit is nothing different from what was done in the old normal of economic development and has little to do with supply-side structural reform. More importantly, given that fiscal deficit must always be made up by the issuance of government bonds. Newly issued government bonds can be replaced and used indefinitely, but there will always be interest payments on debt which must be added to government spending. The sources of funding for all government expenditures, including the interest payments on debt, always include taxes and fees, so at least in the medium and long term, what it brings is not a reduction but an increase in the tax and fee costs for businesses. In the meantime, it will not change the allocation of resources between the government and businesses. Therefore, the only choice left to us should and must be to combine tax and fee cuts with cuts in government spending and reduce the scale of government spending to create possibility for easing the tax and fee burden of businesses. Only such an approach will lead to a real reduction in the burden of taxes and fees on businesses, and a change in the allocation of resources in favor of businesses. It is also a cost-reduction practice that conforms to the new normal of economic development and the focus of supply-side structural reform.

Another example is the entity that lowers costs. In the past, cost cutting was mainly a task for businesses themselves. Today, lowering costs, as one of the tasks in supply-side structural reform, is considered at the level of macroeconomic policies and from the perspective of the country's overall economic development landscape. This may be the first time in Chinese history. The fundamental reason lies in the fact that cost reduction today is mainly targeted at taxes, fees and factor costs, especially government-imposed transaction costs. Taxes and fees are of course the costs imposed on businesses by the government. No matter tax and fee cuts are made by adjusting government functions and reducing the scale of government spending or increasing fiscal deficit without affecting government functions and spending, it has to be done by the government. The reduction of factor costs, though fundamentally relying on businesses, cannot be achieved without the involvement of the government. As for the reduction of government-imposed transaction costs, the government needs to play a bigger role in advancing reform on the macro level.

Therefore, unlike previous cost reduction actions mainly taken by businesses, the government's active involvement in the efforts to lower costs adopting a top-down approach is a very prominent feature of the cost reduction in the context of supply-side structural reform.

As planned by the Central Economic Work Conference, the key task of economic work in 2017 is to deepen supply-side structural reform. Apparently, against such a background, the significance of cost cutting will be even more prominent, and policies and measures in this regard will be placed in a more important position. Likewise, there will be strong demand for research on cost reduction, both in theory and practice.

Proceeding from the cause of the CPC and the country, we should comprehensively and systematically study cost reduction to provide theoretical and methodological support for related actions and base them on accurate analysis. It will be an important task for us in 2017 and beyond.

4 Winning the Tough Battle of Supply-Side Structural Reform[3]

In today's China, one frequently hears about supply-side structural reform. To deepen supply-side structural reform is a key economic task for 2017 defined by the Central Economic Work Conference as well as a key task for deepening reform of the economic system in 2017 recognized by the State Council. Moreover, the topic of supply-side structural reform is frequently discussed by the academic circles, business community and even the general public.

The fundamental reason why supply-side structural reform has captured so much attention is that it is associated with the new normal of economic development, the reform of the economic system, and therefore the deepening of reform across the board. In the cause of the CPC and the country at present, supply-side structural reform is given top priority since it links development with reform.

I. Supply-side structural reform and the new normal of economic development are naturally linked

Since the 18th CPC National Congress, the CPC Central Committee has drawn a major conclusion in due course that China's economic development has entered a new normal amid a series of profound changes in domestic and international economic situations. The word "new" suggests that the economic environment we are in today is very different from that in the past, so that understanding the new normal, adapting to it, and guiding its development constitutes the major theme of China's economic development both at present and in the period ahead.

Since we are facing the new normal of economic development rather than the old normal, we should take into account the fact that the Chinese economy is moving to a more advanced stage marked by complete functions and more balanced structures. Our only choice is to find a new path of economic development that is very different from the past one and to build a new landscape of macroeconomic regulation that also differs widely from the past one.

Since the prominent problems in the functioning of the Chinese economy are mainly caused not by cyclical and total output factors, but by structural factors, or the interrupted flow of economic activities caused by major structural imbalances, the new focus of macroeconomic policies should naturally be on the prominent problems that are quite different from past ones and on finding a way out from the supply side and structural adjustment

Since the fundamental cause of these major structural imbalances lies in institutional obstacles, in the failure of the market to play a decisive role in resource allocation, and in the failure of the government to better play its due role, to break through the obstacles in systems and mechanisms and achieve a new dynamic balance between supply and demand by means of reform is undoubtedly the new focus of macroeconomic policies.

---

[3] * This is a slightly revised article first published in *People's Daily* on July 6, 2017.

The above changes can be summed up as follows: compared with macroeconomic regulation in the past, which was focused on total output adjustment and the demand side and mainly relied on policy-based operations, macroeconomic regulation in the context of the new normal must be based on structural adjustment, focus on the supply side, and be achieved mainly through reform actions.

It is in such as context and based on such an understanding that the idea of supply-side structural reform has formed and evolved into the major theme of economic work. In other words, supply-side structural reform is closely linked to the new normal of economic development. Only when economic development has entered a new normal will supply-side structural reform be needed. Supply-side structural reform will only be effectively carried out only when it is based on the new normal of economic development. Advancing supply-side structural reform is a major innovation in the effort to adapt to the new normal and guide its development. The two are closely associated with each other.

II. **Supply-side structural reform is inseparable from deepening reform across the board**

Standing at a new historical starting point, the biggest difference between deepening reform across the board proposed at the Third Plenary Session of the 18th CPC Central Committee and previous reform policies is that it is not reform in one particular field or a few fields but reform that involves all fields and covers economic, political, cultural, social, and ecological civilization systems. A central issue that has to be addressed in the effort to deepen reform across the board is to set the direction, define priorities and make plans for all-round reform.

Since the reform is all-round, it is necessary to make clear the ultimate purpose of the reform and what results are to be achieved in each and every field. Given that deepening reform across the board involves the transformation of a range of systems and mechanisms, almost every reform initiative will affect other initiatives and require support from other initiatives. The objectives set for deepening reform across the board should cover not just one field or a few fields, but all fields. The ultimate goal of reform in all fields is to improve and develop socialism with Chinese characteristics and to modernize the country's system and capacity for governance.

Since the all-round reform is intended to modernize the country's governance system, it is necessary to sort out the priorities to work on in the process of advancing reform in all fields. As we all know, China's reform has always focused on the economic system. Deepening reform across the board has been initiated at the historic juncture when the reform of the economic system has achieved remarkable results and the framework of socialist market economy has taken shape. The overall effect of reform should be achieved through the coordinated efforts in reforming the economic, political, cultural, social and ecological civilization systems, so as to modernize the country's governance system. All in all, the reform of the economic system remains the top priority. This means that in the endeavor to deepen reform across the board the reform of the economic system should be prioritized while reform in all other fields is advanced.

Now that China has entered a new normal of economic development which is closely connected with supply-side structural reform, we may find that both the reform of the economic system and the deepening of reform across the board cannot be separated from supply-side structural reform. Information collected from various sources also suggests that the focus and challenge of China's current economic reform is on supply-side and structural issues which are intertwined. Therefore, if we recognize that the core issue in the reform of the economic system is to properly handle the relations between the government and the market so that the market plays a decisive role in resource allocation and the government plays a better role and that this core issue is in essence a supply-side and structural issue, we should and must start with and focus on supply-side structural reform while advancing the reform of the economic system for modernizing the country's governance system. We must seek development in the course of reform.

The dynamics between supply-side structural reform, reform of the economic system reform and deepening of reform across the board clearly shows that the only way for us to continue to deepen reform across the board in the new normal of economic development is to further the reform of the economic system focusing on supply-side structural reform, push forward the tasks of cutting overcapacity, reducing excess inventory, deleveraging, cost cutting and strengthening areas of weakness through reform actions, streamline administration and delegate power, enhance regulation and upgrade government services as an important part of supply-side structural reform, and continue to increase the supply of effective systems.

In other words, to advance supply-side structural reform we must promote the deepening of reform across the board and the latter can only be effectively pushed forward with the latter as the focus. The two complement and depend on each other. They are inseparable as a whole.

III. To deepen supply-side structural reform requires adjustments in ideas, thoughts and strategies

At this point, we can immediately draw the conclusion that supply-side structural reform integrates development and reform. It meets the requirements of the economic policy framework for adapting to the new normal of economic development and is also aligned with the overall plan for deepening reform across the board. In today's China, it is not only an important starting point for promoting development and reform in a coordinated way, but also an important way for giving better play to the leading role of reform in promoting development and enabling China to stand at a higher level of development. Therefore, it is crucial to win the tough battle of supply-side structural reform that concerns the whole picture of the CPC and the country's cause.

However, it would be no easy task to further deepen supply-side structural reform against the backdrop of the new normal of economic development and deepening reform across the board. Since the new normal differs from the old one, deepening reform across the board differs widely from the reform of the economic system, supply-side structural reform differs widely from demand management and adjustment, and the reform mechanisms differ widely from past ones since major problems have changed, it is imperative for us to focus on one particular issue, namely to avoid facing the new situation with conventional thinking and dealing with the new problems by copying the old practices. It is an extremely important and urgent task for us to comprehensively adjust the ideas, thoughts and strategies that we have been accustomed to and seek to advance and deepen supply-side structural reform with new ideas, thoughts and strategies that are quite different from old ones.

For example, cutting overcapacity is the first of the five major tasks of supply-side structural reform. It must not be confused with reducing output. We should not blindly rely on administrative intervention by the government either. Since overcapacity is the root cause of all problems and has to be addressed ultimately, the effort to cut overcapacity should and must be based on market adjustment and focus on existing capacity. We should focus on improving the system and mechanism in which the market plays a decisive role in the allocation of resources.

Another example is lowering costs. Since the main purpose of reducing the tax and fee burden of businesses is to lower their costs and improve the quality of supply, which is structural adjustment rather than total output adjustment, and the focus is on the supply side rather than the demand side, tax and fee cuts should not be made by increasing deficit and issuing more government bonds. Instead, we should combine tax and fee cuts with cuts in government spending and reduce the scale of government spending to create possibility for easing the tax and fee burden of businesses. Only such an approach will lead to a real reduction in the burden of taxes and fees on businesses and a change in the allocation of resources in favor of businesses.

As for strengthening areas of weakness, one of the important tasks of supply-side structural reform, we should not simply resort to expedient solutions or focus on maintaining growth and expanding investment. Since the growth and decline of the service and manufacturing industries occur naturally and the government needs to play a better role in ensuring people's basic needs are met, the effort to strengthen areas of weakness should be based on the new normal of economic development and start with the important areas that hinder economic and social development and people's primary concerns. We should focus on the service sector, especially public services represented by education and medical care.

Regarding the composition of macroeconomic policies, since a policy system guided by the new development philosophy and centered on supply-side structural reform has been developed, we should fall back to the old path of adopting austerity policies when the economy is heating and expansionary policies when the economy is cooling down. When it comes to supply-side structural reform, we must go beyond policy adjustment, seek to skillfully combine policy adjustment and institutional arrangements, and achieve a new dynamic balance between supply and demand through reform actions.

Only in this way can we win the tough battle of supply-side structural reform, and thus advance the implementation of the economic policy framework adapting to the new normal of economic development and the deepening of reform across the board with the modernization of the country's governance system as the overall objective. Eventually we will tread a new path of growing the economy that differs widely from the past one.

5 Improving the Quality of Supply System as the Main Task[4]

As socialism with Chinese characteristics has entered a new era and the principal contradiction in Chinese society has changed, the new challenges posed to economic work are mainly embodied in the urgent need to build a modern economic system that effectively meets the people's ever-growing needs for a better life.

Considering the modernization of the economic system an urgent requirement for getting us smoothly through this critical transition or a strategic goal for China's development means that the CPC and the Chinese government need to make a major adjustment to the ideas, thoughts and strategies for guiding economic work. The focus and direction of the major adjustment is certainly to support the supply-side structural reform that puts quality and efficiency first.

I. Supply-side structural reform given more prominence in the stage of high-quality development

Advancing supply-side structural reform is a major decision made in the context of the new normal of China's economic development. Since the 19th CPC National Congress reached an important conclusion that the Chinese economy has shifted from a stage of high-speed growth to a stage of high-quality development, advancing supply-side structural reform, as a major part of economic work in line with the new normal, has not only assumed greater significance, but also gained more prominence in all policy arrangements and institutional design concerning economic development.

The Chinese economy has entered a stage of high-quality development. It means, first of all, that our fundamental goal is to achieve more equitable and sustainable development featuring higher quality and efficiency. This requires us to focus on improving the quality of the supply system, promote reforms for improving the quality, efficiency and impetus of economic development, pursue the sustained and healthy development of the economy, adhere to the principle of putting quality and efficiency first, and shift the focus of economic work to improving the quality and efficiency of economic development.

The Chinese economy's entering a stage of high-quality development also means that we should be more resolved in pursuing innovative, coordinated, green, open and shared development. This requires us to abandon the practice of focusing on the scale and speed of GDP and pursuing high-speed growth. In response to the prominent problems represented by a series of major structural imbalances such as those in industrial structure and regional development, we should pay more attention to the supply side and work harder on structural adjustment. Moreover, we should focus on improving the quality of supply and the supply structure, stimulate the vitality of economic growth, and strive to achieve a new dynamic balance between supply and demand.

[4] * This is a slightly revised version of an article first published in *Qiushi*, No1, 2018.

In addition, the Chinese economy's entering a stage of high-quality development means that we should firmly focus on the real economy in the process of pursuing economic development. This requires that, on the one hand, we should make greater efforts to promote the upgrading of the industrial structure, accelerate the development of advanced manufacturing and modern service industries, and boost the development of infrastructure network so as to push Chinese industries towards the medium–high end of the global value chain. On the other hand, more attention should be paid to accelerating the formation of new drivers of growth, encouraging more people to engage in innovation and business startup initiatives, and creating more sources of growth in such areas as medium–high-end consumption, innovation, green and low-carbon economy, sharing economy, modern supply chains, and human capital services. Moreover, we should focus more on promoting the in-depth integration of the Internet, big data, and artificial intelligence with the real economy, and support the upgrading of traditional industries.

II. Modernizing the economic system by focusing on supply-side structural reform

Modernizing the economic system is a complex, systematic project involving a wide range of fields and exerting wide influences. Focusing on the main task of supply-side structural reform, the report delivered by President Xi Jinping at the 19th CPC National Congress made strategic arrangements in terms of innovation-driven development, rural revitalization, coordinated regional development, economic reforms, and opening up. Since supply-side structural reform runs through all fields and the whole process of the endeavor to modernize the economic system, we should not only aim at satisfying the people's needs for a better life, but also align the endeavor with supply-side structural reform. In other words, our goal should be to focus on supply-side structural reform and build a modern economic system that effectively meets the people's ever-growing needs for a better life.

This actually tells us that to modernize the economic system with supply-side structural reform as the main task poses an unprecedented and grave challenge to us, on both practical and theoretical levels.

First, a new principal contradiction in Chinese society. As the principal contradiction changes, the people's needs for a better life are manifested not only in the upgraded needs for material and cultural products, but also in the growing needs for institutions and policy products in such areas as democracy, the rule of law, fairness, justice, security and the environment. The supply system to meet the people's needs for a better life involves both the market and the government. Not only should the market play a decisive role, but the government should also play a better role. This means that, in the face of the people's ever-growing needs for a better life, we should pay equal attention to the supply of material and cultural products and that of institutional and policy products in the endeavor to modernize the economic system mainly through supply-side structural reform. We should improve supply both by the market and by the government and assign the responsibility of addressing the problem of unbalanced and inadequate development to both the market and the government.

Second, a new perspective of analysis. As the root cause of the prominent problems in the functioning of the Chinese economy has changed to the unsmooth flow of economic activities brought by major structural imbalances, the economic analysis based on cyclical and total output factors appears to be inadequate and limited. This means that the focus of economic situation analysis should naturally turn to the major structural imbalances represented by the imbalances in industrial structure and regional development. Moreover, the endeavor to modernize the economic system mainly through supply-side structural reform should also be aimed at addressing the major structural imbalances.

Third, a new policy focus. As the focus of China's macroeconomic policies has shifted from demand management to supply-side structural reform, short-term counter-cyclical operations on the demand side are no longer the main option. The approach now is structural adjustment on the supply side. This means that the main objective of macroeconomic regulation is to improve the quality of supply and the supply structure. In addition, in the endeavor to modernize the economic system mainly through supply-side structural reform, the top priority is to promote reforms for improving the quality, efficiency and impetus of economic development.

Fourth, the new approach to policy implementation. In the past, macroeconomic regulation aimed at promoting economic development was mainly achieved through policy operations, while macroeconomic regulation centered on supply-side structural reform must be extended to the level of systems and mechanisms. This means that to modernize the economic system mainly through supply-side structural reform we should not stop at policy adjustments, but break through the obstacles in systems and mechanisms through reform, and pave the way for the modernization of the economic system by promoting various basic reforms.

III. **Key points for promoting supply-side structural reform**

Socialism with Chinese characteristics has entered a new era and the principal contradiction in Chinese society has undergone a major change. It is no easy task to advance supply-side structural reform and thus modernize the economic system against such a background Since supply-side structural reform differs widely from demand management, and the reform mechanisms differ widely from past ones since major problems in the functioning of the Chinese economy have changed, it is imperative for us to focus on one particular issue, namely to avoid facing the new situation with conventional thinking and dealing with the new problems by copying the old practices. It is an extremely important and urgent task for us to comprehensively adjust the ideas, thoughts and strategies that we have been accustomed to and seek to advance the endeavor to modernize the economic system mainly through supply-side structural reform with new ideas, thoughts and strategies that are quite different from old ones. In particular, we should pay attention to the tasks of cutting overcapacity, reducing excess inventory, deleveraging, lowering costs, and strengthening areas of weaknesses and seek to improve the allocation of existing resources, increase the supply of high-quality resources, and achieve a dynamic balance between supply and demand.

For example, cutting overcapacity is the first of the five major tasks of supply-side structural reform. It must not be confused with reducing output. We should not blindly rely on administrative intervention by the government either. Since overcapacity is the root cause of all problems and has to be addressed ultimately, the effort to cut overcapacity should and must be based on market adjustment and focus on existing capacity. We should focus on improving the system and mechanism in which the market plays a decisive role in the allocation of resources.

Another example is lowering costs. Since the main purpose of reducing the tax and fee burden of businesses is to lower their costs and improve the quality of supply, which is structural adjustment rather than total output adjustment, and the focus is on the supply side rather than the demand side, tax and fee cuts should not be made by increasing deficit and issuing more government bonds. Instead, we should combine tax and fee cuts with cuts in government spending and reduce the scale of government spending to create possibility for easing the tax and fee burden of businesses. Only such an approach will lead to a real reduction in the burden of taxes and fees on businesses and a change in the allocation of resources in favor of businesses.

As for strengthening areas of weakness, one of the important tasks of supply-side structural reform, we should not simply resort to expedient solutions or focus on maintaining growth and expanding investment. Since the growth and decline of the service and manufacturing industries occur naturally and the government needs to play a better role in ensuring people's basic needs are met, the effort to strengthen areas of weakness should be based on the new normal of economic development and start with the important areas that hinder economic and social development and people's primary concerns. We should focus on the service sector, especially public services represented by education and medical care.

Only in this way can we blaze a new path of economic work that differs widely from the past one. In response to the requirements of the new era, we should strive to change the growth model, improve the economic structure, and foster new drivers of growth to modernize the economic system. In doing so, we will better meet the people's ever-growing needs on economic, political, cultural, social and ecological fronts and better promote all-round human development and social progress.

6 Ensuring Economic Operation Within Proper Range: How to Look at It and What to Do?[5]

The Central Economic Work Conference held at the end of 2019 made all-round plans for economic work in 2020. One of the most important aspects is to ensure that the economy operates within a proper range. This is clearly a strategic choice made for the purpose of achieving high-quality economic development, building a moderately prosperous society in all respects, and reaching all the objectives of the

[5] * This article was published in *Guangming Daily* on January 7, 2020, and slight changes were made when the book was published.

13th Five-Year Plan, and to lay a solid foundation for the country's development during the 14th Five-Year Plan period and the attainment of the second centenary goal.

The question is, given the grave and complicated economic situation at home and abroad, especially the mounting economic downward pressure, how should we look at such a challenge and what should we do to meet it?

I. Correctly understanding the proper range within which the economy operates

What is the proper range within which the economy operates? The answer may vary according to the development stage and the embraced development philosophy. In the stage of high-speed growth, the size and growth rate of GDP are the core objective, so the proper range within which the economy operates should certainly be marked by quantitative growth. From the stage of high-speed growth to the stage of high-quality development, the quality and efficiency of GDP have gradually replaced the size and growth rate of GDP as the core objective. With the change of core objective, the proper range within which the economy operates should no longer be focused on the size and growth rate of GDP. In addition, indicators that reflect the quality and efficiency of GDP, such as employment, price level and improvement of people's lives, should not only be considered, but also be pursued before the size and speed of GDP. This is not only the strategic direction for the stage of high-quality development, but also the concrete embodiment of the new development philosophy.

In other words, as China is turning to the stage of high-quality development, as required by the new development philosophy, both the appropriate growth of quantity and the steady improvement of quality are important marks of the proper range within which the economy operates. Moreover, in the equation between quantity and quality, the latter carries a relatively heavier weight.

Since the implications of "proper range" have changed significantly, the strategy to ensure the economy operates within a proper range should address both quantity and quality. We should be committed to pursuing the appropriate growth of quantity and the steady improvement of quality. This means that we should go beyond assessing the economic situation simply from the dimension of quantity and focus on grasping the proper range within which the economy operates from the dimensions of both quantity and quality. It is not only necessary but also crucial for ensuring the economy operates within a proper range.

We can find that in the context of remaining committed to the new development philosophy, one of the key tasks for 2020 determined by the Central Economic Work Conference, the series of plans made to ensure the economy operates steadily within a proper range, are intended to ensure the economy achieves an appropriate growth in quantity and a steady improvement in quality.

II. Taking stock of all macroeconomic regulatory instruments

Of all the macroeconomic regulation tools in traditional sense, counter-cyclical regulation should be ranked first. In fact, at least after experiencing the Asian financial crisis and the international financial crisis, we know well about how counter-cyclical regulation works out and how to implement it. It is without doubt wise to use this tool which has sufficient theoretical support and has been employed several times.

However, in the context of the new era of socialism with Chinese characteristics and high-quality economic development, we should see that counter-cyclical regulation is subordinate to the policy of demand management in theory, and short-term supply–demand balance is always pursued in practice. It is basically characterized by withstanding the cyclical fluctuations of the economy and the imbalance between supply and demand, with just policy adjustments in most cases. There would be no reform actions that address structural and institutional obstacles. Since the 18th CPC National Congress, one of the important innovations in the China' endeavor to develop socialist economy has been to endow deepening reform with the significance of macroeconomic regulation and regard it as the fundamental way of macroeconomic regulation. Based on that, a major decision was made to implement supply-side structural reform. This means that China's macroeconomic regulation tools today are by no means limited to counter-cyclical regulation. At least one important tool—supply-side structural reform can be added to the pool. Moreover, supply-side structural reform should precede counter-cyclical regulation and be taken as the focus of macroeconomic regulation.

Since the macroeconomic regulatory system has undergone profound changes, macroeconomic regulation efforts to ensure the economy operates within a proper range should give play to the respective roles of counter-cyclical regulation and supply-side structural reform. Moreover, supply-side structural reform should be the main approach and fiscal and monetary policies the main means, supported by policies on employment, industries, investment, consumption and regions.

We may also find that at least two of the four important understandings reached at the Central Economic Work Conference are directly related to the efforts to deepen supply-side structural reform. First, we must prudently manage the intensity of counter-cyclical regulation, invigorate micro entities, and integrate supply-side structural reform into the whole process of macroeconomic regulation. Second, we should be good at removing institutional barriers to development through reform, activating dormant potential for development, and enabling various market players to work hard at the front line of scientific and technological innovation and domestic and international market competition.

III. **Identifying the real cause of problems and implementing targeted solution**

China's current economic performance shows that there may be a long list of problems that lead to or are related to the economic downturn. Among them, there are external and internal problems, cyclical and structural and institutional problems, as well as old and new problems. We need to distinguish carefully between all these problems and take targeted measures accordingly. Counter-cyclical regulation is effective in addressing short-term, external or cyclical problems. Long-term, internal or structural and institutional problems, however, can only be solved by deepening supply-side structural reform.

Since the problems are in many aspects, the cause of the current economic downturn pressure should be analyzed, and countermeasures should be selected from multiple perspectives. We should not only pay attention to short-term economic fluctuations, but also consider long-term structural factors. We should not only pay attention to the balance between supply and demand, but also seek to improve the supply structure. We should not only pay attention to the changes in economic performance, but also dig deep into the fundamental problems in systems and mechanisms. Furthermore, we should not only address short-term, external or cyclical problems through counter-cyclical regulation, but also deepen supply-side structural reform to address long-term, internal or structural and institutional problems.

In other words, there is no such thing as a cure-all remedy in the world. It is impossible to solve all problems together indiscriminately, let alone using just one single means.

We can also see that the Central Economic Work Conference this time reached a basic conclusion that China is now in a pivotal stage for transforming its growth model, improving its economic structure, and fostering new drivers of growth, structural, institutional and cyclical issues are intertwined, and the impact of three overlapping phases continues to deepen. Therefore, we should put stability first, adhere to the policy framework of keeping macroeconomic policies stable, micro policies flexible, and social policies supportive, and make macroeconomic regulation more forward-looking, targeted and effective.

IV. **Balancing short-term and long-term treatments**

The macroeconomic regulation operations aimed at withstanding the economic downward pressure is to achieve a short-term supply–demand balance in the first place, which is undoubtedly consistent with common sense. This is because on the whole the macroeconomic regulation operations for withstanding the economic downturn pressure such as stabilizing growth and making structural adjustment are mainly aimed at the current balance between supply and demand.

However, fundamentally speaking, to ensure that the economy operates within a proper range is to maintain steady growth with sound long-term momentum. Therefore, the effort to withstand the economic downward pressure and ensure the economy operates within a proper range must be sustainable, rather than expedient. In this regard, while short-term supply–demand balance is important, long-term structural balance is also indispensable. Practices over the years have repeatedly reminded us that supply–demand balance in the short term must be based on structural balance in the long term. Without long-term structural balance, short-term supply–demand balance would be unsustainable. Furthermore, compared with the stage of high-speed growth, the main problems in the functioning of the economy in the stage of high-quality development are structural and institutional ones. It is not only a basic principle of materialist dialectics, but also a basic skill for growing the economy well to identify the main problems and take targeted measures to solve them. This means that solving the problems that the supply system does not adapt to the changes in the demand structure and that it is difficult to achieve the smooth flow of economic activities is the most important factor in the stage of high-quality development. Promoting reforms for improving the quality, efficiency and impetus of economic development, putting more efforts into structural adjustment, and finding a way out in removing institutional and institutional obstacles should be the focus of macroeconomic regulation in the stage of high-quality development.

Since both short-term supply–demand balance and long-term structural balance are necessary conditions for ensuring the economy operates within a proper range, and structural and institutional problems are prominent problems in the stage of high-quality development, the efforts to assess the effects of withstanding the economic downward pressure should focus on producing both short-term and long-term effects and addressing immediate and long-term problems together. The purpose is to strike a balance between supply–demand balance and structural improvement. The former would pave the way for the latter while the latter would contribute to the former. In addition, priority should be given to structural and the institutional problems, and the focus should be on advancing basic reforms concerning such problems.

In other words, the short-term and long-term effects of withstanding the economic downturn pressure are interdependent, and the two must be considered holistically to strike a balance between multiple objectives. We should not focus only on the short-term supply–demand balance, ignoring structural improvement in the long term, or make no distinction between major and minor problems.

We may find that, in making plans for economic work in 2020, the Central Economic Work Conference stressed the importance of being comprehensive and coordinated. It was made clear that all-out efforts should be made to ensure stability on six fronts and coordinated efforts should be made to maintain stable growth, promote reform, make structural adjustments, improve people's wellbeing, guard against risks, and ensure stability.

V. **Introducing timely and appropriate counter-cyclical regulation**

In the final analysis, counter-cyclical regulation in the face of economic downward pressure is aimed at ensuring the economy operates steadily within a proper range. Therefore, in addition to choosing the right direction, it is also crucial to be timely and appropriate. To be timely is to introduce counter-cyclical regulation at the right time. Slow response may not be good, but overreaction is also harmful. To be appropriate is to ensure counter-cyclical regulation is not too tight. The regulation is not strict enough, we may intensify it. When it is too tough, however, it would be difficult to make any readjustment and it may bring negative effects. The yardstick is to see whether it can invigorate micro entities and add impetus to economic development.

Since counter-cyclical regulation is to intended to help stabilize economic growth in a proper range, all related operations should be focused on this core objective. We should not only make timely policy adjustments, proactive or minor ones, but also try to introduce targeted measures policy that produce the best results. This is valuable experience we have gained over the years which is also essential for developing a sound macroeconomic regulatory system.

Since timely and appropriate measures are of extreme importance to stabilizing economic growth within a proper range, we should not miss the right time to act and thus fail to reach the objective, or introduce strong stimulus policies that would overdraw future growth.

We may find that the Central Economic Work Conference put forward a clear requirement for counter-cyclical regulation, namely prudently managing counter-cyclical regulation and making macroeconomic regulation more forward-looking, targeted and effective. Therefore, we should intensify efforts to improve the quality and efficiency of proactive fiscal policy and pursue prudent monetary policy that is flexible and appropriate.

VI. **Basic conclusions**

We can draw two conclusions from the above discussion.

The current economic downward pressure comes against the backdrop of the shift to a stage of high-quality development. On the surface, it seems to be no different from the downward pressures that we experienced many times during periods of high growth. However, if we look deeper into the root cause, we will find that behind what seems to be similar, there is something profound that is quite different. At the stage of high-quality development, economic downward pressure may be embodied in insufficient effective demand whose underlying cause is mostly in structural and institutional problems. Macroeconomic regulation operations in response to the economic downward pressure in the stage of high-quality development may be focused on the short-term goal of increasing effective demand, the effect will always evolve along with the continuous changes in structural and institutional problems. Therefore, economic downward pressure means different things in different contexts, so does macroeconomic regulation. We should try to gain more experience from practice and do not rush for quick results. We need to be patient and prepared to "fight a long war".

Macroeconomic regulation for achieving the objective of ensuring the economy operates within a proper range must be carried out according to the changed macroeconomic environment as well as changed ideas, thoughts and strategies. We should not only consider the proper range from the dimensions of quantity and quality, but also take quantitative and qualitative measures. We should give full play to the respective roles of counter-cyclical regulation and supply-side structural reform and give priority to the latter. We should not only introduce counter-cyclical regulation to address short-term, external or cyclical problems, but also deepen supply-side structural reform to deal with long-term, internal or structural and institutional problems. We should not only pay attention to both short-term and long-term effects and address immediate and long-term problems together to strike a balance between supply–demand balance and structural improvement, but also give priority to structural and the institutional problems and focus on advancing basic reforms concerning such problems. We should not only follow the right direction of regulation, but also carry out timely and appropriate counter-cyclical regulation and strive to be precise and effective.

It can be expected that the macroeconomic regulation operations aimed at ensuring the economy operates within a proper range will put our capacity for deepening supply-side structural reform to the test. The final results will also depend, to a large extent, on whether we can turn the economic downward pressure into a driving force for deepening reform.

Chapter 4
Building a Macroeconomic Regulatory System for the New Era

1 Introduction

As China's stage of economic development changes, its macroeconomic regulatory system must also keep pace with the times. This chapter, comprising six articles, is entitled "Building a Macroeconomic Regulatory System for the New Era".

The Third Plenary Session of the 18th CPC Central Committee focused on the reform of the economic system, and drew a conclusion that the market should play a decisive role in resource allocation and that the government should play a better role. Since then, every discussion about the relationship between the government and the market, especially about the building of a macroeconomic regulatory system, has followed two clues. One is that the market plays a decisive role in resource allocation. Another is to give better play to the role of the government. However, in China, the better role of the government is supported by a series of special factors that can be generated only in China's national conditions. Understanding these special factors is crucial to the building of a macroeconomic regulatory system for the new era. The article "How Can the Government Be More Effective?" was written at the invitation of the Theory Department of *People's Daily*.

As China has entered a new normal, its economic situation and macroeconomic policies have undergone substantial changes, posing challenges to macroeconomic analysis. The analysis of the macroeconomic situation concerns the understanding of the present and planning for the future, while the analysis of macroeconomic policies concerns the evaluation of policy effectiveness do their significance cannot be underestimated. Given the complicated economic situation as well as economic and non-economic factors compounded by cyclical and structural ones, we can only devote more energy and effort than ever before to do macroeconomic analysis in a more frequent and detailed way. Given the diverse objectives of macroeconomic policies, we can only focus on the main problems and strive to make policy research

P. Gao, *A Shift Toward High-Quality Development of China*,
Research Series on the Chinese Dream and China's Development Path,
https://doi.org/10.1007/978-981-99-8990-4_4

more relevant and response efforts timelier. It was with based on such an understanding that I wrote the article "Changes and Challenges Facing Macroeconomic Analysis".

There were about two years from 2015 when the CPC Central Committee proposed to push forward supply-side structural reform to 2016 when the need to focus on supply-side structural reform was stressed and the 19th CPC National Congress made the strategic plan for modernizing the economic system. During this period, the biggest change in the field of macroeconomic regulation was that a policy system guided by the new development philosophy and centered around supply-side structural reform took shape. The next task is apparently to establish a macroeconomic regulatory system commensurate with supply-side structural reform according to the changed economic environment, development philosophy, policy focus, and approach to policy implementation in response to the prominent problems. Therefore, I wrote the article "Establishing a Macroeconomic Regulatory System Commensurate with Supply-side Structural Reform".

The Central Economic Work Conference held in December 2017 put forward the idea of Xi Jinping Thought on Socialist Economy with Chinese Characteristics for a New Era. Since then, a series of new ideas, thoughts and strategies on economic work developed since the 18th CPC National Congress have been collectively expressed as Xi Jinping Thought on Socialist Economy with Chinese Characteristics for a New Era. Therefore, it is necessary to formulate the theory of China's macroeconomic system in the new era and to better understand China's practices in this regard on the basis of sorting out the evolution of the new ideas, thoughts and strategies to Xi Jinping Thought on Socialist Economy with Chinese Characteristics for a New Era. The article "Profound Changes in China's Macroeconomic Regulatory System in the New Era", using a comparative approach, examines the changes from five aspects, i.e. analysis perspective, development philosophy, policy focus, approach to policy implementation, and the government's role.

In 2019, in the face of the escalating trade frictions between China and the United States and the mounting economic downward pressure, the Chinese government launched a series of macroeconomic measures with far-reaching efforts to strengthen counter-cyclical regulation. It was necessary but led to much misunderstanding among the general public. One of the most worrying phenomena was that counter-cyclical regulation was equated with demand management and considered as the whole of macroeconomic policies. If this is not corrected in time, supply-side structural reform, as the focus of macroeconomic regulation in the stage of high-quality development, will be reduced to something that exists in name only, which may lead to the reappearance of conventional thinking and thus greater uncertainty and instability in the process of economic development. To ensure that macroeconomic policies are accurate and appropriate and produce the right results, we must set the right direction for the pursuit of macroeconomic policies. In consideration of all these, I wrote the article "Setting the Right Direction for Current Macroeconomic Policies".

As the economic downward pressure continues to grow, the significance of stable growth for macroeconomic policy objectives and the macroeconomic regulatory system has become increasingly prominent. However, there are different understandings and views on how to stabilize growth. Since how to achieve steady growth requires a high level of expertise and the economic and policy environments at home and abroad are quite different from those in the past, it is very important to figure out where to start to stabilize growth in light of the economic reality at the stage of high-quality development.

In the article "Stabilizing Growth: How to Optimize Policy Impact", I proposed efforts on four fronts to maintain stable growth. The strengths of demand management and supply-side structural reform should be both brought into play to complement each other, with the latter playing the main role. The various problems should be addressed with different approaches such as carrying out counter-cyclical regulation and deepening supply-side structural reform. Both short-term and long-term objectives should be considered, so should supply–demand balance and structural improvement. We should embrace the ideas, thoughts and strategies in line with the stage of high-quality development and be prepared to "fight a protracted war".

2 How Can the Government Be More Effective?[1]

China's achievements in economic development are universally acknowledged today, and very few negative comments can be found in this regard. When it comes to why it has achieved so much—the factors that underpin China's economic success, however, views are often differing and some understandings are even superficial. Despite the differences in the angle of observation, methodological basis, the amount of information gathered and the position held, there is a more important, profound and easily overlooked reason for this. The interpretation of anything that happens in China can only and must be based on a comprehensive and systematic understanding of the country's specific realities.

Fundamentally speaking, the sustained and healthy development of the Chinese economy is driven by a series of special factors that exist only in the conditions of China. Looking back on the trajectory of the Chinese economy over the past 30 years, which is different from those of other economies, we can find that, of all the listed special factors that support the sustained and healthy development of the Chinese economy, a very important aspect is the macroeconomic regulation implemented by the government that has been in a proper state.

Furthermore, the Chinese government's proper macroeconomic regulation is apparently directly related to its great capacity for managing economic growth. Given the complexities of domestic and international economic situations, it would be difficult for the Chinese economy to grow in a sustainable and healthy way without such capacity of the Chinese government.

[1] * This is a slightly revised version of an article first published in *People's Daily* on January 30, 2015.

The question is how the Chinese government has developed such capacity. In my view, it has strengths in at least five aspects.

I. **Adeptness at learning**

Historically, attaching importance to and being good at learning is a fine tradition of the CPC. Mao Zedong once called upon the whole Party to keep studying. Since the beginning of reform and opening up, this fine tradition has not only been preserved, but has been carried forward. A system has even been put in place to sustain it.

At the beginning of reform and opening up, very few Party and government officials in China had received economic training. Even fewer understood and were familiar with the mechanisms of market economy. Therefore, China's reform and opening up actually started with studying the theory of the market economy. How the government should play its role in the market economy, in particular, was the most important aspect for Party and government officials at all levels. Since then, focusing on the central task of economic development, it has become a common practice for Party and government officials at all levels to study the theory of the market economy. In addition, for the purpose of guiding economic work and regulating the economy, the study has focused more on macroeconomic activities and macroeconomic regulation operations.

In today's China, macroeconomic analysis is often an important part of various learning activities, such as the collective study sessions of the Political Bureau of the CPC Central Committee as well as core theoretical groups of Party committees at all levels, themed study sessions of People's Congress standing committees, Chinese People's Political Consultative Conference committees, and governments at all levels, regular training sessions for Party and government officials organized by Party schools and administrative colleges at all levels, occasional training sessions for Party and government officials organized by relevant local authorities on their own initiative, as well as various forums, seminars, symposiums and educational tours organized in market-based ways all over the country. Moreover, test questions in the examinations for the public recruitment of civil servants as well as Party and government officials at all levels across the country always involve macroeconomic theories. It is fair to say that macroeconomic theories have become a mandatory course of study for Party and government officials at all levels.

Because of this, a good number of Party and government officials in China are well-versed in economic theories or have received systematic training in economics. Many are experts in economic management. In fact, even among people who did not train as economists or who do not work in economic management many are literate on macroeconomic topics. Therefore, within the Chinese government system, not only do people have a common language when discussing economic issues, but they are also able to discuss the issues at the operational level and reach basic consensus on the basis of in-depth and detailed discussion.

II. **Adeptness at research**

The Chinese government has always attached great importance to research work and based its decision-making on in-depth research, which is vividly reflected in the macroeconomic field.

Before important national Party and government meetings (such as the Party Congress and the Two Sessions) are held, both the CPC Central Committee and the State Council would set up a number of research groups on relevant topics, especially those concerning economic development, to carry out special research nationwide and produce research reports.

Before the annual Central Economic Work Conference, officials at all levels, including members of the Standing Committee of the Political Bureau of the CPC Central Committee, members of the Political Bureau, and members of the State Council, are sent to various localities to conduct field research. In addition, officials of all provinces, autonomous regions and municipalities directly under the Central Government would also make research efforts on a regular basis. Their research results represent first-hand information about the realities of China's economic development.

In fact, in China's Party and government system, there has been continued research on economic situation, economic policies, economic development, economic reform and other issues. Almost all matters concerning major economic issues are brought up to decision-makers based on extensive research for consideration.

The various information gathered in the process of research not only provides an important basis for drafting documents for important meetings of the Party and the government and making important related decisions. It can also make the Chinese government's decision-making on economic issues based on sufficient and accurate information, and help ensure that the Chinese government's plans on economic issues are in line with China's national conditions, thus enhancing the relevance and feasibility of economic decisions.

III. **Adeptness at pooling the wisdom of all people**

The macroeconomic decisions of the Chinese government are not determined by just a few officials, but are made based on the participation of both top decision-makers and ordinary people.

As an important embodiment of the Party's leadership over economic development, the Political Bureau of the CPC Central Committee would consider the assessment of the economic situation and the choice of macroeconomic policies as an important part of its meeting. Strengthening and improving the Party's leadership over economic development, following the overriding trends in development, and constantly improving the macroeconomic regulatory system have always been the central tasks of the top decision-makers.

As a key element to governance, meeting documents concerning important issues of economic development, such as the report on the work of the government and the communiqué of the Central Economic Work Conference, are drafted by a team led by the CPC Central Committee and the State Council. Team members usually include heads and experts from policy research institutions and agencies of the central government, major economic think tanks, and the business community.

As a routine decision-making procedure, the annual report on the work of the government would be presented to a meeting convened by Party and state leaders and attended by representatives from all sectors including economic, social, educational, and business communities and political parties other than the CPC to solicit their opinions for revision, before being finalized and submitted to the Two Sessions.

As an important channel for communicating with economic think tanks and taking up policy suggestions, when it comes to major changes in the economic situation or major economic decisions, Party and state leaders and the heads of relevant government agencies would also convene a meeting of experts mainly from the economic field.

China has also established a regular information disclosure system. National research institutes that serve as think tanks, institutions of higher learning, and even the research teams of businesses can all impart information about the economic situation and offer relevant policy advice to the decision-makers and top leaders at any time by submitting an Important Report, Special Report, or Report on a Specific Situation.

Such effective and extensive intellectual support can not only help us avoid or reduce mistakes in economic decision-making, but also make decision-making more scientific, democratic and law-based.

IV. **Adeptness at grasping the overriding trend**

After more than 30 years of reform and opening up, the Chinese government has a broader vision in dealing with complex and volatile economic issues. A basic model of macroeconomic thinking is to assess the current situation and the future trend based on domestic and international situations for devising macroeconomic policies.

China's response to the Southeast Asian financial crisis in the 1990s and the international financial crisis since 2008 shows that priority is given to the bigger picture in this country and when necessary local interests would be sacrificed for the sustained and healthy development of the economy. Such macroeconomic regulation thinking is embodied not only in the design of macroeconomic policies, but also in a series of practical actions for macroeconomic regulation in various periods. There is a mechanism through which resources can be mobilized on a large scale nationwide and resources are allocated to meet the needs of macroeconomic regulation.

The Chinese economy has been deeply integrated with the world economy and is closely related to the changes in the global political landscape. Recognizing that the Chinese economy has become an important part of the world economy and that the two are closely connected, the Chinese government is not only responsive to the changes in the global economic situation, but also good at planning with a global vision, balancing immediate and long-term interests, seizing various opportunities, and managing the timing, pace and intensity of implementing macroeconomic policies.

V. **Adeptness at summing up experience**

Improvements in China's macroeconomic regulation are attributable to the government's relentless efforts in introducing new, up-to-date approaches to macroeconomic regulation.

The concept of macroeconomic regulation was introduced into China from the West after the beginning of reform and opening up, and China's macroeconomic regulation mechanism has gradually taken shape under the market economy in the process of reform and opening up. China had put forward something similar to macroeconomic regulation, such as the formulation of overall balance, but it was mostly rooted in the soil of planned economy. It was a set of methods characterized by planned adjustment, introduced based on the experience of the Soviet Union and Eastern European countries. However, China has never stopped at learning from Western textbooks when it comes to macroeconomic regulation. Even its macroeconomic regulation mechanism did not stop improving at the early stage of reform and opening up. Its basic trajectory over the past 30 years shows us that China has been keeping pace with the times and seeking to study and improve macroeconomic regulation in the process of practicing it.

Today's China is more focused than ever on economic development and the focus on development has been agreed upon by the whole Party and all sectors of society. Because of that, economic issues are studied not only by government agencies, think tanks and academic institutions, but also by entrepreneurs and ordinary people. Moreover, economic issues are almost inevitably covered in various seminars and forums held by various institutions throughout the country, considered as a theme in various activities organized by the business community, and discussed by ordinary people in their spare time. Amid such nationwide discussions about economic issues, people have been summing up experience, adjusting the direction, and improving their understanding of the laws underlying economic development.

Drawing nourishment from such fertile soil, the Chinese government will naturally increase its capacity for managing economic growth, improve its skills in macroeconomic regulation, and play an increasingly better role in carrying out macroeconomic regulation.

3 Changes in and Challenges Facing Macroeconomic Analysis[2]

Considerable changes have taken place in China's macroeconomic situation and macroeconomic policies, posing strong challenges to the established approach to macroeconomic analysis.

Firstly, take a look at the macroeconomic situation.

Whatever indicators are used to assess the situation and globally or domestically speaking, China's macroeconomic situation in the new normal differs sharply from that in the past. An essential feature is that the current domestic and international

[2] * The is a slightly revised edition of "Macroeconomic Analysis Should Be More Detailed" published in *Economic Daily* on July 18, 2015.

economic situations are getting increasingly complicated. Moreover, economic and non-economic factors are compounded, so are cyclical and structural factors. The full picture is very intricate. For example, it took only seven years for China's economic growth to fall from 14.2% in 2007 to 10.4% in 2010 and 7.4% in 2014.

Another example is the annual growth rate of government revenue. It was 21.3% during the 11th Five-Year Plan period, 24.8% in 2011, and only 8.6% in 2014 despite a series of extraordinary measures, including increasing the profits to be turned in by some financial institutions. Since the beginning of 2015, the economic downturn pressure has been increasing, and government revenue has been declining at a faster pace. Economic growth faces the possibility of falling below seven percent. As one of the most comprehensive economic indicators, the growth rate of government revenue actually dropped to five percent between January and May. Since some government-managed funds were listed into the general public budget, the growth rate was only 3.1%.

The slowdown or decline in the growth rate of the economy and government revenue is actually not a concern. This is because even such a growth rate would be justifiably high when compared with other economies in the world today. Moreover, as the new normal of economic development suggests, some of these elements are what we have always wanted, and we are happy to have them. Some are not what we want and we still have to accept them. Some are caused by cyclical factors, while others are the result of economic restructuring.

Then what are the respective proportions of the elements we are happy to see and those that we have to accept? What are the roles of cyclical and structural factors? What are normal phenomena and what are short-term ones? And so on and so forth. All these questions are apparently major strategic issues concerning China's economic development that must be addressed not in macroeconomic analysis. Only on the basis of a systematic analysis can we get an accurate understanding of the macroeconomic situation.

Secondly, take a look at the macroeconomic policies.

Common sense suggests that the graver and more volatile the economic situation becomes, the more the government needs to strengthen macroeconomic regulation. However, the macroeconomic regulation that has entered a new normal is also so different from that in the past. In addition to the above-mentioned changes in the macroeconomic situation, the changes on at least three levels must be considered in the process of macroeconomic regulation.

First, people's understanding of the situation has changed. With the change of the economic situation both at home and abroad, people's understanding of the situation has also changed, which is true in the academic and business communities, and among the decision-maker and the general public. The term "new normal" is actually used to reflect the understanding that today's macroeconomic situation is different from that in the past. Given the new understanding that the Chinese economy is moving to a more advanced stage marked by complete functions and more balanced structures, the choice of macroeconomic policies must be aligned with the new normal and based on the initiative to adapt to the new normal and guide its development.

Second, the thinking on governance has changed. With the changes in the situation and the understanding of the situation, the new leadership of the CPC Central Committee has also changed their way of guiding economic work, and developed a series of new macroeconomic regulation ideas that are quite different from past ones. For example, the market should play a decisive role in resource allocation. What businesses can decide on their own should be left to the market to decide. The government should take the initiative to do its job well and know clearly what to do and what not to do. What should be pursued is sustainable development featuring high quality and efficiency and development supported by full employment, improved productivity, better returns on investment and higher efficiency in resource allocation. Maintaining a certain economic growth rate is mainly to ensure employment. Macroeconomic policies should stay focused to send out a signal to the general public about promoting economic restructuring. As long as the economy operates within a proper range, macroeconomic policies should remain stable. The side effects of strong stimulus policies on economic development should be avoided. Therefore, since the thinking on governance based on the new situation and understanding has changed, the choice of macroeconomic policies must be linked to the new ideas guiding economic work and the macroeconomic regulatory system and methods should be improved according to the new ideas.

Third, the macroeconomic policy landscape has changed. Given the changes in the situation, the understanding of the situation and the thinking on governance, the role of macroeconomic policies has covered both counter-cyclical regulation and structural adjustment and their objectives have included stabilizing growth, ensuring employment, guarding against risks, adjusting the structure, stabilizing prices, improving people's wellbeing, and promoting reform. This means that we have to allocate the limited resources of macroeconomic regulation to play the dual role and achieve multiple objectives at the same time. This also means that less room is left for us to use macroeconomic regulation, which makes it inevitable to frequently adjust the objectives or focus of macroeconomic regulation. Therefore, even if it is urgent to make macroeconomic policies more expansionary, we should properly devise the new composition of macroeconomic policies centering on the dual role of counter-cyclical regulation and structural adjustment, while considering the multiple objectives of stabilizing growth, ensuring employment, guarding against risks, adjusting the structure, stabilizing prices, improving people's wellbeing and promoting reform.

In the face of all these changes, we should frankly acknowledge that the current macroeconomic situation, which is very complex and different from that in the past, is in many ways unfamiliar to us. It is difficult to make a clear explanation by based on previous knowledge structure and research experience. We should also acknowledge that we are not very clear about the new path of macroeconomic regulation and the new composition of macroeconomic policies in line with the new normal of economic development. As for what exactly should be adjusted or changed, we still need to explore further and gradually get on the right track.

In the face of all these challenges, we should recognize that for the analysis of the macroeconomic situation concerning the understanding of the current situation and planning for the future, we should, first of all, devote energy and efforts more than ever to tread a new path of frequent and detailed analysis. We should also recognize that for the analysis of macroeconomic policies concerning the effectiveness of the current policy of stabilizing growth, we should be calm and adopt a clear-headed approach, focus on the main problems, and strive to make policy research more relevant and response efforts timelier.

To sum up, we should adjust in a comprehensive and timely manner the ideas and thoughts that we used to take for granted, and promote the transformation of macroeconomic theories and practices with different new ones. On that basis, we should develop a new approach to macroeconomic analysis that adapts to the new normal and guides its development.

4 Establishing a Macroeconomic Regulatory System Commensurate with Supply-Side Structural Reform[3]

In recent years, China's macroeconomic regulatory system has undergone a series of unprecedented major changes. In 2013, the idea of three overlapping phases was put forward. In 2014, a major conclusion that China's economic development has entered a new normal was drawn. In 2015, the idea of pursuing innovative, coordinated, green, open and shared development was framed and a major decision was made to promote supply-side structural reform. In 2016, it was proposed to continue deepening supply-side structural reform. In 2017, a strategic plan was made for modernizing the economic system at the 19th CPC National Congress.

I. Different assessment of the situation

In the past, we would assess the economic situation from the perspective of cyclical and total output factors, attributing changes in the economic situation to the impact of cyclical or total output factors. We would compare the changes in the economic situation to fever that would occur periodically in the course of a person's life. The economy always moves forward amid cyclical fluctuations, downturn or overheating. Economic downturn and overheating would be attributed to the imbalance between total demand and supply. Economic downturn is caused by excess supply while overheating is caused by excess demand.

However, as China's economic development enters a new normal, the analysis mainly based on cyclical and total output factors is becoming increasingly insufficient. As President Xi Jinping said, "The outstanding problems facing the functioning of the Chinese economy are partially cyclical and total output factors, but mainly major structural imbalances."[4] However, since the outstanding problems are no longer cyclical or total output factors, a change in the economic situation is no

[3] * This is a slightly revised version of an article first published in *Economic Daily* on December 18, 2017.

[4] Xi (2017, p. 113).

longer as simple as "a cold or fever". It could be a combination of "cold, fever and cardiovascular disease"—a complex mix of "acute and chronic diseases". Since the root cause of the outstanding problems lies in the unsmooth flow of economic activities caused by major structural imbalances, the "acute diseases" of cyclical fluctuations and imbalances between total supply and demand are no longer the main concern. Instead, priority should be given to the "chronic diseases" represented by a series of major structural imbalances, such as imbalances in the industrial structure and regional development.

II. **A different development philosophy**

The economic development thinking we used to embrace focused on either GDP or growth rate. The growth rate of GDP was often considered the only yardstick for assessing the economic situation. A fast growth rate would mean a good situation while a slow one would mean a bad situation. A faster growth would suggest the effectiveness of our efforts while a slower one would suggest ineffectiveness. The pursuit of high-speed growth and the only focus on GDP were seen everywhere.

However, in the face of the historical change that the Chinese economy has shifted from a stage of high-speed growth to a stage of high-quality development, the economic development thinking we uphold today is different from that. As President Xi said, "the ideas, thinking and focus of economic work should be adjusted."[5] "Our development must be sound development. We must pursue with firmness of purpose the vision of innovative, coordinated, green, open and shared development…and strive to achieve higher-quality, more efficient, fairer and more sustainable development."[6] Since the blind pursuit of high-speed growth has given way to high-quality development, GDP growth rate should not be the only yardstick for assessing the economic situation and economic work. In addition, quality and efficiency indicators should be introduced and considered as the key issue. Since the goal is to achieve higher-quality, more efficient, fairer, and more sustainable development, it is no longer an important option for us to adopt stimulus policies for achieving short-term economic growth and overdrawing future growth. Instead, we should "implement the new development philosophy and modernize the economic system", guide the economy towards sustained and healthy development, follow the principle of putting quality and efficiency first, and shift the focus to improving the quality and efficiency of economic development.

III. **Different policy focuses**

The focus of our macroeconomic policies used to be demand management. Keeping a close eye on demand, we would carry out counter-cyclical regulation for short-term stability in response to the cyclical fluctuations of the economy and the increase or decrease in total demand. Whenever the economy suffered a downturn and total demand was insufficient, we would take measures to increase total demand. Whenever the economy was overheating and total demand was excess, we would act to

---

[5] Xi (2017, p. 112).

[6] Xi (2017, pp. 21–35).

reduce total demand. Such a simple way of managing total demand is well-known even to non-economic professionals after nearly 40 years of reform and opening up.

However, the focus of China's macroeconomic policies at present is supply-side structural reform. As President Xi said, "The CPC Central Committee has proposed to promote supply-side structural reform. This is a major adjustment to China's economic development thinking and focus of efforts made based on a comprehensive analysis of the long cycle of the world economy and the new normal of China's economic development… Promoting supply-side structural reform should be the focus of the efforts to grow the economy at present and in the period ahead."[7] Since the focus of macroeconomic policies has shifted from the demand side to the supply side, our efforts should be concentrated on the supply side. The starting point is to focus on stimulating the vitality of economic growth and to strive for a new dynamic balance between supply and demand. Since the focus of macroeconomic policies is to address structural rather than total output problems, increasing and reducing demand may be a method, but the main approach has been changed to structural adjustment. Short-term counter-cyclical operations are also no longer the main option. Since the main objective of macroeconomic policies is to improve the quality and structure of supply, "acute diseases" such as cyclical fluctuations and imbalances between total supply and demand needed to be "treated", but priority should still be given to "chronic diseases" represented by a series of major structural imbalances such as those in industrial structure and regional development. The focus of efforts should be promoting reforms for improving the quality, efficiency and impetus of economic development.

IV. **Different approach to policy implementation**

In the past, China's macroeconomic regulation was mainly based on or reflected in policy operations. Various policy arrangements were made to achieve the objectives of macroeconomic regulation. This was apparently in line with the assessment of the situation mainly based on cyclical and total output factors. As mentioned earlier, we would address the problems arising from cyclical fluctuations and imbalances between total supply and demand as "acute diseases". The main approach was to introduce short-term counter-cyclical operations. Such operations would be completed on the policy level, without affecting related systems and mechanisms.

However, the macroeconomic regulation that we carry out now must go beyond policy operations and be extended to the level of systems and mechanisms. We should mainly rely on reform actions and skillfully combine policy adjustment with institutional arrangements. This is directly related to a profound change in our assessment of the economic situation. As President Xi said, "The cause of structural problems on the supply side is the distorted allocation of factors, which is an institutional obstacle."[8] Therefore, "the fundamental way to advance supply-side structural reform… is to

[7] Xi (2017, p. 107).

[8] Xi (2017, p. 106).

deepen reform".[9] Since the outstanding problems we face have changed from supply–demand imbalance to structural imbalances, short-term counter-cyclical operations are no longer as effective as they used to be and we should continue to address the imbalance between supply and demand while focusing on solving structural imbalances. Since the root cause of supply-side structural problems lies in institutional obstacles, in the failure of the market to play a decisive role in resource allocation, and in the failure of the government to better play its due role, policy operations targeted at institutional obstacles would naturally become less effective and we can only reform the systems and mechanisms. While taking supply-side structural reform as the focus of macroeconomic policies, the fundamental approach is to break through institutional obstacles by means of reform and to pave the way for supply-side structural reform by promoting various basic reforms.

V. A complete shift in ideas, thoughts and strategies

In this context, we can see clearly that the macroeconomic environment we face in China as we enter a new era is already very different from that in the past. A macroeconomic regulatory system that is guided by the new development philosophy, centered on supply-side structural reform, and adapts to the new normal of economic development has taken shape. The outstanding feature of this system is focusing not only on the scale of development, short-term regulation, demand management, and policy operations, but more on the quality of development, sustained driver of growth, supply-side structural improvement, and reform actions.

Since the new normal of economic development differs from the old one, the new development philosophy differs widely from the old one, supply-side structural reform differs widely from demand management, and the reform mechanisms differ widely from past ones since major problems have changed, it is imperative for us to focus on one particular issue, namely to avoid facing the new situation with conventional thinking and dealing with the new problems by copying the old practices. It is an extremely important and urgent task for us to comprehensively adjust the ideas, thoughts and strategies that we have been accustomed to and seek to advance and deepen supply-side structural reform with new ideas, thoughts and strategies that are quite different from old ones and put in place a sound macroeconomic regulatory system commensurate with supply-side structural reform.

Only in this way can we blaze a new trail of economic work that differs widely from the past one. In response to the requirements of the new era, we should strive to change the growth model, improve the economic structure, and foster new drivers of growth to modernize the economic system. In doing so, we will better meet the people's ever-growing needs on economic, political, cultural, social and ecological fronts and better promote all-round human development and social progress.

[9] Xi (2017, p. 115).

5 Profound Changes in China's Macroeconomic Regulatory System in the New Era[10]

Since the 18th CPC National Congress, a series of profound changes have taken place in China's macroeconomic regulation theories and practices amid the formation of Xi Jinping Thought on Socialist Economy with Chinese Characteristics for a New Era. As a result of such profound changes, a macroeconomic regulatory system for the new era has taken shape in China.

It would be good if we adopt a before-and-after approach in examining these changes and find out the essential aspects.

I. Perspective of analysis: from cyclical and total output factors to the compounding of multiple factors

The professional analysis and accurate assessment of the economic situation is undoubtedly the prerequisite for the implementation of macroeconomic regulation and is also a very important basic task.

In the past, our analysis of the economic situation was carried out in the context of traditional macroeconomics. According to the principles of traditional macroeconomics, the changes in the economic situation would be compared to fever that would occur periodically in the course of a person's life. The economy always moves forward amid cyclical fluctuations, downturn or overheating. Economic downturn and overheating would be attributed to the imbalance between total demand and supply. Economic downturn is caused by excess supply while overheating is caused by excess demand. Therefore, whenever there was a change in the economic situation, while focusing on the outstanding problems, we would always analyze it from two basic perspectives, namely cyclical and total output factors. We would attribute the change to the impact of cyclical factors, or regard it as the result of total output factors. In the former case, both economic downward and overheating would be considered cyclical or short-term. In the latter case, the main problem was believed to be total supply and demand, and the main aspect of the problem on the demand side. Both excess supply and excess demand can be alleviated or solved by increasing or reducing total demand.

However, as China's economic development enters a new normal, we are faced with new issues such as slower growth, structural adjustment and change of growth drivers as well as the resulting changes. The analysis mainly based on cyclical and total output factors is becoming increasingly insufficient and disconnected from China's economic realities.

As Xi Jinping clearly noted, "The outstanding problems facing the functioning of the Chinese economy are partially cyclical and total output factors, but mainly major

[10] * This is an excerpt from "Understanding China's Macroeconomic Regulatory System in the New Era" published in *Social Sciences in China,* No, 9, 2018.

structural imbalances.[11]" "Structural problems are the most prominent and the main aspect of the problems is on the supply side."[12]

This is clearly an important and innovative conclusion.

First, since the outstanding problems in the functioning of the economy are not or no longer cyclical and total output factors, but short-term cyclical fluctuations amid long-term trends and total output problems intertwined with structural problems, a change in the economic situation would not be as simple as "a cold or fever", but a combination of "cold or fever and cardiovascular disease"—a complex mix of "acute and chronic diseases".

Second, since the root causes of the outstanding problems are not or no longer cyclical fluctuations and the imbalance between total supply and demand, but the unsmooth flow of economic activities caused by major structural imbalances, the changes in the economic situation may be not short-term, cyclical changes but long-term development trends, or a combination of cyclical changes and development trends as well as short-term and long-term changes.

Third, since structural problem is the most prominent and the main aspect of the problem is on the supply side, total supply and demand is not or no longer the main problem, and the demand side is not or no longer the main aspect of the problem. The method of increasing or reducing total demand is not or no longer an effective way to alleviate or solve the problem.

This suggests that it is imperative to expand the perspective of economic situation analysis under the new normal of economic development. We should pay attention not only to short-term economic fluctuations, but also long-term structural factors, and skillfully combine the effort to iron out short-term fluctuations on the demand side with that to address long-term structural problems on the supply side. We should not only pay attention to the balance between total supply and demand, but also improve the supply structure. The effort to treat "acute diseases" manifested in supply–demand imbalances should be closely linked with that to treat "chronic diseases" represented by a series of major structural imbalances such as those in industrial structure and regional development.

II. Development philosophy: from high-speed growth to high-quality development

An accurate assessment of development stage is the starting point of doing economic work well, and different development stages would naturally require different guiding principles for economic work—the development philosophy. As the fundamental factor that concerns the bigger picture and long-term interests, development philosophy is a crystallization of development ideas, especially those about the direction and focus of development.

The development philosophy we used to uphold was developed in and agreed with the stage of high-speed economic growth. Rooted in the special context of the stage of high-speed growth, economic work would naturally focus on the total economic

[11] Xi (2017, p. 113).

[12] Xi (2017, p. 105).

output and growth rate, or the size and speed of GDP. Therefore, the growth rate of GDP was often considered the only yardstick for assessing the economic situation. A fast growth rate would mean a good situation while a slow one would mean a bad situation. A faster growth would suggest the effectiveness of our efforts while a slower one would suggest ineffectiveness. The pursuit of high-speed growth and the only focus on GDP were seen everywhere.

However, in the face of the historical change that the Chinese economy has shifted from a stage of high-speed growth to a stage of high-quality development, the traditional development philosophy that may have become conventional thinking has met strong challenges on the levels of both economic indicators and policy considerations.

Under the new normal of economic development, in response to the new changes in the environment, conditions, tasks and requirements for China's economic development, President Xi Jinping said that "the ideas, thinking and focus of economic work should be adjusted".[13] "Our development must be sound development. We must pursue with firmness of purpose the vision of innovative, coordinated, green, open and shared development…and strive to achieve higher-quality, more efficient, fairer and more sustainable development."[14]

The adjustment here is by no means literal, but substantial change.

First, since the economy has shifted from high-speed growth to high-quality development, the assessment of the economic situation and economic work does not exclude the consideration of GDP growth rate, but it is not the only nor the most important yardstick. In addition, we should introduce quality and efficiency indicators and put them first in doing economic work, making them the centerpiece of the entire assessment system. In assessing the results of economic development, we should look at not how fast GDP grows, but how good the quality and efficiency are.

Second, since the goal is to achieve higher-quality, more efficient, fairer and more sustainable development, to promote economic development in the current stage may still require an effort to increase total demand but it can only be at a moderate level. It is not or no longer our top option to adopt stimulus policies for short-term economic growth and overdraw future growth. Instead, we should guide the economy towards sustained and healthy development, follow the principle of putting quality and efficiency first, and consider the improvement of the quality and efficiency of economic development as the ultimate purpose.

Third, since we must pursue innovative, coordinated, green, open and shared development, development remains the key to solving all the problems in China. However, what we seek is not or no longer development in the traditional sense, but development that embodies the new development philosophy. In other words, innovation is the primary driving force, coordination is inherent, eco-friendliness is universal, opening up is the only way, and sharing is the fundamental purpose of economic development.

This means that since China has entered a stage of high-quality development, the focus on scale and speed has given way to that on quality and efficiency and

[13] Xi (2017, p. 112).

[14] Xi (2017, pp. 21–35).

promoting high-quality development has become essential for maintaining sustained and healthy economic development. Correspondingly, on the practical level, guided by the new development philosophy, we should develop a set of indicators, policies, and standards, a statistical system, and performance evaluation methods that will help promote high-quality development and make them the fundamental driving force behind the economic work that has been set in stone.

III. **Policy focus: from demand management to supply-side structural reform**

Macroeconomic policies always have a focus that determines the central element of macroeconomic regulation as well as its target, approach and priority. It is the soul of macroeconomic policies.

The focus of China's macroeconomic policies used to be demand management. Its basic feature was to focus on the demand side and practice counter-cyclical regulation for short-term stability amid cyclical economic fluctuations. Whenever the economy went down and total demand was insufficient, actions would be taken to increase total demand. Whenever the economy was overheating and total demand was excess, actions would be taken to reduce total demand. Such a simple way of managing total demand is well-known even to non-economic professionals after nearly 40 years of reform and opening up.

However, as the new idea of supply-side structural reform was creatively put forward and replaced demand management as the focus of macroeconomic policies, the rules about how macroeconomic policies work out and are implemented, which have been well known and used for many years, are no longer applicable and must be adjusted accordingly.

As President Xi said, "We should take advancing supply-side structural reform as the focus of economic development and economic work at present and in the period ahead, change the growth model, and foster innovation to build a new engine and support for sustained and healthy economic development."[15] "We must focus on improving supply-side structure, proceed from the production side, improve the quality and efficiency of the supply system, expand effective and medium–high-end supply, and make the supply-side structure more responsive to changes in demand."[16]

This is in essence a radical adjustment to demand management and also means a change in the direction of macroeconomic regulation.

First, since the structural reform is on the supply side, demand may not be excluded in our consideration, but efforts will be mainly on the supply side. We should pay more attention to the supply side, stimulate the vitality of economic growth, and strive to achieve a new dynamic balance between supply and demand.

Second, since the focus of supply-side structural reform is to solve structural rather than total output problems, demand management may not be excluded, but the main approach will be structural adjustment. Short-term counter-cyclical operations are still needed but are no longer the main option.

[15] Xi (2017, pp. 107–108).

[16] Xi (2017, p. 119).

Third, since the main objective of supply-side structural reform is to improve the quality of supply and the supply structure, "acute diseases" such as cyclical fluctuations and the imbalance between supply and demand should still be treated, but we should promote the reforms for improving the quality, efficiency and impetus of economic development and put more effort into structural adjustment.

This reminds us that the major adjustment in the focus of macroeconomic policies means that the focus of macroeconomic regulation has changed along with its target, approach and main objective. Recognizing that such a change is irreversible, it is an important task for us in the new era to continue to manage demand properly and at the same time explore a new path of macroeconomic regulation with supply-side structural reform as the focus.

IV. Implementation mechanism: from policy operations to the combination of policy operations and reform actions

Macroeconomic regulation must be achieved with specific operations. Different compositions of macroeconomic policies would require different implementation mechanisms.

Macroeconomic regulation in China used to be achieved mainly through policy operations. Various policy variables and arrangements were used to reach the objectives of macroeconomic regulation. One of the items on the agenda of the annual Central Economic Work Conference would be to devise the macroeconomic policies for the next year. This was apparently in response to the assessment of the situation mainly based on cyclical and total output factors. As mentioned earlier, the problems arising from cyclical fluctuations and imbalances between total supply and demand would be "treated as acute diseases". The main approach was to introduce short-term counter-cyclical operations which would be simply on the policy level, without affecting related systems and mechanisms.

However, as the economic situation has undergone profound changes, especially since supply-side structural reform has become the focus of macroeconomic policies, the implementation of macroeconomic regulation should go beyond policy operation and be extended to the level of systems and mechanisms, mainly relying on reform actions.

As President Xi once said, "The cause of structural problems on the supply side is the distorted allocation of factors, which is an institutional obstacle."[17] Therefore, the fundamental way to advance supply-side structural reform "is to deepen reform… It means to improve the system and mechanism in which the market plays a decisive role in resource allocation, deepen the reform of the administrative system, break up monopoly, improve the factor market, and give play to the role of the price mechanism in guiding resource allocation".[18]

This is a very important shift.

First, since the outstanding problems we face have changed from supply–demand imbalance to structural imbalances and "acute diseases" have given way to "chronic

[17] Xi (2017, p. 106).

[18] Xi (2017, p. 115).

diseases", short-term counter-cyclical operations are no longer as effective as before. While continuing to treat "acute diseases"—the imbalance between supply and demand, we should focus on treating "chronic diseases"—structural imbalances.

Second, since the fundamental cause of supply-side structural problems lies in the institutional obstacles, the failure of the market to play a decisive role in resource allocation, and the failure of the government to better play its due role, the policy operations targeted at the obstacles in the systems and mechanisms are surely insufficient and we can only carry out a reform of the systems and mechanisms.

Third, the core and key of supply-side structural reform is reform. On the basis of identifying the supply-side structure and the imbalances in it, reform should be used to improve the overall supply structure and improve the capacity and quality of total supply.[19] We must deepen reform across the board to advance supply-side structural reform. The fundamental approach should be to break through the obstacles in systems and mechanisms with reform and focus on paving the way for supply-side structural reform by pushing forward various basic reforms.

This actually reminds us that, as a focus of economic work that supports high-quality development, supply-side structural reform is still within the scope of macroeconomic policies, but it should not be limited to the policy level. It also includes institutional reform, and even more importantly, it is driven by reform. In other words, it is necessary to skillfully combine policy adjustment with reform actions and integrate the long-term and long-term effects of reform with the short-term effects of macroeconomic policies to gather momentum for stable and sustainable economic growth.

V. **The government: from cleaning up to being more effective**

Adopting a problem-oriented approach and focusing on the principal contradiction is not only a Marxist methodology, but also a valuable asset for us to do our work in economic and other fields well.

In the past, in the face of the principal contradiction between the people's ever-growing material and cultural needs and backward social production and the main aspect of the contradiction lies in the reality of backward social production. The focus of economic work was to address insufficient supply and increase GDP. Therefore, availability and quantity were at the center of problems, and the main goal was to increase the supply of material and cultural products. The central task was to develop the business sector and market system. The purpose of macroeconomic regulation was to give full play to the decisive role of market in resource allocation. The government would step in only in the case of market failure.

However, since the principal contradiction in Chinese society has changed to the contradiction between the people's ever-growing needs for a better life and unbalanced and inadequate development and the main aspect of the contradiction has changed to unbalanced and inadequate development, both the focus of economic work and the role of the government have changed.

---

[19] Fang (2017).

As President Xi pointed out, "The evolution of the principal contradiction facing Chinese society represents a historic shift that affects the whole landscape and that creates many new demands for the work of the Party and the country. Building on continued efforts to sustain development, we must devote great energy to addressing development's imbalances and inadequacies, and push hard to improve the quality and effect of development. With this, we will be better placed to meet the ever-growing economic, political, cultural, social, and ecological needs of our people, and to promote well-rounded human development and all-round social progress."[20]

A series of new requirements have been set out in response to this major shift. Their significance to macroeconomic regulation should never be underestimated.

First, the needs for a better life mean upgraded material and cultural needs and the expansion from material and cultural needs to the needs for democracy, the rule of law, fairness, justice, security and the environment. The needs for a better life should be met with not only material and cultural products, but also institutional and policy products. We should not only upgrade material and cultural products, but also institutional and policy products.

Second, the focus of efforts to meet the needs for a better life is different. The upgrading of material and cultural products mainly depends on the market and the central issue has changed from availability and quantity to quality so the focus should be on vigorously improving the quality and efficiency of material and cultural products. It is the government's responsibility to consider institutional and policy products and attention should be given to not only quality, but also availability and quantity. The focus should be placed on the effective satisfaction of the people's needs for institutional and policy products as a new source of growth.

Third, both the market system and the government system are indispensable to meet the people's growing needs for a better life, and both have the responsibility to address the problem of unbalanced and inadequate development. While attaching equal importance to the supply of material and cultural products and that of institutional and policy products, we should improve both market supply and government supply and assign the responsibility of addressing unbalanced and inadequate development to both the market and government systems. We should make sure that "the market plays a decisive role in resource allocation" and "the government plays a better role".[21] The government should not only make up for the deficiencies in the field of material and cultural products, but also play a leading role in the field of institutional and policy products.

Fourth, since the people's ever-growing needs for a better life are more reflected in the needs for institutional products and policy products and the major constraint on such needs is the unbalanced and inadequate supply of the government system, greater importance should be given to developing the government system and addressing the unbalanced and inadequate supply of the government system. On the basis of identifying the main factors that affect the people's aspiration and needs for a better life, we should gather speed in modernizing the country's governance system and seek

[20] Xi (2017, pp. 11–12).

[21] Xi (2017, p. 21).

to establish a modern governance system that better meets the people's ever-growing economic, political, cultural, social and ecological needs.

This shows that, given the historical change in the principal contradiction in Chinese society, it is particularly important to improve the macroeconomic regulatory system by building an economic system that gives full play to the role of the market and better play to the role of the government. Therefore, the ultimate purpose of macroeconomic regulation and economic work in the new era should be to continue focusing on economic development and properly handle the dialectical relationship between improving the quality of development and achieving all-round development to meet the people's growing needs for a better life with more balanced and adequate supply.

We can see that the macroeconomic and policy environments we are now facing in China are very different from those in the past. There is already a macroeconomic regulatory system for the new era that is guided by the new development philosophy, closely follows the change in the principal contradiction in Chinese society, focuses on supply-side structural reform, adapts to the new normal of economic development, and meets the requirements of high-quality development.

It should be noted that all the profound changes in China's macroeconomic regulatory system involve major, rather than general, adjustments in the thinking and focus of China's economic development. Such adjustments are both profound and fundamental. They are not short-term but would last a fairly long period of time. This concerns not only macroeconomic policies, but also the macroeconomic theories underlying the policies.

Since the new normal differs sharply from the old one, the stage of high-quality development differs widely from the stage of high-speed growth, the new development philosophy differs sharply from the old one, the people's needs for a better life differ widely from material and cultural needs, supply-side structural reform differs widely from demand management, and the reform mechanisms differ widely from past ones since major problems have changed, it is imperative for us to focus on one particular issue, namely to avoid facing the new situation with conventional thinking and dealing with the new problems by copying the old practices.

Therefore, an extremely important and urgent task ahead of us is to take the initiative to meet the requirements of high-quality development. Guided by Xi Jinping Thought on Socialist Economy with Chinese Characteristics for a New Era, we should further comprehensively adjust the ideas, thoughts and strategies that we used to take for granted in the past and push forward and deepen supply-side structural reform with very different new ones to ensure that China's macroeconomic regulatory system for the new era functions well.

Only in this way can we remain focused, cope with the complex economic situation calmly and find a new path that differs widely from the past one for macroeconomic regulation and economic work in the new era.

6 Setting the Right Direction for Current Macroeconomic Policies[22]

It is particularly important today for China to set the right direction for the country's macroeconomic policies. Why is that?

With profound changes in the external environment and new economic downward pressure, demand management is playing an increasingly prominent role in China's macroeconomic regulation. The centerpiece of demand management has changed from moderately increasing total demand and continuously increasing domestic demand to strengthening counter-cyclical regulation. Moreover, a series of macroeconomic measures have been introduced to strengthen counter-cyclical regulation. Thus, in fact, the pursuit of macroeconomic policies has shown a dual direction, namely supply-side structural reform and demand management.

The dual direction is, of course, a choice that should be made in the face of the complex situation marked by an increasing number of difficult problems for many years. However, even though the policymakers have a clear understanding of the reasons for the current composition of macroeconomic policies and have repeatedly stressed that there should be no mass stimulus, there is still much misinterpretation and misunderstanding in the general public, particularly one-sided understanding of macroeconomic policies. In addition to the repeated expressions of "relaxing control again" and "restarting easing", some people have compared the current counter-cyclical regulation to the demand stimulus measures taken in response to the international financial crisis. Some people often equate macroeconomic policies with counter-cyclical regulation. When it comes to counter-cyclical regulation, they would talk so much about it. As for supply-side structural reform, which is the focus of macroeconomic policies, they would simply mention the principles without going into the details.

The problem is that macroeconomic policies must be implemented on the primary level after all. In the end, the policy objectives must be achieved through a series of coordinated actions taken by both market entities and government departments at all levels. If macroeconomic policies are understood as counter-cyclical regulation and supply-side structural reform is put aside, it would be against the current purpose of macroeconomic regulation and may even lead to the reappearance of conventional thinking, adding to the uncertainty and instability in the process of economic development. In light of that, Premier Li Keqiang stressed in delivering the Report on the Work of the Government in 2019 that "we will ensure that the right direction is set for the pursuit of our macroeconomic policies".

Therefore, the issue of policy understanding eventually boils downs to the issue of policy implementation and effect. How well the policies are understood concerns the direction, intensity and pace of implementation efforts. To ensure proper intensity, accurate pace, and desired results, we must set the right direction for the current pursuit of macroeconomic policies.

---

[22] * This is a slightly revised version of an article first published in *Economic Daily* on March 20, 2019.

Then, how to set the right direction for the current pursuit of macroeconomic policies?

First, we should understand the current pursuit of macroeconomic policies from the two dimensions of supply-side structural reform and demand management. In the face of mixed new and old problems as well as cyclical and structural problems, we should not concentrate on long-term development and structural adjustment but respond slowly to short-term fluctuations and economic downturn pressure, which would make economic indicators slip out of a proper range. Likewise, we should not adopt strong short-term stimulus policies that will undermine long-term development for the purpose of achieving short-term balance and withstanding economic downturn pressure, thus causing new risk hazards. Therefore, it is necessary to strengthen counter-cyclical regulation and demand stimulus in response to the economic downward pressure. It is also imperative to deepen supply-side structural reform based for long-term development and continuously focus on the reality that the supply system does not adapt to the changes in the demand structure. We should consider both strengthening counter-cyclical regulation and advancing supply-side structural reform as a long-term strategy. The two should complement each other and be pushed forward at the same time.

Second, we should understand the current pursuit of macroeconomic policies from the perspective of the high-quality development stage. In the stage of high-speed growth, GDP was the top priority, and all efforts were intended to increase GDP growth rate. At that time, demand management characterized by counter-cyclical regulation was the focus of macroeconomic policies. In the stage of high-quality development, quality and efficiency have replaced GDP growth as the core objective, structural problems have replaced total output problems as the main problems, and the main task is to improve the supply structure and the quality of supply. Correspondingly, supply-side structural reform has replaced demand management as the focus of macroeconomic policies. At this time, counter-cyclical regulation may be necessary, but its purpose is to pave the way for supply-side structural reform. In other words, in the context of pursuing high-quality development, demand management plays a supporting role while supply-side structural reform plays a leading role. Working on both supply and demand does not mean that the efforts on the two fronts are parallel, or the same weight should be given to them.

Third, we should understand the current pursuit of macroeconomic policies from the perspective of maintaining strategic focus. Given the changes in a generally stable economic performance, some of which cause concern, the repeated emphasis on maintaining strategic focus is to prevent frequent and excessive policy adjustments from causing panic and negative impacts on the economy. The strategic focus to be maintained is, in the final analysis, to advance supply-side structural reform as the main task, and stabilize expectations with a stable macroeconomic policy environment. We should not change our basic conclusions about the stage of economic development and the economic situation, or our resolve to further deepen supply-side structural reform because of any external shocks. We should not replace the pursuit of quality with that of speed, jump from the supply side to the demand side, put aside structural problems and focus on total output problems whenever there is economic downturn. Nor should we change policy, introduce fiscal stimulus, and encourage the central bank to relax regulation. In this sense, the current strengthening of counter-cyclical regulation is an expedient measure, rather than a change in the overall landscape of macroeconomic policies. It is not that demand management would replace supply-side structural reform and become the focus of macroeconomic policies. According to the policy of consolidating the gains in the five priority tasks, strengthening the dynamism of micro entities, upgrading industrial chains, and ensuring unimpeded flows in the economy, to deepen supply-side structural reform is the fundamental purpose of macroeconomic regulation in the current stage.

We can come to a very clear conclusion that the change of era, development stage, principal contradiction, and focus of macroeconomic policies requires a change in our understanding of the direction set for the current pursuit of macroeconomic policies. Macroeconomic regulation in the context of high-quality development is different form that in the context of high-speed growth. Under the guidance of Xi Jinping Thought on Socialist Economy with Chinese Characteristics for a New Era, we should fully understand the current composition of macroeconomic policies with changed ideas, thoughts and strategies. On this basis, we should balance total output and structure, immediate and long-term interests, and domestic and foreign affairs, strengthen policy coordination, and do economic work well at present and in the period ahead.

7 Stabilizing Growth: How to Optimize Policy Impact[23]

As the economic downward pressure continues to grow, the significance of stabilizing growth to macroeconomic policy objectives and the macroeconomic regulatory system becomes increasingly prominent, and it is undoubtedly extremely important to do a good job in stabilizing growth at present and in the period ahead. However, the graver the situation is, the more sober we should remain; the more complicated the problems are, the more clear-headed we should be. Since stabilizing growth is, after all, a highly professional and delicate task, and the economic and policy environments at home and abroad are quite different from those in the past, the efforts to stabilize growth must be made prudently. The most important is to figure out where to start to stabilize growth on the basis of thoroughly understanding the reality of economic performance in the stage of high-quality development.

In the face of the current economic downward pressure, it is imperative to place steady growth in a more important position. However, if we look at the theoretical and practical innovations that have focused on steady growth since the 18th CPC National Congress, we can see the substantial measures taken to stabilize growth in China as it shifts to a stage of high-quality development are not limited to demand management represented by counter-cyclical regulation. At least supply-side structural reform is

[23] * This is a slightly revised version of an article first published in *Economic Daily* on November 19, 2019.

also one of them. Moreover, in the macroeconomic regulatory system commensurate with high-quality development, supply-side structural reform plays the leading role while demand management plays a supporting role. The former has been introduced and implemented in response to the prominent problems in the stage of high-quality development, which is a radical adjustment to the latter. Therefore, in the effort to stabilize growth we should leverage the respective strengths of demand management and supply-side structural reform and prioritize the latter. The macroeconomic regulation in the new era should be characterized by the focus on supply-side structural reform, the leading role of fiscal and monetary policies, as well as the supporting role of employment, industry, investment, consumption and regional policies. We should not focus all our hopes on strengthening demand stimulation or forget that supply-side structural reform is the long-term strategy and a permanent solution.

In the face of the current economic downward pressure, it is imperative to strengthen counter-cyclical regulation. However, if we sort out the problems that cause or are related to the economic downturn, it would be easy to find out that there are external and internal problems, as well as cyclical, structural and institutional problems. For short-term, external or cyclical problems, counter-cyclical regulation would undoubtedly be effective. However, for long-term, internal or structural and institutional problems, counter-cyclical regulation will not be targeted, and it is very likely to be insufficient. Therefore, the efforts to stabilize growth must be well-targeted. While implementing counter-cyclical regulation in response to short-term, external or cyclical problems, we should address long-term, internal, or structural and institutional problems by deepening supply-side structural reform. We should neither address all problems indiscriminately nor expect that counter-cyclical regulation can solve all the problems.

In the face of the current economic downward pressure, it is imperative to achieve a short-term balance between supply and demand. However, if we look beyond the scope of short-term and total output problems to long-term and structural problems, we will find that long-term structural balance is also indispensable. Practices over the years have repeatedly reminded us that the short-term supply–demand balance must be based on long-term structural balance. Without long-term structural balance, short-term supply–demand balance would be unsustainable. Moreover, compared with the stage of high-speed growth, the main problems in the functioning of the economy in the stage of high-quality development are structural problems and the main aspect of the problems are on the supply side. Therefore, to stabilize growth, on the one hand, we should consider both short-term and long-term objectives and seek to achieve supply–demand balance and improve structures at the same time. Supply–demand balance should be used to facilitate structural improvement and the latter should be used to make the former sustainable. On the other hand, it is necessary to distinguish between primary and secondary problems, focus on structural and supply-side problems, and prioritize supply-side structural reform. Our efforts should be concentrated on advancing various basic reforms concerning supply-side structural problems. We should neither consider only short-term supply–demand balance or long-term structural improvement, nor mistake non-primary problems for primary ones.

The current economic downward pressure comes against the backdrop of the shift to a stage of high-quality development. Economic downturn or downward pressure may appear to be similar at different stages of development, but the internal causes and how the effect would spread are quite different. Behind total output and demand-side problems are structural and supply-side problems on deeper levels. Economic downward pressure may mean different things in different contexts and the effort to stabilize growth in the stage of high-quality is different from that in the stage of high-speed growth. If we simply copy the practices in the stage of high-speed growth to cope with the economic downward pressure in the stage of high-quality development, it is likely to backfire and even lead to opposite results. Likewise, if we try to achieve all objectives through regulation, we are likely to introduce mass stimulus in which case we will lose all the hard-won results of supply-side structural reform. Therefore, on the one hand, the efforts to stabilize growth should be consistent with the theme of the new era and the mission of the new development stage, as well as the ideas, thoughts and strategies that are in line with the stage of high-quality development. On the other hand, we should be prepared for a long battle on thinking. We should neither adhere to the old path and pursue the goal of stabilizing growth with conventional thinking, nor expect to achieve a quick success.

In conclusion, it is clear that in today's China, the efforts to stabilize growth must be made on the two fronts of policy adjustment and deepening reform, with the latter being the mainstay. This will put our capacity for deepening supply-side structural reform to the test. The effectiveness of such efforts will also depend largely on whether we can translate the economic downward pressure into a driving force for deepening reform. Focusing on stabilizing growth through supply-side structural reform should never and cannot be empty talk.

Chapter 5
New Interpretations of Proactive Fiscal Policy

1 Introduction

This chapter, comprising eight articles, is entitled "New Interpretations of Proactive Fiscal Policy". The "new interpretations" here implies offering new explanations about proactive fiscal policy or redefining proactive fiscal policy.

Fiscal policy has always played a leading role in macroeconomic regulation. This is true not only in the stage of high-speed growth with demand management as the focus, but also in the stage of high-quality development. However, with the change in the stage of economic development and that in the focus of macroeconomic regulation brought about by it, the design of fiscal policy must be changed accordingly. Such a change would certainly not happen overnight, but require a gradual process. The initial adjustment was made in 2013. In the face of the shift in China's economic situation, what should we do about the proactive fiscal policy that has been implemented for 5 years? The article "Drawing a Roadmap for Proactive Fiscal Policy" makes an analysis from three aspects in answering the question.

There has been a blind spot in the calculation of China's fiscal deficit for quite a long time. This is certainly related to the complicated evolution of the government budget system since the beginning of reform and opening up. An important reason is that the reform of the current government budget system is not in place yet and there is still something uncertain. Since fiscal deficit is a basic indicator of fiscal expansion, its calculation concerns not only the design of proactive fiscal policy, but also the assessment of such aspects as fiscal security and the effectiveness of macroeconomic regulation, which needs to be analyzed from a professional perspective. Therefore, right before the Central Economic Work Conference of the year, I wrote the article "Full-scope Budget Deficit: A Benchmark for Assessing the Implementation and Potential of Proactive Fiscal Policy".

As a defense for fiscal and even economic security, the ratio of fiscal deficit to GDP should be no more than 3% which was prescribed in the agreement on the EU's establishment. Although this ratio has not been clearly proven to be scientific

P. Gao, *A Shift Toward High-Quality Development of China*,
Research Series on the Chinese Dream and China's Development Path,
https://doi.org/10.1007/978-981-99-8990-4_5

or fully adopted within the EU, China has always used it as a cautionary indicator since the day it was introduced and the ratio in the country has been said to be less than 3%. Therefore, the fact has evolved into a worst-case scenario that people would accept. As China's economic development enters a new normal and efforts are made to build a macroeconomic regulatory system mainly through supply-side structural reform, there have been differing views about whether the 3% ratio should still be considered part of proactive fiscal policy. The article "Keeping Budget Deficit below Three Percent of GDP" was written in early 2017. At the time, greater importance was given to proactive fiscal policy and there was a heated discussion about whether the fiscal deficit should be limited to 3% of GDP.

Proactive fiscal policy has always been equated with expansionary fiscal policy, which is common sense in the eyes of many people. However, profound changes have taken place in China's economic environment and macroeconomic regulation as China moves to a stage of high-quality development. In such a context, the definition and implementation path of proactive fiscal policy have in fact been adjusted accordingly. Understanding proactive fiscal policy from a single perspective of expansion not only goes against the changed reality, but also will lead to deviations in policy implementation. Therefore, we must redefine proactive fiscal policy in light of the changed macroeconomic environment and macroeconomic regulation, and clearly explain the proactive fiscal policy in the shift to a stage of high-quality development. In view of that, I wrote two articles, namely "Four Profound Changes in Proactive Fiscal Policy" and "Proactive Fiscal Policy during the Shift to High-quality Development".

In 2019, in the face of new problems and challenges brought about by the escalating trade frictions between China and the United States, China gathered pace in adjusting the design of proactive fiscal policy after years of continuous exploration. The clearest sign was that the meeting of the Political Bureau of the CPC Central Committee held in July 2018 proposed that "fiscal policy should play a bigger role in increasing domestic demand and facilitating structural adjustment". Since then, the role of proactive fiscal policy has been clearly expanded from simply increasing demand to both increasing demand and facilitating structural adjustment. Correspondingly, a series of important adjustments have also been made in the basic operations of proactive fiscal policy. It was against this background that I wrote the article "2019: Profound Changes in the Design of Proactive Fiscal Policy". The basic idea of this article is that, compared with previous theoretical analysis and practices, the design of proactive fiscal policy in the shift to a stage of high-quality development has changed and its implications have changed. Therefore, we should not try to understand the current proactive fiscal policy simply based on past theories and practices.

Based on the adjustment in 2019 and facing a more complex and graver economic situation, the design of proactive fiscal policy in 2020 seemed to be more mature both in theory and in practice. At this point, it is not only necessary but also possible to give a comprehensive and systematic explanation of the changes in the design of proactive fiscal policy. At the invitation of *Economic Daily* and *Qiushi* magazine, I wrote two articles, namely "2020: What Kind of Proactive Fiscal Policy Do We Need?" and

"Reshaping Proactive Fiscal Policy", according to the plans made regarding proactive fiscal policy at the Central Economic Work Conference. The former is a short article intended to briefly analyze the direction of proactive fiscal policy in 2020. The latter is a longer one intended to explain as clearly as possible the evolution of proactive fiscal policy so far and then draw some logical conclusions.

2 Drawing a Roadmap for Proactive Fiscal Policy[1]

On the basis of fully assessing the economic situations at home and abroad, the Central Economic Work Conference in 2012 made the decision to continue implementing a proactive fiscal policy and a prudent monetary policy. Therefore, the combination of these two macroeconomic policies entered its third consecutive year in China. However, the past trajectory of China's macroeconomic policies tells us that there is something different in the combination this time. Proactive fiscal policy and prudent monetary policy may mean different things, or even significant adjustments or changes in the new context.

Properly grasping these adjustments and changes is undoubtedly very important for us to understand the guiding principles of the Central Economic Work Conference and do a good job in performing economic tasks in 2013.

I. **Giving due consideration to needs on two fronts and focusing on multiple objectives**

Starting from 2008, with the outbreak and evolution of the global financial crisis, China's macroeconomic policy mix can be roughly divided into two stages. One is characterized by the combination of proactive fiscal policy and moderately loose monetary policy and the other by the combination of proactive fiscal policy and prudent monetary policy. However, both combinations show an expansionary tendency. The only difference lies in the intensity and structure of expansion. The combination of proactive fiscal policy and prudent monetary policy in 2013 is certainly an expansionary operation of macroeconomic regulation on the whole.

Five years have passed since such an expansionary operation was launched in 2008. Compared to that of previous years, the expansionary operation of 2013 has at least three differences. First, under the law of diminishing marginal utility, the effectiveness of expansionary operations has decreased. Even with mass expansionary measures like those introduced in 2008, the effect will not be as good as it was in that year. Second, as a result of the expansionary policy, the negative impact on structural adjustment has appeared. Compared with the years before the crisis, today we are facing greater pressure and heavier and more urgent tasks on the front of structural adjustment. Third, as the global economy continues to fluctuate and the issues of imbalances and unsustainability become more prominent, an increasing number of

[1] This is a slightly revised version of "2013: Roadmap for Proactive Fiscal Policy", published in *People's Daily* on January 21, 2013.

people realize that it would be impossible to achieve recovery in the true sense on the basis of the existing economic structure. To keep the economy on the track of sustainable and healthy development, we must intensify efforts to make strategic adjustments in the economic structure and change the growth model thoroughly.

This means that even if the slow growth of the world economy will continue, the imbalance between the downward pressure on economic growth and relative overcapacity has intensified, and the fundamental aspects of macroeconomic policies still need to maintain an expansionary tendency, we cannot simply adopt mass expansionary measures like those of 2008 or seek to achieve economic growth targets at the expense of structural adjustment. This also means that to achieve economic growth with quality, efficiency and sustainability through continuous transformation of growth model and improvement of the economic structure, we must give due consideration to the needs for both steady growth and structural adjustment, and tread a path of coordination between counter-cyclical regulation and structural adjustment.

Because of that, the macroeconomic policies of 2013 are aimed at both counter-cyclical regulation and structural adjustment, in contrast to the previous focus simply on counter-cyclical regulation. Moreover, the macroeconomic regulation of 2013 is intended to attain multiple objectives such as stabilizing growth, adjusting the structure, controlling prices and guarding against risks, instead of simply maintaining or stabilizing growth.

Therefore, faced with the needs on two fronts and multiple objectives, China has to strike a proper balance between them in selecting macroeconomic policies for the current stage.

II. **Starting with deficit increase, tax reduction and expenditure increase**

In the composition of macroeconomic policies, proactive fiscal policy is certainly intended mainly to implement expansion. As an expansionary operation of macroeconomic regulation, proactive fiscal policy boils down to three measures, namely increasing deficit, reducing tax revenue, and increasing expenditure. In other words, fiscal expansion always starts with deficit increase, tax reduction and expenditure increase. The proactive fiscal policy of 2013 is naturally no exception.

First, increasing deficit. It is necessary to increase deficit because the extent of fiscal expansion is directly determined by the size of fiscal deficit and its marginal effect. Only when fiscal deficit is large will the expansionary effect be strong. To be specific, only when the fiscal deficit of 2013 is larger than that of 2012 is it likely to produce expansionary effect in reality. If the fiscal deficit of 2013 is the same as that of 2012, the fiscal policy of 2013 will tend to produce neutral effect. If the fiscal deficit in 2013 is smaller than that of 2012, the fiscal policy of 2013 will tend to produce tightening effect. To implement fiscal expansion, the fiscal deficit of 2013 should naturally increase from the 2012 level. Considering the eight hundred billion yuan in government bonds and the 270 billion yuan used to replenish the Central Budget Stabilization Fund, the total fiscal deficit of 2012 was 1.05 trillion yuan. Given the economic trend and the needs to implement fiscal expansion and in other aspects in 2013, the Central Budget Stabilization Fund is already made smaller and the increase in the fiscal deficit of 2013 is expected to be in hundred billion yuan.

Second, reducing tax revenue and increasing expenditure. When fiscal deficit is set, there are two types of operations to reach the target, namely reducing tax revenue and increasing expenditure. A fiscal deficit of a certain amount can support either tax reduction or expenditure increase, or both of them. This depends on proactive fiscal policy's extent of expansion. Common sense also tells us that, given the multiplier difference between tax revenue and expenditure, increasing expenditure would produce a stronger and more immediate expansionary effect than reducing taxes. Considering the current macroeconomic policies intended to meet needs on two fronts and multiple objectives as well as the interests of all stakeholders, we can conclude that the proactive fiscal policy of 2013 should and must focus on structural tax reduction.

We should focus on structural tax reduction rather than on increasing government spending because tax reduction produces expansionary effect mainly through the increase of people's disposable income rather than the increase of direct government investment. On the one hand, this helps to stabilize growth as a result of counter-cyclical adjustment. On the other hand, this allows the market to play a greater role in investment, that is, in resource allocation. It also helps to avoid the trap of direct government investment and give better play to the role of proactive fiscal policy in promoting structural adjustment. It was for this reason that structural tax reduction already became the central part of proactive fiscal policy in 2012, especially in the second half of 2012. In 2013, this approach will not and should not change substantially, and given the needs on two fronts and multiple objectives, the role of structural tax reduction in fiscal expansion will become increasingly prominent. It may even become a major factor that determines the success of macroeconomic regulation this time. This means that at least half or more of the fiscal deficit in 2013 should be used to support structural tax reduction.

Increasing government spending is undoubtedly also necessary for fiscal expansion. It used to play a major role in the composition of macroeconomic policies. It was precisely because of the increase of government spending that we were able to take the lead in achieving recovery and growth in the wake of the international financial crisis. However, given the important changes in the macroeconomic situation, major adjustments have been made to the composition of macroeconomic policies and the need to balance counter-cyclical regulation and structural adjustment has become increasingly prominent. The effort to increase government spending in 2013 will have to be curbed. Governments at all levels should practice economy. They should strictly control general expenditures and spend money on important work that must be done. Moreover, even for the public investment expenditure that must be increased, the private sector investment should be increased, and priority should be given to infrastructure that concerns people's wellbeing and long-term development. This means that portion of fiscal deficit in 2013 to support government spending should be less than that in previous years, or at least less than the proportion used to finance structural tax reduction.

III. **Replacing BT with VAT as the focus of macroeconomic regulation**

The specific plans for structural tax reduction as the main component of proactive fiscal policy will certainly be the most distinctive feature of the macroeconomic policy landscape in 2013. This is because macroeconomic regulation in the current stage must accommodate the needs on two fronts and focus on multiple objectives and structural tax reduction is an appropriate choice that can accommodate all factors in such a context. This is also because structural tax reduction is a macroeconomic regulation measure that most people would agree on. In a sense, structural tax reduction has stood at the center of China's macroeconomic operations.

There are certainly many options when it comes to promoting structural tax reduction. For example, the eighteen taxes in the current tax system can all be cut. However, if we want to align the current tax system with the tax reform during the 12th Five-Year Plan period or develop a balanced tax revenue system, the priority of the efforts to promote structural tax reduction is undoubtedly to cut indirect taxes rather than direct taxes and to cut major indirect taxes in which income account for a large share. For this reason, the Central Economic Work Conference in 2012 used the expression "improving the structural tax reduction policy in combination with the tax system reform" when discussing the issue of structural tax reduction.

Furthermore, in the current tax system, major indirect taxes include VAT, BT and excise tax. In 2011, the share of these three taxes was 41.1%, 15.25% and 8.79%, respectively. If we look at the three taxes in the context of tax reform and the progress in this regard, we will find that only VAT is the best choice for structural tax reduction. The reason is not hard to explain.

First, according to the plan for tax reform during the 12th Five-Year Plan period, BT will eventually be replaced by VAT. It will be included in the VAT system by the end of the 12th Five-Year Plan period. Second, excise tax is levied on luxury goods and goods related to energy and resource consumption. It is always difficult to reach a consensus on cutting excise tax since it concerns the government's income distribution policy and policy arrangements for energy saving and emission reduction. Third, VAT is the largest tax in China's current tax system. Even a slight change in this tax will greatly affect the government's total tax revenue, and maximum tax reduction is likely to be achieved. Thus, comparatively speaking, reducing VAT, or mainly reducing it, is apparently almost the only right option for structural tax reduction.

It is gratifying that the pilot program on replacing BT with VAT, which is being carried out in Shanghai and other parts of the country, is a structural tax reduction initiative featuring the largest scale and widest impact. It has offered a good platform for reducing the VAT burden. Firstly, with the replacement of BT with VAT, double taxation caused by no deduction of BT will tend to be reduced by the inclusion of relevant industries in the scope of VAT. Thus, the original tax burden borne by the relevant industries will be reduced. Secondly, with the replacement of BT with VAT, the imbalance between the two taxes brought about by the VAT reform—the decrease of VAT burden will cause the relative rise of BT burden. This will tend to be mitigated by the inclusion of relevant industries in the VAT coverage. Thus, the original tax burden borne by the relevant industries will be reduced. Third, a higher overall VAT tax burden was caused by the wide application of the two higher tax rates, 17% and 13%. With the replacement of BT with VAT and the addition of two lower tax rates,

11% and 6%, the average VAT rate and the overall tax burden will be reduced by applying the two lower tax rates to the relevant industries.

In fact, Shanghai's pilot program on replacing BT with VAT over the past year has shown that the tax reduction effect brought by it has far exceeded expectations. The pilot program has been extended to include Beijing, Jiangsu, Anhui, Fujian, Guangdong, Tianjin, Zhejiang and Hubei. Given that the pilot program will eventually be promoted across the country and all service industries, the most conservative estimate of taxes reduced would be at least in hundreds of billions of yuan.

Therefore, in 2013, we will focus on the main task of structural tax reduction, in particular the reduction of VAT. There are two paths we can choose.

Option One is to gather pace in extending the coverage of the pilot program on replacing BT with VAT. The more areas and industries are covered in the pilot program, the greater economies of scale structural tax reduction will achieve. Taking effective actions to involve more areas and industries will apparently help produce the desired results of structural tax reduction.

Option Two is to reduce the standard rate of VAT while extending the coverage. To include the service sector in the VAT system originally designed based on the characteristics of the manufacturing sector, it is necessary to take the characteristics of the service sector into account and make corresponding adjustments and restart institutional arrangements under the condition that the two sectors are integrated. To meet the needs of both sectors and achieve long-term development, while extending the coverage, we should also reduce the standard rate of VAT so that the average tax burden will be reduced more substantially.

3 Full-Scope Budget Deficit: A Benchmark for Assessing the Implementation and Potential of Proactive Fiscal Policy[2]

At the end of the year, facing the severe economic downward pressure in China, people are calling for further strengthening proactive fiscal policy, and even high expectations have been formed.

Common sense tells us that fiscal deficit and the deficit-to-GDP ratio are the basic yardstick for assessing the implementation of proactive fiscal policy. Apparently, the assessment of the current implementation of proactive fiscal policy and the further strengthening of its implementation must be based on an accurate understanding and scientific calculation of fiscal deficit and the deficit-to-GDP ratio.

I. **Deficit in the general public budget is not the whole of fiscal deficit**

Ordinarily, the size of China's fiscal deficit is determined on the basis of the annual budget report approved by the National People's Congress. For example, in 2016,

[2] This article was published in *Securities Times* on November 28, 2016, and slight changes were made when the book was published.

China set a budget deficit of 2.18 trillion yuan, an increase of 0.56 trillion yuan over the previous year, including a central government budget deficit of 1.4 trillion yuan and a local government budget deficit of 0.78 trillion yuan, with the deficit-to-GDP ratio rising to 3%.

However, looking at these figures from the perspective of modern budgeting, and particularly in light of the new Budget Law, we can see at least three problems.

First, both the deficit of 2.18 trillion yuan and the deficit-to-GDP ratio of 3% are the results of calculation based on the general public budget.

Second, according to international practice, in calculating fiscal deficit we should consider all government revenues and expenditures, not just some of them.

Third, China has implemented the new Budget Law since 2015. Compared with the old Budget Law, the biggest change is that in addition to the general public budget it also covers three other types of budgets, namely a budget for government-managed funds, a budget for social security funds, and a budget for state-owned capital operations.

It means that the current fiscal deficit of 2.18 trillion yuan, as is known by the general public, does not cover all deficits in government budgets across the country in 2016. The deficit-to-GDP ratio of 3% does not reflect the real level of China's fiscal deficit in 2016, and should and must be re-calculated based on all deficits in government budgets.

II. **There is a need to do some addition**

To calculate the fiscal deficit of 2016 accurately and scientifically, we should do some addition in at least three aspects on the basis of the above-mentioned deficit and deficit-to-GDP ratio.

First, the local government special bonds of four hundred billion yuan listed under the 2016 budgets of government-managed funds are in fact a form of local government debt. According to the Interim Measures for Managing the Issuance of Special Bonds by Local Governments, special bonds are mainly used to raise funds for public projects that would generate certain income and the sources of repayment are the government-managed funds or special income corresponding to the projects, which should be included in the budgets of government-managed funds. As it is impossible for the public projects to generate income in the current period, the debt can only be repaid with the income obtained after the project is completed. This will directly result in a deficit of government-managed funds in the current period.

Second, in 2016, China's central government set a 5.27 trillion-yuan limit for the issuance of local government bonds for debt swap. In theory, a debt swap would not result in a net increase in debt, and thus would not affect deficit. However, in China, such swapped local debts had never been recognized as deficit or included in the deficit of the current period. Since they were given legitimacy, they have been recognized as deferred deficit.

Third, as of the end of August 2016, the National Development and Reform Commission (NDRC) had issued 1.8 trillion-yuan long-term special development bonds through policy banks. On the surface, these long-term special development bonds are financial bonds, and the special development funds formed thereof are also invested in the development projects, which seems to have nothing to do with government bonds. However, they receive a 90% interest subsidy from the government, which makes them a kind of quasi-government bonds and apparently debt in the form of bonds.

In addition, local efforts to promote public–private partnerships (PPPs), in fact, imply that there are many government debts. To attract more private sector investors, local governments would sign contracts with project-related companies through industrial investment funds and make commitments in terms of repurchase (guaranteed principal), guaranteed income (a fixed return at a certain rate each year), and installment payments (expenditures from the budget each year in the name of services purchased by the government). They may even issue a letter of guarantee through the National People's Congress. The resulting deficit in this case should not be underestimated.

With all these factors considered, China's fiscal deficit in 2016 is bound to be much larger than 2.18 trillion yuan and the deficit-to-GDP ratio will surely be higher than 3% by a considerable margin.

III. There is a need to prudently assess the implementation and potential of proactive fiscal policy

The annual Central Economic Work Conference is about to be held. The design of macroeconomic policies for 2017 must be based on an assessment of the implementation of proactive fiscal policy in 2016 and the potential of proactive fiscal policy in 2017. There is no doubt that this assessment should be based on an exhaustive fiscal deficit rather than the deficit in the general public budget.

However, once we change the criterion of assessment from deficit in the general public budget to exhaustive fiscal deficit, we will definitely find that the implementation of China's proactive fiscal policy in 2016 has been stepped up on a level higher than that people are aware of. Likewise, the room left for China to further strengthen the implementation of proactive fiscal policy in 2017 is not as ample as people think. Therefore, in the current period, it is very important to carefully assess the implementation and potential of proactive fiscal policy.

This means that, in the context of China's economic development entering a new normal and its effort to push forward supply-side structural reform, we should, on the one hand, implement more proactive fiscal policies to ensure the economy operates within a proper range, and on the other hand, carefully assess its possible benefits and costs and stay alert to the potential fiscal risks. Proactive fiscal policy has in fact shown a sign of diminishing marginal utility and its implementation should focus on both stimulating demand and structural adjustment, which is a policy-specific plan and a major measure of institutional reform. It is, therefore, imperative to properly address issues concerning fiscal deficit and local government debt on the basis of properly assessing the implementation and potential of proactive fiscal policy. While ensuring steady economic growth, we should keep in mind worst-case scenarios and strive to prevent regional and systemic risks.

4 Keeping Budget Deficit Below Three Percent of GDP[3]

When it comes to the current composition of macroeconomic policies, popular expectations for fiscal policy are apparently rising. In recent years, the Central Economic Work Conference has changed the stress on proactive fiscal policy from "making it stronger and more effective" to "making it stronger" and then "making it more proactive and effective". The changes show that since the effectiveness of monetary policy has been impaired repeatedly, people are expecting fiscal policy to play a major role in withstanding the economic downward pressure and maintaining steady economic growth.

As considerable weight is given to fiscal policy, more and more attention has been paid to the deficit-to-GDP ratio since the ratio is often seen as an indicator of how much room is left for fiscal policy to play its role. Because of that, there has been heated discussions about keeping budget deficit below 3% of GDP.

However, since we are talking about the deficit-to-GDP ratio in the context of the new normal of economic development and supply-side structural reform, four issues need to be clarified.

First, a deficit-to-GDP ratio of 3% is certainly not the golden rule, nor is it the product of a theoretical study. It is simply a bargain made in the early years of the EU for the purpose of unified management. Indeed, even within the EU, there are more than a few member states that are not following the rule. However, internationally, it is used to measure the level of a country's fiscal risks. Over the years, China has been working to keep the deficit-to-GDP ratio lower than 3% to prevent fiscal risks. Therefore, people are so used to it as a cautionary indicator related to fiscal risks and even consider it unacceptable to have a ratio higher than 3%. How the rule is followed influences not only people's assessment of the current fiscal situation, but also people's expectations for future trends in this regard.

Second, there have been both nominal and real fiscal deficits in China. The nominal fiscal deficit refers to the difference between revenue and expenditure in the general public budget. The real fiscal deficit refers to the difference between government revenue and expenditure listed in the general public budget, budgets of government-managed funds, budgets of social security funds, and budgets of state capital operations. Interestingly, before 2016, China's nominal fiscal deficit was usually larger than the real fiscal deficit. In 2015, for example, although the nominal deficit-to-GDP ratio was 2.4%, the real ratio was much lower than 2.4%. At the time, proactive fiscal policy was not proactive enough and its role was not brought into full play, so people would often talk about it. In 2016, the opposite began to happen—the real fiscal deficit is much larger than the nominal fiscal deficit. Although the nominal deficit-to-GDP ratio is controlled at 3%, the real ratio is definitely much higher than 3%. Since 3% is a ratio set based on the general public budget instead of all types of government revenue and expenditure, we should look beyond the nominal fiscal deficit and take the real fiscal deficit as the yardstick for assessing the fiscal situation.

---

[3] This is a slightly revised version of an article first published in *Guangming Daily* on March 21, 2017.

This means that in today's China, even if the nominal fiscal deficit is controlled at 3%, the real fiscal deficit is likely to exceed the level. Furthermore, if the nominal fiscal deficit exceeds the level, the real fiscal deficit may be even larger.

Third, the focus of proactive fiscal policy differs according to the economic situation and policy objectives. Unlike the previous proactive fiscal policy that was implemented on the demand side and through total output adjustment, proactive fiscal policy in the context of the new normal of economic development and supply-side structural reform must be finally implemented on the supply side and through structural adjustment and should be promoted mainly by means of reform. This means that today's China still needs the support of fiscal deficit but what it means and how it works have changed—the focus must be on paving the way for supply-side structural reform. Even if it is still connected with the demand side and total output adjustment and be used to support expenditure increase and tax and fee cuts, it is after all an intermediate link and plays a supporting role. All the objectives must ultimately be reached through efforts on the supply side and structural adjustment. It plays a moderate role in helping increase total demand and an auxiliary role in promoting supply-side structural reform. Therefore, the use of fiscal deficits can and should be moderated.

Fourth, although the new Budget Law enacted in 2015 began to allow the issuance of local government bonds neither the old Budget Law nor the new one allow any deficit in local budgets at all levels. In fact, local governments have been having a fiscal deficit and it has been growing since the beginning of reform and opening up. Between 2008 and 2010, in particular, a huge quantity of debts arose from financing platforms, which still poses a serious threat to China's fiscal security. As the issuance of local government bonds and the swap of matured local government bonds became allowed in 2015, we can see the long-standing tradition of using fiscal deficit on the local level and the huge demand for the swap and issuance of local government bonds. Previously "invisible" fiscal deficits have been made public, and the scale of issuing various forms of local government bonds, including bonds for debt swap, has been increasing rapidly. The situation must be addressed carefully, or it may get too tricky to cope with.

In conclusion, we should and must limit fiscal deficit to 3% of GDP. At lease this makes us stay alert to deficit and fiscal risks. It also shows to all sectors that we are paying attention to economic growth while not relaxing our vigilance against economic risks. This is certainly important for further deepening supply-side structural reform, doing economic work well at present and in the period ahead, and especially stabilizing people's expectations for economic trends and policy developments.

5 Four Profound Changes in Proactive Fiscal Policy[4]

Since 1998 when China began to use the term "proactive fiscal policy", the adjective "proactive" has been considered synonymous with "expansionary". People would equate proactive fiscal policy with expansionary fiscal policy. Therefore, as the stress on proactive fiscal policy has been changing in recent years, people have been interpreting it centering around expansion.

If we look at the formulations made by the Central Economic Work Conference about plans for proactive fiscal policy, we can see that before 2014, the formulation used was either "implementing a proactive fiscal policy" or "continuing to implement a proactive fiscal policy". In 2014, it was proposed to make proactive fiscal policy "strong"; in 2015, it was proposed to make the policy "stronger"; in 2016, it was proposed to make the policy "more proactive and effective".

Since "proactive" is equated with "expansionary", making the policy strong, stronger or more proactive and effective would be correspondingly interpreted as expanding further based on the previous year, or as being dissatisfied with the effects of fiscal expansion of the previous year and thus requiring greater expansionary efforts.

However, it should be noted that 2014 was exactly the first year after the major conclusion on China's economic development entering a new normal was drawn. The formulations about proactive fiscal policy after that have been obviously based on the new normal and aimed at understanding and grasping the new normal and guiding its development. This means that then changed stress on proactive fiscal policy has been placed in a very different context.

First, the economic situation has been assessed differently. As President Xi said, "The outstanding problems facing the functioning of the Chinese economy are partially cyclical and total output factors, but mainly major structural imbalances".[5] Since the outstanding problems are no longer cyclical or total output factors and the root cause of the outstanding problems lies in the unsmooth flow of economic activities caused by major structural imbalances, proactive fiscal policy may still need to include counter-cyclical operations and efforts to stimulate demand, but short-term regulation and total output expansion are no longer, or should not be, its main objectives. Instead, we should focus on the outstanding problems that differ widely from past ones and shift our focus to structural adjustment, stimulate the vitality of economic growth and strive to achieve a new dynamic balance between supply and demand while seeking to increase total output.

Second, the development philosophy has changed. As President Xi said, under the new normal of economic development, "the ideas, thinking and focus of economic work should be adjusted"[6]. The Fifth Plenary Session of the 18th CPC Central Committee proposed the new development philosophy of pursuing "innovative,

---

[4] This is a slightly revised version of an article first published in *Guangming Daily* on September 1, 2017.

[5] Xi (2017b, p. 113).

[6] Xi (2017b, p. 112).

coordinated, green, open and shared development". President Xi's Report at the 19th CPC National Congress stressed the need to lead the economy towards higher-quality, more efficient, fairer, and more sustainable development. Since the purpose of economic development is no longer to achieve high-speed growth and GDP is no longer the only focus, proactive fiscal policy may still include measures to stabilize growth, but adopting stimulus policies for short-term economic growth and over-drawing future growth is no longer or should no longer be its focus and developing projects is no longer or can no longer be the main approach. Instead, we should implement the new development philosophy, lead the economy towards sustained and healthy development, shift our focus to improving the quality and efficiency of economic development while supporting steady growth, and take decisive measures to change the growth model, adjust the structure and alleviate overcapacity.

Third, the thinking on and focus of economic work have changed. As President Xi said, "The CPC Central Committee has proposed to promote supply-side structural reform. This is a major adjustment to China's economic development thinking and focus of efforts made based on a comprehensive analysis of the long cycle of the world economy and the new normal of China's economic development... Promoting supply-side structural reform should be the focus of the efforts to grow the economy at present and in the period ahead."[7] Since the focus of economic work is on the supply side and its main objective is to solve structural problems, proactive fiscal policy may still require demand-side management and efforts to increase demand, but demand-side management and increasing demand are no longer or should no longer be its main task, and quantitative easing and mass stimulus are no longer or should no longer be its main options. Instead, we should focus on improving the quality of supply and moderately increase total demand while continuing with the main task of advancing supply-side structural reform.

Fourth, the approach to policy implementation has changed. As President Xi said, "The cause of structural problems on the supply side is the distorted allocation of factors, which is an institutional obstacle."[8] Therefore, "the fundamental way to advance supply-side structural reform... is to deepen reform".[9] Since the root cause of supply-side structural problems lies in institutional obstacles, in the failure of the market to play a decisive role in resource allocation, and in the failure of the government to better play its due role, proactive fiscal policy may remain within the scope of macroeconomic policies and still require policy operations, but simply increasing demand is no longer or should no longer be the main approach to its implementation. Instead, while taking supply-side structural reform as the focus of macroeconomic policies, we should adopt the fundamental approach of removing institutional obstacles by means of reform and promoting various basic reforms to pave the way for supply-side structural reform.

All these changes lead to one simple conclusion. Compared with proactive fiscal policy under the old normal of economic development, proactive fiscal policy under

---

[7] Xi (2017a).

[8] Xi (2017f).

[9] Xi (2017b, p. 115).

the new normal should focus on not only short-term regulation, increasing total demand, the scale of development, and policy operations, but also the continued momentum for growth, structural adjustment on the supply side, the quality of development, and reform actions.

It is in the process of all the changes that we have initially established an economic policy framework to adapt to the new normal of economic development. Only by incorporating proactive fiscal policy into this new policy framework and aligning it with the features of the new normal can we acquire a thorough understanding of proactive fiscal policy's design so far and accept and applaud the intentions behind such design.

6 Proactive Fiscal Policy During the Shift to High-Quality Development[10]

To keep the Chinese economy moving steadily towards a sustainable future, we need to give play to the supporting role of proactive fiscal policy. It is even more important to the endeavor to ensure stability on six fronts, namely employment, finance, foreign trade, foreign investment, domestic investment, and market expectations.

It should be noted that proactive fiscal policy is not an entirely foreign product, and the use of this policy name and related practices have all occurred in the high-speed growth stage of the Chinese economy. A proactive fiscal policy means fiscal expansion that focuses on tax and fee cuts and increasing expenditure and deficit. Such an understanding shared by many has also been developed in the stage of high-speed growth. As the Chinese economy shifts from a stage of high-speed growth to a stage of high-quality development, is there any change in the implications and implementation of proactive fiscal policy as a special concept closely associated with China's economic reality and national conditions in the stage of high-speed growth? If the answer is yes, what are the changes then?

On the basis of asking the above questions, China should figure out how to design its proactive fiscal policy in the face of the complex and volatile domestic and international situations, especially the new problems and challenges brought about by the continuous escalation of China–U.S. trade frictions.

I. **A very different macroeconomic environment**

A careful examination of the current macroeconomic and policy environments in China and a comparison with the stage of high-speed growth show us that a series of profound changes, which are quite different from those in the past, are gradually taking place.

In contrast to the stage of high-speed growth, the Chinese economy shifting to the stage of high-quality development faces structural problems rather than total output

[10] This is a slightly revised version of an article first published in *Economic Daily* on October 15, 2018.

problems, and the main aspect of the problems is on the supply side rather than the demand side. Although the economic downturn pressure caused by the China–U.S. trade frictions is mainly reflected in the total demand and the demand side, the problems about total demand and the demand side are secondary compared with structural problems and the supply side.

In contrast to the stage of high-speed growth, the focus of China's macroeconomic policies as it moves into the stage of high-quality development is supply-side structural reform rather than demand management. Although the economic downturn pressure caused by China–U.S. trade frictions is mainly reflected in the necessity of implementing demand management, increasing demand is just a secondary objective compared with improving the supply structure and the quality of supply and the efforts to increase demand should be moderate.

In contrast to the stage of high-speed growth, China's fundamental approach to macroeconomic regulation when shifting to the stage of high-quality development is to deepen reform rather than to make policy arrangements. The economic downturn pressure brought about by China–U.S. trade frictions calls for timely policy choices, but the effectiveness of short-term counter-cyclical operations is no longer sufficient compared with the reform of systems and mechanisms and the promotion of various basic reforms.

If we look at proactive fiscal policy in the above-mentioned macroeconomic and policy contexts, it is fair to say that although the policy name remains unchanged, what it means and how to implement it are absolutely different now.

II. **Very different tax and fee cuts**

In contrast to the tax and fee cuts for fiscal expansion in the stage of high-speed growth, the tax and fee cuts made in China now are mainly aimed at reducing costs rather than increasing demand and focused on the supply side rather than the demand side.

Since cost reduction is the main objective, especially for the real economy, tax and fee cuts are mainly targeted at businesses rather than individuals and the taxes and fees to be reduced are mainly those related to businesses. Therefore, tax and fee cuts are structural—the cuts are clearly targeted rather than indiscriminate.

Taking the supply side as the focus, the efforts to cut taxes and fees should cause a substantive rather than nominal decrease in the costs of businesses and should be embodied in the substantive rather than nominal transfer of resource allocation power by the government. Therefore, the decrease in government revenue caused by such tax and fee cuts should be made up by reducing government expenditure, rather than by increasing deficit and issuing more government bonds.

Taking cost reduction as the main objective, tax and fee cuts is in essence structural reform rather than quantitative adjustment. It is mainly driven by reform actions rather than policy arrangements. Therefore, tax and fee cuts should be combined with the reform of tax and fee system. carried out as part of the reform.

This tells us that in the face of the economic downturn pressure brought about by the escalating trade frictions between China and the United States, we should certainly further step up efforts and gather pace in tax and fee cuts, but tax and fee cuts at the stage of high-quality development should not deviate from cost reduction, the supply side, and reform. The effort to increase demand should be skillfully combined with or based on that to reduce costs. Demand-side operations should be linked to the reduction of government spending. We should not seek the short-term increase of total demand at the cost of increasing the future burden of businesses. In addition, we should focus on the reform of the tax and fee system. Taxes and fees should not be cut indiscriminately, nor should the reform of the tax and fee system be replaced with policy adjustment.

III. **Very different expenditure increase**

The effort to increase government expenditure under a proactive fiscal policy is mainly manifested in the increase of government investment. Quite different from what happens at a stage of high-speed growth, China's effort to increase government investment at present is combined with that to adjust the structure and strengthen areas of weakness.

When combined with structural adjustment, the effort to increase investment is not only to increase the total demand, but also to adjust the economic structure. Since the main problems are structural ones, the effort to increase government investment should be aimed at the two objectives of increasing demand and adjusting the structure. Moreover, we must focus on adjusting the economic structure rather than increasing the total demand, and give full play to the crucial role of government investment in improving the supply structure.

When combined with the effort to strengthen areas of weakness, increasing government investment should cover both the demand side and the supply side. Since the main aspect of the problems is on the supply side, the effort to increase government investment should not only address demand and supply differently according to their characteristics, but also be focused on precisely strengthening areas of weakness to tap the potential of effective demand and improve medium- and long-term supply.

In fact, combining the effort to increase government investment with that to adjust the structure and strengthen areas of weakness is to make sure that the former serves the main task of supply-side structural reform. On the one hand, we should not repeat the mistake of relaxing regulation for increasing the total demand and thus disrupting the adjustment of economic structure. On the other hand, we should not overlook the progress of reform due to discretionary policy choices, suspending or even canceling developed reform plans.

This tells us that in the face of the economic downturn pressure brought by the escalating trade frictions between China and the United States, we should certainly further increase scale and pace in promoting government investment, but doing it at the stage of high-quality development should not deviate from combining it with making structural adjustment and strengthening areas of weakness. In particular, strengthening areas of weakness is the key task. In the effort to increase government investment, we should not only focus on strengthening areas of weakness, but also aim at increasing demand and adjusting the structure. Moreover, when the balance between increasing demand and adjusting the structure cannot be maintained, it is necessary to ensure progress in the latter by intensifying efforts to strength areas of weaknesses. The main focus of the effort to increase government investment is to make up the deficiencies in core technologies and infrastructure for which China still has to depend on others.

IV. **Very different deficit increase**

For a very long time, increasing fiscal deficit was regarded as the basic feature of proactive fiscal policy. Both tax and fee cuts and the increase of government spending would ultimately result from the increase of fiscal deficit. However, this practice, which prevailed in the stage of high-speed growth, has changed significantly in the shift to a stage of high-quality development. The decision to increase fiscal deficit has been increasingly constrained by the need to mitigate financial risks.

Given the need for risk prevention, the decision to increase deficit should be based on a consideration of not only the needs of macroeconomic policies, but also the requirement of financial risk mitigation. In view of the fact that the financial risks facing China today are not the same as those in the past, and preventing and defusing major risks is one of the three tough battles that must be won in order to build a moderately prosperous society in all respects, we should not only set a limit on the increase of deficit, but also strive to ensure the limit is never exceeded.

The need for risk prevention also requires us to stay fully alert to deficit. The scale and extent of deficit increase should be based on the established thinking of the Chinese people. Since keeping budget deficit below 3% of GDP is an international practice that has also long been accepted by the Chinese people and China has been striving to keep the ratio lower than 3%, we should set the limit on deficit increase as 3% and thus stabilize the expectations of the Chinese people.

Given the need for risk prevention, deficit increase should play a moderate role in helping increase total demand. Even if deficit is increased to promote supply-side structural reform, its role in improving the quality of supply and the supply structure must be defined as "auxiliary".

This tells us that in the face of the economic downturn pressure brought by the escalating trade frictions between China and the United States, we should certainly further increase the size of fiscal deficit and its proportion in GDP, but it should not undermine the efforts to mitigate financial risks. We should not relax our vigilance against financial risks while focusing on economic growth. No expansionary measures should be taken regardless of cost and no money should be spent without considering the capacity to repay.

V. **Thorough understanding of proactive fiscal policy**

The results of looking at proactive fiscal policy in the context of the stage of high-quality development and analyzing tax and fee cuts, expenditure increase, and deficit increase suggest that it has become inopportune to interpret China's proactive fiscal policy based on ideas and understandings of the past.

It should be noted that the recent meeting of the Political Bureau of the CPC Central Committee specified the fiscal policy's task as "playing a bigger role in increasing domestic demand and adjusting the structure", at least indicating that proactive fiscal policy is more than helping to increase demand. It is fair to say that, as China moves into a stage of high-quality development, proactive fiscal policy should be understood from two dimensions, namely increasing domestic demand and adjusting the structure. It is imperative to make a comprehensive and brand-new interpretation of proactive fiscal policy.

Furthermore, since being proactive is no longer equal to being expansionary, the practices of proactive fiscal policy, mainly including tax and fee cuts and increasing expenditure and deficit, are no longer synonymous with fiscal expansion. We should redefine proactive fiscal policy and adopt a proactive attitude and take proactive actions in different fields of macroeconomic regulation, including increasing domestic demand and adjusting the structure. This may be the right thing to do to figure out what proactive fiscal policy means and how to implement it in a new context.

In fact, it is something essential to do. It will not only ensure that proactive fiscal policy meets the need for high-quality development and prevent people from addressing new issues with old practices, but also help to introduce practical and effective measures to deal with a series of new problems and challenges brought about by China–U.S. trade frictions. It will lay the foundation for us to maintain our strategic focus and self-confidence and blaze a new path for pursuing steady and healthy economic development.

7 2019: Profound Changes in the Design of Proactive Fiscal Policy[11]

Facing new economic downward pressure and in the context of making positive fiscal policy stronger and more effective, China has launched a series of unprecedented fiscal expansion measures in 2019. These measures were undoubtedly essential to China's good economic performance in the first quarter of 2019.

However, a comparative analysis of the theories and practices concerning proactive fiscal policy indicates that there are some profound changes in the design of proactive fiscal policy for 2019. The practices are different from we have experienced repeatedly and know very well and the related opinions and suggestions are different from previous ones.

There is a need to discuss the main policy variables involved in this issue.

I. **Fiscal deficit**

The fiscal deficit set for 2019 is 2.76 trillion yuan, an increase of 380 billion yuan over the previous year. On this basis, the deficit-to-GDP ratio is 2.8%, up 0.2

[11] This is a slightly revised version of an article titled "Grasping Deep Changes in the Configuration of Proactive Fiscal Policy" first published in *Economic Daily* on May 17, 2019.

percentage point over the previous year. Increasing fiscal deficit and the deficit-to-GDP ratio is obviously a fiscal expansion measure in response to the new economic downward pressure.

However, the basic principles of macroeconomics tell us that the strength of fiscal expansion does not depend on whether there is a fiscal deficit or how large the fiscal deficit is, but on the marginal change of fiscal deficit. The increase of fiscal deficit by 380 billion yuan and that of the deficit-to-GDP ratio by 0.2 percentage point are intended to offset the new economic downward pressure. Regardless of how effective the move is, at least two facts are crystal clear.

First, compared with the practices in response to the international financial crisis over ten years ago and the Asian financial crisis over twenty years ago, the mass stimulus policies in particular, increasing the size of fiscal deficit and the deficit-to-GDP ratio for 2019 is apparently a much less desperate measure. This indicates that the increase in fiscal deficit and the deficit-to-GDP ratio can be regarded as a sign of fiscal expansion, or a sign of positive fiscal policy. In general, however, this is well-controlled fiscal expansion and a well-managed effort to improve the policy's intensity and performance.

Second, compared with the suggestions of many people on increasing fiscal deficit and the deficit-to-GDP ratio on a large scale, especially those about exceeding the cautionary ratio of 3%, the increase in fiscal deficit and the deficit-to-GDP ratio for 2019 is indeed much smaller. This indicates that the increase of fiscal deficit and the deficit-to-GDP ratio does reflect the requirement of achieving fiscal expansion or pursuing a proactive fiscal policy with greater intensity and better performance. In general, however, this is to achieve fiscal expansion and improve the policy's intensity and performance with a well-controlled fiscal deficit.

To put it mildly, even if the 2.15 trillion-yuan local government special bonds listed in the budgets of government-managed funds are taken into account, we may find that the real deficit-to-GDP ratio has exceeded 3%, but this is actually an ingenious arrangement to ensure that the nominal deficit-to-GDP ratio calculated based on the general public budget does not exceed 3%. The purpose is to stabilize expectations by controlling the nominal deficit-to-GDP ratio. Ultimately, this arrangement is the result of thinking on well-controlled fiscal expansion and well-managed fiscal deficit.

Responding to the complicated and strong economic downward pressure with well-controlled fiscal expansion and a well-managed fiscal deficit is undoubtedly a marked change in the design of proactive fiscal policy for 2019.

This suggests that it may be more appropriate to understand the fiscal deficit and deficit-to-GDP ratio for 2019 from two dimensions rather than one. On the one hand, we should see that an increase of fiscal deficit by 380 billion yuan and an increase of deficit-to-GDP ratio by 0.2 percentage point are in response to the new economic downward pressure. On the other hand, we should see that the increase is controlled at the level of 380 billion yuan and 0.2 percentage point respectively for the purpose of preventing financial risks. In other words, the consideration about increasing deficit and the deficit-to-GDP ratio is on the basis of a full assessment of financial risks facing China and is directly linked to the effort to mitigate major risks. Such an arrangement is actually a result of striking a balance between stabilizing growth and preventing risks.

II. **Tax and fee reduction**

Tax and fee cuts planned for 2019 amount to as much as two trillion yuan, which is undoubtedly unprecedented in the history of the People's Republic of China. However, if we look beyond the scale and further at how the taxes and fees are cut, we can find the practices as a fiscal expansion measure to cope with the new economic downward pressure are different from previous ones and those advocated or suggested by many people before.

First, it should be noted that VAT, rather than corporate income tax, payments constitute a major part of the two trillion-yuan cuts. Different from previous practices and the suggestions of many people, the tax and fee cuts in 2019 are mainly to reduce the costs of businesses, not to increase demand. It should also be noted that the reduction in VAT is mainly achieved by lowering the tax rate, which in turn is mainly reflected in the standard tax rate applicable to the manufacturing sector (from 16 to 13%). To be more specific, the main purpose of the tax and fee cuts in 2019 is to reduce costs in the real sector, not in other sectors.

Second, it should be noted that there is a huge difference between the two trillion-yuan tax and fee cuts and the 380 billion-yuan increase in fiscal deficit. Different from previous practices and the suggestions of many people, the tax and fee cuts in 2019 are mainly supported not by increasing deficit or issuing more government bonds. It should also be noted that while taxes and fees are cut, actions in other aspects have been successively launched, such as reducing general expenditures of the central government by more than 5%, lowering the three public expenditures by about 3%, recovering long-standing idle funds, increasing the profits contributed by specific financial institutions and central enterprises, tapping the potential of local governments, and improving the expenditure structure. To be more specific, the tax and fee cuts in 2019 is mainly achieved by reducing government expenditure, promoting the government's frugality for the benefit of businesses.

Third, it should be noted that the two trillion-yuan tax and fee cuts are achieved through reform of the tax and fee system rather than policy adjustment. Different from previous practices and the suggestions of many people, tax and fee cuts in 2019 is not a temporary measure, but a sustained and effective action; it is based on a long-term strategy, rather than expediency. It should also be noted that all reform actions are linked to certain reform plan and follow the direction of the reform. To be more specific, the tax and fee cuts in 2019 are not based on short-term arrangements for ironing out cyclical fluctuations, but on the long-term strategy of solving the structural problems in the functioning of the economy and achieving the sustained, healthy and steady economic development.

Coping with the complicated and strong economic downturn pressure by reducing the costs of the real economy, practicing fiscal frugality, and implementing institutional reform is apparently another marked change in the design of proactive fiscal policy for 2019.

This suggests that the tax and fee cuts in 2019 should be understood from two dimensions rather than one. On the one hand, in response to the new economic downward pressure, tax and fee cuts have reached as high as two trillion yuan, which is an unprecedented scale. On the other hand, the two trillion-yuan tax and fee cuts are made in different ways rather than indiscriminately. In other words, the main objective of tax and fee cuts is not only to increase demand, but also to reduce costs, with the latter as the mainstay. Such an arrangement is a concrete reflection of attaching importance to stabilizing demand by means of supply-side structural reform.

III. **Expenditure increase**

The effort to increase government expenditure in the context of proactive fiscal policy is mainly manifested in the increase of government investment. In 2019, the investment specified in the central government budget is 577.6 billion yuan, an increase of forty billion yuan over the previous year. In addition, special local government bonds amount to 2.15 trillion yuan, an increase of eight hundred billion yuan over the previous year, and most of them can be used to fund key projects. The amount of government investment on the two levels is not small. Two marked changes can be identified if we look deeper into the specific areas and projects where the investment goes and compare them with past practices and investment promotion plans proposed by many people before.

First, in 2019, special emphasis is placed on increasing effective investment and canceling all unnecessary expenditure, with a focus on investment in key projects. As part of the initiative to closely follow national development strategies and accelerate the progress on key projects, a number of projects have been identified as effective investment and the focus of investment promotion for 2019, such as railway projects involving an investment of eight hundred billion yuan, road and water transportation projects involving an investment of 1.8 trillion yuan, a new series of major water conservancy projects, projects for accelerating the planning and construction of the Sichuan-Tibet Railway, projects on infrastructure such as intercity transportation, logistics, municipal administration, disaster prevention and control, civil aviation and general aviation, and projects for developing new-generation information infrastructure.

Second, in 2019, special emphasis is placed on combining the effort to increase investment with that to strengthen areas of weakness, with a focus the structural feature of investment. As part of the initiative to gather pace in strengthening important areas of weakness in economic and social development, a number of projects have been identified as areas of weakness and included in the scope of investment promotion for 2019, including those recognized as projects of effective investment or key investment projects as well as areas of serious weaknesses in the field of infrastructure such as intercity transportation, logistics, municipal infrastructure, agricultural infrastructure and public service facilities.

Defining the focus of investment promotion efforts as increasing effective investment and strengthening areas of weakness to cope with the complicated and strong economic downturn pressure is surely the third marked change in the design of proactive fiscal policy for 2019.

This suggests that the investment promotion efforts of 2019 should be understood from two dimensions rather than one. On the one hand, it should be noted that the size of increased government investment in response to the new economic downward pressure is not small. On the other hand, it should also be noted that investment increase is targeted at projects of effective investment and areas of weakness, rather than any random areas or projects. In other words, the effort to increase investment is no longer purely focused on quantity but linked to supply-side structural reform and implemented in structural adjustment projects. Such an arrangement is actually a move to give play to the key role of government investment in stabilizing demand and improving the supply structure.

IV. **A different positive fiscal policy**

From increasing fiscal deficit to tax and fee cuts and then increasing expenditure, the closer we look at the main policy variables involved in proactive fiscal policy, the more we find that the current design of proactive fiscal policy is different compared with previous theories and practices.

Although the policy name remains unchanged and the policy's intensity and performance are to be further improved, in the context of entering the stage of high-quality economic development and focusing on supply-side structural reform, the adjective "proactive" is no longer simply equal to "expansionary", but makes fiscal policy play a bigger role in increasing domestic demand and adjusting the structure at the same time.

Since today's proactive fiscal policy is different, it is not right to understand the policy using theories and practices of the past. In a word, guided by Xi Jinping Thought on Socialist Economy with Chinese Characteristics for a New Era, we should incorporate proactive fiscal policy into the bigger picture of promoting high-quality development and supply-side structural reform and understand it with changed ideas, thoughts and strategies. This is the only way to do the economic work well in the current stage.

8 2020: What Kind of Proactive Fiscal Policy Do We Need?[12]

At the beginning of the New Year, people are full of expectations for proactive fiscal policy, facing the complex and grave economic situations at home and abroad. What should we do with proactive fiscal policy in 2020?

---

[12] This is a slightly revised version of an article first published in *Economic Daily* on January 5, 2020.

The recently concluded Central Economic Work Conference explained what it means to continue implementing a proactive fiscal policy: "The quality and efficiency of proactive fiscal policy should be improved. We should pay more attention to structural adjustment, resolutely cut general expenditures, ensure spending in key areas, and provide financial support to guarantee local governments' ability to pay salaries, maintain normal government functions, and meet basic living needs." It should be noted that this is a major plan made for the purpose of promoting high-quality economic development and achieving the goal of building a moderately prosperous society in all respects and the objectives of the 13th Five-Year Plan, placing proactive fiscal policy in the bigger picture of economic work. It can be expected that proactive fiscal policy in 2020 will undergo many marked and profound changes.

I. **Seeking an increase in both quantity and quality**

As one of the two major means to implement macroeconomic regulation, proactive fiscal policy should certainly be coordinated with monetary, employment, industrial, investment, consumption and regional policies to ensure economic indicators within a proper range. However, the proper range here does not cover just a single indicator of GDP growth. It also involves indicators that reflect the quality and efficiency of GDP, such as the adequacy of employment and the improvement of people's lives. In the context of "remaining committed to the new development philosophy" at the Central Economic Work Conference, an appropriate growth of quantity and a steady improvement of quality are both important signs of maintaining economic indicators within a proper range.

In other words, in line with the further understanding of economic indicators within a proper range, the practices of proactive fiscal policy should also be aimed at ensuring the economy achieves an appropriate growth of quantity and a steady improvement of quality. Moreover, in the balance between quantity and quality, priority should be given to the latter.

Therefore, different from the stress on proactive fiscal policy in previous years such as "making it strong", "making its stronger", and "making it more proactive" and "making it stronger and more effective" in 2019, the new stress placed by the Central Economic Work Conference on proactive fiscal policy for 2020 is "improving its quality and efficiency".

II. **Focusing on both increasing demand and adjusting the structure**

Proactive fiscal policy which is based on the theory of demand management and launched in 1998 against the impact of the Asian financial crisis, has always been focused on increasing demand. However, as the Chinese economy shifts from a stage of high-speed growth to a stage of high-quality development, proactive fiscal policy needs to go beyond the single dimension of increasing demand and cover structural adjustment. Since the main problems in the functioning of the economy in the current stage are structural ones and the economic downward pressure is mainly caused by the mix of structural, institutional and cyclical problems, and in light of the focus on promoting high-quality development proposed at the Central Economic Work Conference, proactive fiscal policy should help to increase effective demand through counter-cyclical regulation on the one hand and push forward structural adjustment with stronger and more proactive actions on the other hand.

In other words, in the critical period of changing the growth model, improving the economic structure and transforming growth drivers, proactive fiscal policy should be aimed at both increasing demand and adjusting the structure and a greater focus should be placed on the latter.

Therefore, different from the single focus of proactive fiscal policy on increasing demand in previous years and following the proposal made by the Political Bureau of the CPC Central Committee in July 2018 that "fiscal policy should play a bigger role in increasing domestic demand and adjusting the structuring", the new design of proactive fiscal policy for 2020 made by the Central Economic Work Conference is to focus more on structural adjustment.

III. **Resolutely cutting general expenditures**

To increase demand or adjust the structure, proactive fiscal policy would include no more than two practices, namely tax and fee cuts and increasing investment spending. The problem is that both practices must be supported by a fiscal deficit. However, as supply-side structural reform replaces demand management and becomes the focus of China's macroeconomic policies, increasing fiscal deficit is not the only source of funding for the implementation of proactive fiscal policy. Other sources are also emerging, such as improving and adjusting the structure of fiscal expenditure and cutting general expenditures to boost tax and fee cuts and investment increase. As the Central Economic Work Conference has proposed to win the three tough battles and do a good job in stabilizing six fronts, the significance of cutting general expenditures has become even greater. The decision to increase deficit should be constrained by the need to ensure stable overall leverage ratio and to mitigate financial risks so that no systemic financial risks would be incurred.

In other words, based on risk awareness and in line with the principle of "keeping government spending low and enriching the people", the implementation of proactive fiscal policy must be supported by dual sources of funding. While moderately increasing fiscal deficit, we should also focus on cutting government spending for the benefit of the people.

Therefore, different from the previous practice of closely connecting tax and fee cuts and investment increase with the increase of fiscal deficit and in the context of consolidate and expanding progress in tax and fee cuts, maintaining certain expenditures and increasing transfer payments, the new plan made by the Central Economic Work Conference for proactive fiscal policy of 2020 is to resolutely cut general expenditures.

IV. **Ensuring improvement of people's lives and support for key areas**

As a policy arrangement concerning the cause of the Party and the country, it is undoubtedly an important purpose of proactive fiscal policy to advance the coordinated efforts to maintain stable growth, promote reform, make structural adjustments, improve people's wellbeing, guard against risks, and ensure stability. This is relatively easy to achieve when the growth in fiscal revenue is quite strong. However, given the increasing economic downward pressure and declining growth in fiscal revenue, China is faced with a growing imbalance between fiscal revenue and expenditure. Since this is not only the reality we have to accept, but also a result of the laws underlying economic development, making good use of limited financial resources and ensuring the sustainability of fiscal operations has increasingly become a key option in the implementation of proactive fiscal policy. The Central Economic Work Conference has made it clear that social policies must ensure basic needs are met and that people's wellbeing must be improved and especially the basic needs of people in difficulty are met. In such a context, the allocation of government funds or the planning of fiscal expenditure should be made on the premise of balancing multiple objectives and be focused on meeting basic needs and creating inclusive benefits as well as strengthening areas of weakness.

In other words, in the implementation of proactive fiscal policy, government funds should be properly allocated, the efficiency in using funds should be improved, and priority should be given to the improvement of people's wellbeing and the key areas.

Therefore, unlike in the past when specific expenditures were seldom addressed, the Central Economic Work Conference has made a new plan for proactive fiscal policy in 2020, namely to ensure spending in key areas and provide financial support to guarantee local governments' ability to pay salaries, maintain normal government functions, and meet basic living needs.

In conclusion, it is clear that from a new historical starting point, we have to fully understand the design of proactive fiscal policy for 2020 based on the changed ideas, thoughts, and strategies. Only in this way can we truly meet the requirements for pursuing high-quality development, respond to the new problems and challenges in the functioning of the economy with practical and effective fiscal measures, and ensure that economic indicators stay within a proper range.

9 Reshaping Proactive Fiscal Policy

Since the 18th CPC National Congress, as the Chinese economy shifts from a stage of high-speed growth to a stage of high-quality development, China's proactive fiscal policy has undergone a series of extremely profound and important changes, under the guidance of Xi Jinping Thought on Socialist Economy with Chinese Characteristics for a New Era. These changes, from both theoretical innovation and developments in practices, are the result of the close integration of theory and practice.

The design of proactive fiscal policy for 2020 is a concentrated reflection of the changes so far. It differs widely from the past theories and practices of proactive fiscal policy that we are very familiar with. The Central Economic Work Conference held in December 2019 explained what it means to continue implementing a proactive fiscal policy. "The quality and efficiency of proactive fiscal policy should be improved. We should pay more attention to structural adjustment, resolutely cut general expenditures, ensure spending in key areas, and provide financial support to guarantee local governments' ability to pay salaries, maintain normal government functions, and meet basic living needs."

To correctly understand China's proactive fiscal policy, it is undoubtedly necessary to proceed from the design of the policy for 2020 and seek to identify the main aspects of the changes on the basis of making comparative analysis.

I. Goal: Focus shifted from quantity to both quality and quantity

China began to use the term "proactive fiscal policy" in response to the Asian financial crisis in 1998. For a long time since then, the adjective "proactive" has been considered synonymous with "expansionary". Here, being expansionary is in quantitative terms and refers to the increase of total demand. People would equate proactive fiscal policy with expansionary fiscal policy, namely practices of fiscal expansion mainly including tax and fee cuts and expenditure increase aimed at increasing total demand. Therefore, in the face of changes in the economic situation, people tend to understand and interpret the stress on proactive fiscal policy, such as making the policy strong, stronger, more proactive or stronger and more effective, from the perspective of quantitative expansion.

All these have been facing increasingly great challenges, as the Chinese economy shifts from a stage of high-speed growth to a stage of high-quality development and the new development philosophy is used to guide economic work. Unlike previous efforts focusing on the size and growth rate of GDP, the idea of innovative, coordinated, green, open and shared development focuses more on the quality and efficiency of GDP and on improving the quality and efficiency of economic development. In response to this change in the development philosophy, in addition to the size and growth rate of GDP, indicators that reflect the quality and efficiency of GDP, such as adequate employment and improvement of people's lives, should not only be considered in the design of proactive fiscal policy, but also be pursued as the top priority. Quality and efficiency should always be put first.

This means that proactive fiscal policy should not focus on achieving quantitative growth. Achieving qualitative improvement is also an indispensable and even more important goal. Shifting from quantitative growth to qualitative improvement at the right time and making efforts on both qualitative and quantitative fronts is a major adjustment in the goal of proactive fiscal policy and also an inevitable choice to reshape the policy.

Furthermore, with the new development philosophy guiding practices, an appropriate growth of quantity and a steady improvement of quality are both important signs of the economy operating within a proper range. In line with such an understanding, proactive fiscal policy, as one of the two major means of macroeconomic regulation in the new era, must certainly be implemented for achieving dual objectives—an appropriate growth of quantity and a steady improvement of quality. Moreover, in the balance between quantity and quality, we should tilt towards the latter and take improving the quality and efficiency of economic development as the core objective.

In fact, as far as how fiscal policy works is concerned, quantity and quality are considered at the same time. However, the focus is different in different stages of development. The prevailing trend is that quality has been assuming growing significance and taking up an increasingly large share. The practices of proactive fiscal policy in 2019 show that the effort to cut taxes and fees is not only about the scale of reduction but also about what effects are produced and the effort to increase expenditure is not only about the amount of money spent or how much work is done with the money but also about what practical results are achieved. The evaluation of effects, assessment of performance, and cost-effectiveness analysis should all be done from the two dimensions of quantity and quality, and arrangements should also be made to ensure related work is well done and improved. Such a process of shifting from quantitative to qualitative growth and gradually focusing on quality in the goal of proactive fiscal policy is inevitable for solving the major problems of China's development in the new era and also natural in the Chinese economy's shift to a stage of high-quality development.

It is against such a background that the Central Economic Work Conference has used the expression of "vigorously improving quality and efficacy" in defining the goal of proactive fiscal policy for 2020. The expression used in 2019 is "making it stronger and more effective". Such a change is sending us a clear message that proactive fiscal policy now pays more attention to quality and efficacy and works on both quality and quantity.

II. **Role: From increasing demand to adjusting the structure and increasing demand**

The role of proactive fiscal policy underpinned by demand management theory has been mainly defined as increasing demand. On all occasions when proactive fiscal policy is involved or discussed, people would mostly talk about the role or task of proactive fiscal policy as increasing total demand. This is because of the understanding that the main problems in the functioning of the economy are about total supply and demand, and the main aspect of the problems is on the demand side. Therefore, focusing on the balance between supply and demand and making short-term counter-cyclical adjustments mainly through increasing or reducing total demand in response to cyclical economic fluctuations becomes the basic course of action for proactive fiscal policy and even macroeconomic regulation as a whole.

As the Chinese economy shifts from a stage of high-speed growth stage to a stage of high-quality development and supply-side structural reform replaces demand management as the focus of economic work, the practices mentioned above have become increasingly against the reality of economic development on both the levels of economic operation and policy implementation. Different from situation in the stage of high-speed growth stage, in the stage of high-quality development, the main problems in the functioning of the Chinese economy are structural ones and the main aspect of the problems is on the supply side. In response to the changes in main problems and the main aspect of the problems, in addition to total output and demand-side problems, structural and supply-side problems should not only be considered in the design of proactive fiscal policy, but also be addressed as the top priority. Different from demand management, supply-side structural reform focuses more on structural and supply-side problems rather than total output and demand-side ones and places greater emphasis on achieving the objectives of macroeconomic regulation through reform actions rather than policy adjustments. In response to the change in the focus of economic work, proactive fiscal policy should not only be aimed at balancing the demand side and the supply side, but also address total output and structural problems with counter-cyclical regulation and supply-side structural reform and advance supply-side structural reform throughout the whole process of macroeconomic regulation.

This means that proactive fiscal policy should not stop at playing a role only in increasing demand. Promoting structural adjustment is also an indispensable and even more important role to play. Advancing from increasing demand to adjusting the structure in due course and thus playing a role on both fronts is a major adjustment in the role of proactive fiscal policy and also the key to reshaping the policy.

Furthermore, given supply-side structural reform as the focus of economic work and the task of keeping economic indicators within a proper range, it is not right to address all problems indiscriminately or expect to solve all problems with a single means. In line with such an understanding, proactive fiscal policy, as one of the two major means of macroeconomic regulation in the new era, should certainly play a dual role of adjusting the structure and increasing demand. Moreover, in the balance between increasing demand and adjusting the structure, we should tilt towards the latter and take improving the supply-side structure as the main task.

In fact, fundamentally speaking, the role of proactive fiscal policy has always been multifaceted, not just one dimension of increasing demand. In terms of promoting structural adjustment, proactive fiscal policy also has significant comparative advantages. It is just that such a role and advantages become more prominent and important today as we move to a stage of high-quality development and focus on supply-side structural reform. Take the proactive fiscal policy of 2019 as an example. While large-scale tax and fee cuts and the increase of government investment, directly or indirectly, contributed to the increase of total demand, we should also see that tax and fee cuts was well-targeted. Most taxes cut were VAT and most fees cut were social insurance premiums, both of which are mainly paid by businesses. The purpose is apparently to reduce costs for businesses, especially those in the manufacturing sector and micro and small enterprises. This is undoubtedly a structural adjustment effect. The increase of government investment focused on projects of effective investment and areas of weakness, rather than any random projects or areas. The key areas of investment included railways, road and water transportation, major water conservancy projects, infrastructure and new-generation information infrastructure. This is also undoubtedly a structural adjustment effect.

Given such a change, the Central Economic Work Conference has used the expression "focusing more on structural adjustment" in defining the role of proactive fiscal policy for 2020. It should be noted that the policy's role has been limited to increasing demand in the past years. The Political Bureau of the CPC Central Committee proposed for the first time that "fiscal policy should play a bigger role in increasing domestic demand and promoting structural adjustment" in July 2018. The change from "increasing demand" to "playing a bigger role in increasing domestic demand and promoting structural adjustment" and then "focusing more on structural adjustment" sends us a clear message that proactive fiscal policy should not only work on both increasing demand and promoting structural adjustment, but also be more vigorous and proactive on the latter front.

III. Approach to policy implementation: from making policy adjustments to deepening reform and making policy adjustments

In the past, the implementation of China's proactive fiscal policy was mainly based on or reflected in policy adjustments. Policy variables and policy arrangements were used to respond to cyclical fluctuations and the imbalance between total supply and demand and achieve the objectives of macroeconomic regulation. The difference between policy adjustment and institutional change is that it is effective in the short term, rather than sustainable and stable. As far as the two main practices of proactive fiscal policy—tax and fee cuts and increasing expenditure are concerned, there is always a period of application which lasts for 1–3 years. Once the period of application ends, everything would return to what it was before. On the one hand, this approach meets the needs for counter-cyclical regulation to iron out cyclical economic fluctuations and achieve short-term stability, which is part of policy adjustments. On the other hand, it is also consistent with the requirement that proactive fiscal policy focuses on quantitative growth and increasing demand, which was how proactive fiscal policy worked in the past.

As the Chinese economy shifts from a stage of high-speed growth to a stage of high-quality development, and especially as the goal and role of proactive fiscal policy have changed, policy adjustments have become increasingly insufficient and there is a growing need to initiate institutional reform. On the one hand, as the focus shifts from simply quantity to both quality and quantity, the efforts centering on improving quality and efficiency are bound to meet problems in systems and mechanisms. On the other hand, as the role shifts from increasing demand to promoting structural adjustment and increasing demand, the efforts to improve the economic structure or industrial structure would also naturally start from solving the problems in systems and mechanisms. In the face of the problems mainly rooted in institutional obstacles, policy adjustments may be necessary, but institutional obstacles can only be removed through institutional reform. In response to the change in the goal and role of proactive fiscal policy, we should not only strike a balance between making policy adjustments and deepening reform, but also take deepening reform as the fundamental approach and focus on promoting various basic reforms to pave the way for supply-side structural reform.

This means that proactive fiscal policy should not be implemented simply through policy adjustment but must also include institutional reform or even be driven mainly by reform. Advancing from making policy adjustments to deepening reform in due course and thus leveraging their respective strengths is a major adjustment necessary for the implementation of proactive fiscal policy and also an essential step to reshape the policy.

Furthermore, deepening reform as a fundamental approach to macroeconomic regulation requires us to take well-targeted actions. In line with such an understanding, proactive fiscal policy, as one of the two major means of macroeconomic regulation in the new era, should certainly be implemented through both making policy adjustments and deepening reform. Moreover, in the balance between making policy adjustments and deepening reform, we should tilt towards to the latter and promote the reforms for improving the quality, efficiency and impetus of economic development.

In fact, China's proactive fiscal policy has never been divorced from the support of reform since the day it was put into use. In particular, since the CPC Central Committee made the major decision to promote supply-side structural reform, almost every measure introduced as part of proactive fiscal policy has something to do with reform. The proactive fiscal policy of 2019 is an outstanding example. As far as tax and fee cuts is concerned, all measures such as reducing VAT rates, increasing special additional deductions for personal income tax, reducing social insurance premiums, and reviewing and standardizing administrative charges and payments to government-managed funds, were achieved through reforms in the tax and fee system. It is because of institutional reform rather than policy adjustment that the effect of tax and fee cuts is sustainable and stable. As mentioned above, the efforts to increase expenditure focused on the projects of effective investment and areas of weakness on the basis of improving the expenditure structure. To do that, the related systems and mechanisms would have to be reformed. As far as the sources of funding supporting tax and fee cuts and expenditure increase are concerned, increasing deficit was not the only option and more efforts were made to reduce general expenditures to keep government spending low and enrich the people. This is not only a reform of the government itself, but also a reform of the fiscal management system based on the consideration of preventing and defusing major risks.

On the basis of that, regarding the implementation of proactive fiscal policy for 2020, the Central Economic Work Conference proposed something different, such as "consolidating and expanding the gains in tax and fee cuts" and "resolutely cutting general expenditures". A clear message we get from this is that tax and fee cuts should be consolidated and expanded in the further reform of the tax and fee system and expenditure increase should be strengthened by further clarifying the priorities of fiscal expenditure and strengthening structural adjustment. Even the efforts to achieve fiscal balance must be made on the basis of ensuring fiscal deficit stays below the cautionary level and the government practices frugality in exchange for people's better life. In short, proactive fiscal policy should take deepening reform as the fundamental approach to implementation.

IV. Policy mix: From coordination with monetary policy to combination with other policies

Proactive fiscal policy has always been combined with other regulatory measures in macroeconomic regulation. However, in most cases fiscal policy has been coordinated with monetary policy, such as the combination of a tight fiscal policy and a loose monetary policy, the combination of a loose fiscal policy and a loose monetary policy, and a combination of a tight fiscal policy and a tight monetary policy. This has something to do with the fact that the entire macroeconomic regulatory system focuses on quantity-oriented objectives and the function of increasing demand. The main policy means involved in the macroeconomic regulation around quantity and increasing demand are certainly fiscal policy and monetary policy which have natural advantages on these two fronts.

As the Chinese economy shifts from a stage of high-speed growth to a stage of high-quality development and especially as the principal contradiction in Chinese society has changed, people's pursuit has changed from more quantitative growth to higher quality and their focus has shifted from material and cultural needs to the needs for a better life marked by material, cultural and ethical, social, political and ecological progress. To meet the needs of a better life, advancing the efforts to stabilize growth, promote reform, adjust the structure, improve people's wellbeing, guard against risks, and maintain stability and focusing on solving various problems of unbalanced and inadequate development have been increasingly considered in macroeconomic regulation and even become its focus. In response to this change in the landscape of macroeconomic regulation, the policy mix needed for proactive fiscal policy should apparently go beyond monetary policy and include various policies such as employment, industrial, investment, consumption, and regional policies.

This means that proactive fiscal policy should be combined not just with monetary policy, but also with other policies. Expanding the combination of fiscal policy and monetary policy to that of fiscal policy and various policies for macroeconomic regulation is not only a major adjustment in the policy mix of proactive fiscal policy, but also a key option to reshape the policy.

Furthermore, in the context of the endeavor to modernize the country's governance system and governance capacity, there is a strong possibility that fiscal management as the foundation and an important pillar of governance will see its boundary of activities extended and its functions gradually increased. It is very important to understand this point. At least it tells us that, as a policy instrument that bears on the cause of the Party and the country, proactive fiscal policy must show a broader vision and be implemented in combination with not only monetary policy but also other policies. It should be in coordination with the policies in economic, political, cultural, social and ecological fields to achieve the objectives of macroeconomic regulation.

In fact, at least since the CPC Central Committee introduced the major measure to ensure stability on six fronts, namely employment, finance, foreign trade, foreign investment, domestic investment, and market expectations, an important focus of proactive fiscal policy has been to coordinate policies in all fields to ensure that the economy operates within a proper range, which is intended to serve the cause of the Party and the country. Take the proactive fiscal policy of 2019 as an example. It was combined with prudent monetary policy and the deficit-to-GDP ratio was moderately increased to 2.8%. Related structural policy was also adopted. Central and local governments were required to cut general expenditures by an average of 10% and 5%, respectively. Moreover, in coordination with social policy, financial support was provided to guarantee local governments' ability to pay salaries, maintain normal government functions, and meet basic living needs. In coordination with regional policy, the central government would increase transfer payments to local governments, especially central and western regions and areas in need, at a growth rate of 9%.

In 2020, the imbalance between fiscal revenue and expenditure is sure to become increasingly prominent as the growth of fiscal revenue declines and that of fiscal expenditure increases due to a mix of factors such as mounting economic downward pressure and the sudden COVID-19 outbreak. Advancing the cause of the Party and the country by strengthening coordination with other policies and spending limited government funds on important matters in a sustainable way is the focus and also a challenge in the design of proactive fiscal policy. Therefore, in the principle of ensuring macro policies are stable, micro policies are flexible, and social policies ensure basic needs are met, the Central Economic Work Conference has made the plan about ensuring spending in key areas and providing financial support to guarantee local governments' ability to pay salaries, maintain normal government functions, and meet basic living needs. In contrast to the past when specific expenditures were seldom addressed, we can get a clear message that strengthening the coordination of policies in multiple aspects and seeking a dynamic balance between multiple objectives is the only choice of policy mix for proactive fiscal policy.

In short, compared with previous theories and practices, a series of important changes have taken place in the design of China's proactive fiscal policy. The current proactive fiscal policy is different. It is not right to simply understand it using past theories and practices. We should understand it thoroughly using changed ideas, thoughts and strategies. Only in this way can we truly meet the requirement of high-quality development and address the new problems and challenges in the functioning of the economy with pragmatic and effective fiscal measures to achieve the goal of steady and healthy economic and social development.

Chapter 6
New Policies on Tax and Fee Cuts

1 Introduction

This chapter, comprising six articles, is entitled "New Policies on Tax and Fee Cuts". Its basic purpose is to explain the significant differences between this round of tax and fee cuts and previous ones in ideas, measures, theoretical support, and methodological support, thus creating an analytical framework for understanding tax and fee cuts in the shift to high-quality development.

This round of tax and fee cuts started with the replacement of BT with VAT which was first piloted in Shanghai in 2012. In 2013, the Third Plenary Session of the 18th CPC Central Committee made it a key step in tax reform and included it in the overall plan for deepening tax reform. In both the piloting phase and after being included in the overall plan, the initial goal of replacing BT with VAT was not directly linked to tax reduction. Instead, it was positioned as an important measure to improve the tax structure. However, different from the past, this round of efforts to improve the tax structure were based on the basic idea of "reducing indirect taxes and increasing direct taxes". With the launch of the initiative to replace BT with VAT, VAT as the largest indirect tax and BT as the third largest indirect tax were merged and thus tax cuts were considerable. In the meantime, the direct tax reform lagged behind, and the proportion of direct taxes did not increase as expected. As a result, indirect taxes decreased while direct taxes failed to increase. In 2015, the growth rate of tax revenue dropped sharply, and people seemed to recognize the real purpose of replacing BT (BT) with value-added tax (VAT). As a result, some doubts emerged about the progress and pace of the initiative. It was against this background that I wrote the article "Showing Determination and Confidence in China's VAT Reform".

Unlike in the past, tax reduction driven in the context of supply-side structural reforms involves both policy adjustments and reform actions, which is far more complex than imagined. China's overall tax burden only covers the government's revenue from taxation. Other sources of government revenue are excluded. Therefore, we must carefully change the overall tax burden to overall tax and fee burden

P. Gao, *A Shift Toward High-Quality Development of China*,
Research Series on the Chinese Dream and China's Development Path,
https://doi.org/10.1007/978-981-99-3990-4_6

according to international practices. China should cut both taxes and fees. Only in this way can we achieve the purpose of reducing costs for businesses. China's tax and fee burden is basically assumed by businesses, and the taxes and fees paid by them are mainly indirect taxes and fees. Therefore, the focus of tax reduction should be on businesses and indirect taxes. The taxes paid by businesses should be cut before those paid by individuals. Compared with direct tax reduction, indirect tax reduction is a better choice. The collection of taxes is better regulated than the charging of fees but the heaviest burden on businesses is the payment of fees. Therefore, fee reduction should be given priority over tax reduction. It was based on such an understanding that I wrote the article "Cutting Taxes in China: More than Meets the Eye".

In the beginning, tax and fee cuts was understood as one of the measures to increase demand. However, if we follow the sources of revenue for tax and fee cuts and see that this round of tax and fee cuts has gone from "borrowing to reduce taxes and fees" to "borrowing and cutting spending to reduce taxes and fees", we will find that tax and fee cuts in the context of supply-side structural reform is aimed not only at increasing demand, but also at reducing costs. The methods include both increasing deficit and cutting government spending, with the latter being the fundamental approach. Putting the best option of "cutting spending to reduce taxes and fees" on the agenda in due course and then shifting from "borrowing and cutting spending to reduce taxes and fees" to "cutting spending to reduce taxes and fees" is the best way for tax and fee cuts in line with supply-side structural reform. I offered a comprehensive explanation about this understanding in the article "Accurately Grasping the Objectives of and Approach to The Latest Round of Tax and Fee Cuts".

According to the arrangements made at the Third Plenary Session of the 18th CPC Central Committee, one of the objectives of direct tax reform was to "gradually increase the proportion of direct taxes" and thus "gradually reduce the proportion of indirect taxes" on the premise of "stabilizing the tax burden". Therefore, direct tax reform, one of the two components of tax reform this time, can be regarded as the precondition of reducing indirect taxes and be linked to indirect tax reform that plays a significant role in tax reduction. With such an understanding, the direct tax reform, which mainly includes the establishment of a personal income tax system based on adjusted gross income and the introduction of real estate tax, not only affects the improvement of the tax structure, but also concerns the country's financial security. It should be noted that the tax reform and tax and fee cuts initiative supported by increasing deficit and issuing more government bonds is after all hard to sustain and the direct tax reform is a fundamental and supportive measure that must be accelerated. We must take decisive measures so that the direct tax reform, where the focus and main challenge of this round of tax reform lies, can truly be carried through in China. This issue is fully discussed in the article "Direct Tax Reform: A Discussion from the Perspective of Financial Risk Mitigation".

There is no need to elaborate on the significance of building the local tax system. However, there were obviously special considerations when building the local tax system was included in the report delivered at the 19th CPC National Congress and defined in the context of the new era of socialism with Chinese characteristics. On the one hand, the change in the principal contradiction in Chinese society increasingly called for fairness and justice in the distribution of tax burden and the promotion of social equity and justice through tax regulation. It also made the imbalances in the structure of the tax system and the resulting unbalanced distribution of tax burden increasingly serious. On the other hand, there was barely progress in the direct tax reform mainly featuring personal income tax and real estate tax and targeted at VAT. As a result, the tax reform to include them in the local tax system as the main type of tax was also lagging behind. The basic understanding is that the reform of personal income tax and real estate tax lags behind means slow progress in the local tax reform or the development of local tax system. Therefore, it is a practical and theoretical necessity for socialism with Chinese characteristics entering a new era to start the reform of direct taxes represented by personal income tax and real estate tax and thus to promote the improvement of local tax system. This issue is comprehensively expounded in the article "Improving the Local Tax System: A Tough Fight We Must Win".

Tax and fee reduction was undoubtedly at the top of the list of macroeconomic regulation operations in 2018. There were also various views and propositions about tax and fee cuts. Since tax and fee cuts is a task that requires a high level of expertise and must be based on the reality of the shift to high-quality development, there is an urgent need to make an overall plan for it. Therefore, I wrote the article "What Kind of Tax and Fee Cuts Do We Really Need?" This article is intended to answer five questions. Why do we cut taxes and fees? For whom do we cut taxes and fees? What taxes and fees should we cut? What do we use to support tax and fee cuts? How do we cut taxes and fees? The purpose is to compare the different focuses and priorities of tax and fee cuts in the stage of high-speed growth and the stage of high-quality development. On this basis, a basic conclusion is reached that there is a difference of real and nominal reduction. In China's shift to a stage of high-quality development, what we need most is real tax and fee cuts with cost reduction as the main objective, businesses as the key beneficiaries, turnover taxes and fees as the category to be cut, government spending as the source of financial resources, and institutional reform as the approach to implementation.

2 Showing Determination and Confidence in China's VAT Reform[1]

When it comes to replacing BT with VAT (VAT), people who have been following this reform know the plan to implement it in all sectors across the country and thus abolish BT by the end of the 12th Five-Year Plan period. Now the reform is in countdown. The time left for us to finish it is no more than 8 months.

[1] Originally entitled "Replacing Business Tax with Value-added Tax: A Task to Be Completed in the Next Eight Months", the article was published in *China Tax News* on May 13, 2015, and slight changes were made when the book was published.

However, two interrelated views that have been widely debated recently have cast a cloud over this reform in progress.

First, on the premise of stabilizing the tax burden, the replacement of BT with VAT, which helps to reduce indirect taxes, is connected with the move to increase the proportion of direct taxes. The real estate industry plays a special role in driving economic growth and the levying of real estate tax will help to increase direct taxes. In the face of increasing economic downward pressure, however, the introduction of real estate tax is likely to be postponed. If the decrease of indirect taxes does not come along with the increase of direct taxes, it would be difficult to ensure that the tax burden is stabilized which is the premise of this round of tax reform. Moreover, it may hinder the attainment of the objective—improving the tax structure. Once such a situation arises, it will add uncertainty to the current round of tax reform focusing on improving the tax structure.

Second, with the economic downturn, the growth rate of the revenue in national general public budget and tax revenue in particular in the first quarter of 2015 decreased to 2.4% and 1.2% respectively on a year-on-year basis. Such a low growth rate has been rarely seen since 1994. Moreover, the average annual growth rate of revenue in the national general public budget during the 11th Five-Year Plan period was 21.3%, and even reached 25% just 4 years ago in 2011. Such a rapid decline was a surprise and also raised concerns about fiscal revenue and expenditure in 2015 and the coming years. Given the worrying signs of fiscal situation which may become even worse, the replacement of BT with VAT in all sectors will undoubtedly further increase the existing pressure on fiscal revenue and expenditure and even worsen the fiscal situation.

The two views may seem to make sense to some extent. However, they are just one-sided views if we compare them to the bigger picture of economic and social development. It is necessary to look at the greater significance of replacing BT with VAT in the context of the new normal of economic development.

Firstly, deepening reform across the board is undoubtedly a major "battle" concerning the great cause of the Chinese nation. Quite different from previous rounds of reform, the overall goal of deepening reform across the board is to modernize the country's governance. As the foundation and pillar of governance, the reform of the fiscal and tax systems should certainly be carried out first and play a fundamental and supportive role in the modernization of the country's governance system and capacity. As one of the most sound, thorough, effective and practical and least controversial measures for the reform of the fiscal and tax systems, the replacement of BT with VAT is in fact a breakthrough in such reform. The replacement of BT with VAT was first piloted in Shanghai early in 2012. Its development over the past 3 years shows that the direct tax reform, featuring the introduction of real estate tax and the establishment of a personal income tax system based on adjusted gross income and specific income types, has been put on the agenda. Moreover, gradually increasing the proportion of direct taxes as the focus of this round of tax reform was recognized for the first time at the Third Plenary Session of the 18th CPC Central Committee. Thanks to the influence of efforts to replace BT with VAT, the fiscal relationship between central and local governments has started to be readjusted. In addition, for the first time in at least 20 years, Chinese people are reconsidering giving full play to the initiative of both central and local governments, a basic direction of this round of fiscal and tax reforms. Apparently, we can see a roadmap for China to deepen reform across the board, namely from replacing BT with VAT to fiscal and tax reforms and then to the reform of economic, political, cultural, social, ecological and Party building systems. Therefore, if we consider fiscal and tax reforms a fundamental project for deepening reform across the board, then replacing BT with VAT is the essential part of this fundamental project.

Secondly, the current macroeconomic situation is apparently graver and more complex than we expected. Since economic growth is likely to be out of a proper range, the government should not only intervene, but also adopt regulatory measures that are strong and more effective. However, it should be noted that this round of macroeconomic regulation is an expansionary action aimed at stimulating the economy in the context of the new normal of economic development, and the related thinking and efforts should be different from previous ones. In other words, in light of the new situation and tasks, this round of macroeconomic regulation should follow a path that differs widely from the past one. With other factors put aside, the new path here should at least include three aspects. First, any decision about macroeconomic regulation should be made to help adapt to the new normal and guide its development. Second, any decision about macroeconomic regulation should be in line with the new thinking of the new central leadership on economic work. According to the new idea of "making the market play a decisive role in resource allocation", innovations should be developed in the macroeconomic regulatory system and related approaches. Third, any decision about macroeconomic regulation should be made to help reach the objectives of stabilizing growth, promoting reform, adjusting the structure, improving people's wellbeing, and guarding against risks. The new design of macroeconomic policies should be around counter-cyclical regulation and structural adjustment. In today's China, the operation of macroeconomic regulation that best meets the above requirements, is most well-targeted and produces the least side effect is to cut taxes and fees. Furthermore, of all available tax and fee cuts measures, replacing BT with VAT is the best choice for its special advantage of involving the first and third largest taxes in the current tax system and being connected with the main task of the current round of tax reform. Therefore, if we consider the institutional innovation in macroeconomic regulation under the new normal of economic development as a key step in the endeavor to build a moderately prosperous society in all respects and the tax and fee cuts as a priority measure of macroeconomic regulation in the current stage, replacing BT with VAT is surely the first priority in this key step.

Thirdly, the world today is undergoing complex and profound changes and the Chinese economy has been closely integrated with the world economy. The Belt and Road Initiative proposed by China in line with the trends of a multi-polar world, economic globalization, cultural diversity and IT application is not only what China needs to open up wider to the outside world, but also for the purpose of creating a new structure of all-round opening-up and deeply integrating into the world economic system. Needless to say, the Belt and Road Initiative is a systematic project. We should adhere to the principles of extensive consultation, joint contribution and shared benefits and actively promote the alignment of development strategies of all countries involved. As one of the basic and key projects in this initiative, the coordination between tax systems should be taken into account and carried out as soon as possible. Moreover, in China's current tax system, the proportion of indirect taxes is too high and that of direct taxes is too low. The serious imbalance between the two has become an important factor that prevents the functions of modern taxation from being fulfilled. Since it is quite different from the tax structure of major economies in the world today, this has posed a series of obstacles to international trade and investment activities. Without correcting the imbalance between indirect and direct taxes and bringing China's tax structure closer to that of major economies, the Belt and Road Initiative will lack the foundation to be pushed forward. It was based on such an understanding that the Third Plenary Session of the 18th CPC Central Committee defined the main task of this round of tax reform as "gradually increasing the proportion of direct taxes". It was also based on the consideration that "gradually increasing the proportion of direct taxes" and "gradually reducing the proportion of indirect taxes" should be advanced at the same time that replacing BT with VAT, which plays a significant role in reducing indirect taxes, was first introduced as the first measure in the current round of tax reform. Therefore, if we consider the Belt and Road Initiative as a new opportunity for China's economic development and a new strategy for comprehensively improving the open economy, then replacing BT with VAT is the centerpiece of this new opportunity and new strategy.

At this point, a logical conclusion we can draw is that replacing BT with VAT in all sectors is essential for China as it enters a new normal of economic development. In the next 8 months, it is an important task that must be completed on schedule to ensure all relevant measures are implemented.

In this regard, we should be determined and confident.

3 Cutting Taxes in China: More Than Meets the Eye[2]

In today's China, supply-side structural reform is undoubtedly a concept that is used frequently. When it comes to how this reform should be carried out and especially how the government should promote it, there are only two basic solutions, namely streamlining administration and delegating power and cutting taxes. The former certainly needs to be achieved through reform measures, while the latter is often reflected in the choice of macroeconomic policies. Given that the former would unavoidably affect vested interests and would not produce results in the short term while the latter is mainly limited to policy adjustments and would have an effect in a short time, tax reduction has been considered as a preferred measure of supply-side structural reform, and even as a solution to many problems in the current stage.

[2] This article was published in the first issue of *International Taxation in China* in 2016, and slight changes were made when the book was published.

However, if we look closer at China's national conditions and taxation, we will find that the reality is not as simple as what it is in theory and its complexity may be far beyond the imagination of many people.

Tax reduction naturally involves an assessment of China's tax burden. The internationally used indicator for assessing tax burden is overall tax burden—the proportion of tax revenue in GDP. Once this indicator is used to assess China's tax burden, the first issue we may encounter is to change overall tax burden to overall tax and fee burden.

This is because, in today's China, what the government collects from taxpayers is not always called a tax. In addition to taxes, there are various charges, funds, fines, etc. The budget prepared by the government is not just the general public budget. In addition to the revenue listed in the general public budget, there are also other sources of revenue, including budgets of government-managed funds, budgets of state capital operations, and budgets of social security funds. Since there are so many types and sources of government revenue, there has been a debate about which one or which ones should be included in the assessment of overall tax burden. For different considerations and positions, some people prefer a "narrow scope"—to include only the government revenue nominally called taxes in the scope of overall tax burden while some prefer a "medium scope"—to include only the revenue listed in the general public budget in the scope of overall tax burden and others prefer a "broad scope"—to include all types of government revenue in overall tax burden. The debate about the three different scopes have been going on for years. In such a context, people's understanding of China's overall tax burden has been mixed and there are no widely recognized statistical indicators for assessing overall tax burden.

Encouragingly, as the new Budget Law was enacted in January 2015, it seems that the debate over overall tax burden can be put to an end. Unlike the old Budget Law, the new law clearly stipulates that all government revenues and expenditures shall be included in the budget. Government budget comprises the general public budget, budgets of government-managed funds, budgets of state capital operations, and budgets of social security funds. Since the four types of government revenue are, in nature, the revenue collected by the government from taxpayers and the only difference is the name, including all types of government revenue into the statistical scope of overall tax burden is a move that conforms to the laws underlying reform and human development.

Once China's tax burden is assessed using a broad scope, it will be further found that in 2014, for example, the ratio of government revenue referred to as taxes to government revenue denominated in other names was about fifty-three to forty-seven. The ratio shows that the government's revenue from outside taxation is surprisingly considerable. Excluding it from the statistical scope of overall tax burden will not only hinder the proper assessment of China's tax burden, but also lead to confusion among the general public and distortion in the government's decision-making. To prevent such a situation from arising again, it is undoubtedly necessary to refer to the various non-tax sources of revenue collectively as fees, change overall tax burden to overall tax and fee burden, and use the latter as the applicable indicator for assessing China's tax burden.

Based on the 2014 figures, considering both tax and non-tax revenue, or all the revenue listed in the general public budget, budgets of government-managed fund, budgets of state capital operations, and budgets of social security funds with double-counted parts excluded, government revenue totaled 22.557 trillion yuan and accounted for 35.42% of GDP in the year. Compared with the average tax burden of the industrialized countries at around 39%, this figure suggests an upper-middle level in today's world.

Moreover, for tax reduction we need to decide on what taxes to cut and taxes paid by whom to cut. This is because tax revenue is a general term and it is composed of taxes paid by different people and those of different natures. In today's China, the two aspects show distinctive features related to national conditions and the tax situation.

In terms of taxpayers, in 2014, for example, of the total national tax revenue of 11.9158 trillion yuan, 90% were from taxes paid by state-owned enterprises, collective enterprises, joint-stock cooperative enterprises, joint-stock companies, and private enterprises. In addition, < 10% of tax revenue was collected from individuals. The ratio of revenue from businesses to that from individuals was roughly nine to one. If the revenue from self-employed people counted as revenue from individuals is excluded, the share of revenue purely attributable to individuals was only about 6%. Therefore, the ratio of revenue from businesses to that from individuals was roughly 94 to six.

Such an unbalanced structure of tax revenue tells us that although China's overall tax and fee burden is only at an upper-middle level, corporate tax and fee burden in the country ranks much higher than the overall tax and fee burden. One of the important reasons is that China's overall tax and fee burden is approximately equal to the corporate tax and fee burden. Putting aside the fact that taxes and fees paid by businesses must be passed on through various channels, it is fair to say that China's tax and fee burden is basically borne by businesses alone.

In terms of tax types, in 2014, for example, of the total national tax revenue of 11.9158 trillion yuan, 64.2% were from indirect taxes such as domestic VAT, domestic excise tax, BT, VAT and excise tax on import goods, and vehicle purchase tax. If other local taxes with distinct indirect tax features are also included, indirect taxes contributed to more than 70% of total tax revenue. In addition, the proportion of direct taxes such as corporate income tax and personal income tax was only 26.2%. The ratio of indirect tax revenue to direct tax revenue was roughly seven to three. It is fair to say that the majority of China's tax revenue are from indirect taxes.

Such an unbalanced structure of tax revenue shows us that although China's overall tax and fee burden is at an upper-middle level, most of China's tax revenue can be used as a component of the prices of a variety of goods and factors. This part of tax revenue is seemingly invisible and intangible. Its tax burden can be counted as the same but it has a large impact on commodity and factor prices due to its high share. The prices of commodities and factors will be raised by a large margin, which will inevitably reduce their competitiveness. In addition, the price changes are closely connected to those in the tax system and the level of tax burden. This will unavoidably distort the normal mechanism of price formation.

Furthermore, different from how direct taxes work, indirect taxes are not directly related to profit and loss, so even if businesses are in a loss, they should still pay indirect taxes as usual. This is nothing less than adding insult to injury for loss-making businesses that urgently need to find a way to survive and get out of the predicament.

On the one hand, the tax burden in China is basically borne by businesses alone; on the other hand, the major part of the tax burden is from indirect taxes. From the standpoint of supply-side structural reform, although China's overall tax and fee burden has not reached a relatively high level in today's world, if we calculate it carefully and look beyond the total size and deeper into the internal structure, there are serious imbalances in terms of sources and types. An inevitable result of this unbalanced structure is that the levels of tax and fee burden between relevant taxpayers and different types and sources of taxes and fees are either too heavy or too light. Specifically, compared with individuals, businesses are faced much heavier tax burden. Compared with direct taxes, the burden from indirect taxes is much heavier.

In conclusion, it is desirable to make a brief summary of the discussion.

First, tax reduction, which may seem to be within the scope of macroeconomic policy arrangements, is actually a major measure concerning supply-side structural reform that needs to be implemented through both policy arrangements and reform actions. Therefore, we should make various arrangements for tax reduction on the levels of macroeconomic policy arrangements and deepening reform across the board and from both the demand side and the supply side. It is a proper choice to ensure that tax reduction is achieved through supply-side structural reform.

Second, in the process of advancing supply-side structural reform, we should not only cut taxes, but also lower fees. It should be noted that there are great differences between the tax and fee mechanisms in China. The collection of taxes is much better regulated than that of fees and the problems brought by fees are much more serious, so it is more important to lower fees. Therefore, seizing the opportunity presented by the adoption of the new Budget Law, we should continue the tax and fee reform that began in the late 1990s, and make new breakthroughs in regulating the collection of government revenue and its mechanism. This will contribute largely to advancing supply-side structural reform.

Third, as part of the tax and fee cuts initiative, it is necessary to prioritize the items or types of taxes and fees involved to make clear what the priorities are. For example, in terms of taxes and fees on the whole, compared with tax reduction, the reduction of fees should take precedence. For tax reduction, the reduction of taxes paid by businesses should be placed before the reduction of those paid by individuals. The reduction of indirect taxes is a better option compared with the reduction of direct taxes. In other words, this tax reduction initiative, which is centered on supply-side structural reform, should and must focus on the reduction of fees, corporate taxes and indirect taxes.

4 Accurately Grasping the Objectives of and Approach to the Latest Round of Tax and Fee Cuts[3]

I. The core factor of supporting funding sources

Tax and fee reduction is definitely a frequently discussed topic in China's macroeconomic circle, and is also the focus of attention in all sectors of society. This is because tax and fee cuts affect millions of households and have always been a widely welcomed measure. It should be taken as the policy focus because the heavy tax burden on businesses is indeed an outstanding problem in the functioning of the Chinese economy. More importantly, in today's China, in the face of various potential and real fiscal and financial risks, both monetary policy featuring quantitative easing and traditional fiscal policy operations focusing on increasing investment and expenditure have encountered challenges again and again. Addressing all macroeconomic policy objectives and centering around supply-side structural reform, tax and fee cuts has in fact evolved into the main battlefield of macroeconomic regulation.

However, if we look beyond the surface and into the depth of tax and fee cuts, we will find that the central issue is that what sources of funding can be used to pay for it.

Taxes and fees are both collected as sources of revenue to meet the government's spending needs. From the equation of "taxes + fees = government expenditure", it is not difficult to see that tax and fee cuts directly affect the balance between government revenue and expenditure. The sources of funding used to fill the gap in government revenue after tax and fee cuts are important to rebalance government revenue and expenditure. Moreover, they concern the practical effect of tax and fee cuts and the ultimate direction of macroeconomic policies.

In other words, the effect of tax and fee cuts and the direction of macroeconomic policies would be greatly different with the support of different sources of funding. What sources are used actually determines the practical effect of tax and fee cuts as well as the direction of related macroeconomic policies.

It should be noted that this round of tax and fee cuts is carried out in the context of supply-side structural reform rather than demand management. Therefore, the analysis of its effect and related macroeconomic policies should not exclude the core factor of supporting funding sources.

II. From "borrowing money" to "borrowing money and spending less"

The current round of tax and fee cuts implemented in China against the background of supply-side structural reform has gone through two stages so far, namely the stage of "borrowing money to reduce taxes and fees" and the stage of "borrowing money and spending less to reduce taxes and fees".

Supply-side structural reform was officially launched in 2016. In the context of focusing on the five major tasks of cutting overcapacity, reducing excess inventory,

[3] This is a slightly revised version of an article first published in *Economic Daily* on August 11, 2017.

deleveraging, lowering costs, and strengthening areas of weakness, tax and fee cuts, as a main task of lowering costs, began to be implemented on a large scale. Tax and fee cuts amounted to 573.6 billion yuan in the year. The sources of funding supporting such tax and fee cuts were the increase of deficit and the issuance of government bonds to make up for the deficit. The main reason for setting fiscal deficit in the general public budget of the year as 2.18 trillion yuan, an increase of 560 billion yuan over the previous year, and increasing the deficit-to-GDP ratio to 3% was to support tax and fee cuts. As the Report on the Work of the Government delivered by Premier Li Keqiang explained, "moderately increasing fiscal deficit is mainly to cut taxes and fees and further reduce the burden on businesses". The Report on the Execution of the Central and Local Budgets for 2015 and on the Draft Central and Local Budgets for 2016 submitted by the Ministry of Finance also explained that the increased deficit was intended to bring an appropriate increase in necessary fiscal expenditure and mainly to make up for the reduction in revenue brought by tax and fee cuts. This kind of operation can be called "borrowing money to cut taxes and fees".

2017 has been defined as the year for deepening supply-side structural reform. In the context of cost cutting with various measures, tax and fee cuts have been continuously promoted. As planned, the taxes and fees cut would amount to 350 billion yuan and 200 billion yuan respectively, making a total of 550 billion yuan. Such tax and fee cuts would be naturally by the increase of deficit and issuance of more government bonds. This is exactly why the fiscal deficit in the general public budget has been set as 2.38 trillion yuan, an increase of two hundred billion yuan over the previous year, and keeping the deficit-to-GDP ratio at 3%. As Premier Li Keqiang said in the Report on the Work of the Government, "The main reason for keeping this year's deficit-to-GDP ratio unchanged is to allow for further reductions in taxes and fees.... to benefit market entities." In addition, cutting government spending is another way to pay for tax and fee cuts. A concrete manifestation is that reduction in non-priority spending and general expenditures and no increase in spending on official overseas visits, official vehicles, or official receptions are all listed in the general public budget. As Premier Li Keqiang said in the Report on the Work of the Government, "We will scale down non-priority spending and cut budgets for projects that do not deliver desired outcomes. Governments at all levels should tighten their belts, and central government departments should take the lead by cutting their general expenditures by no < 5%. No increase in spending on official overseas visits, official vehicles, or official receptions is permitted; and we will squeeze out more funds to cover cuts in taxes and fees. We will keep government spending low and enrich our people." This kind of operation can be called "borrowing money and spending less to reduce taxes and fees".

III. **A very positive change**

The shift from the combination of deficit increase and issuance of government bonds to that of deficit increase, issuance of government bonds, and expenditure decrease to pay for tax and fee cuts should be regarded as a very positive change. This is because this round of tax and fee cuts in the context of supply-side structural reform has a much different objective than that in the past.

Unlike previous tax and fee cuts aimed at increasing total demand, this round of tax and fee cuts is targeted at lowering costs. The practice of "borrowing money to reduce taxes and fees" may help to reduce businesses' tax and fee burden in the short term, but the principal and interest would eventually need to be repaid in the medium to long term. Even if government debt can be extended indefinitely or even never repaid, the interest expense brought about by the additional issuance of government bonds will always be added to the government expenditure, which will certainly add to the future tax and fee burden of businesses. Therefore, costs are lowered in the short term but increased in the medium to long term. Tax and fee reduction in this way is not a good choice for cost cutting and it is unsustainable and risky.

In contrast, the practice of "borrowing money and spending less to reduce taxes and fees" may still increase the tax and fee burden of businesses in the future and lead to cost reduction in the short term about rising costs in the medium to long term because of borrowing money. However, since the crucial factor of "spending less" is included, some of the pressure from borrowing money can be reduced, along some of the interest expenses added to government expenditure. As a result, the growth in future tax and fee burden of businesses will be reduced, along with associated risks. Therefore, compared with the former practice, the latter is of substantive significance for cost reduction and is in line with the requirements of supply-side structural reform.

Furthermore, spending less for tax and fee cuts and benefiting the people is the real way of cost cutting through tax and fee cuts. Since the public and private sectors are in a competitive relationship when it comes to GDP distribution. Only a substantial reduction in government spending can bring about a substantial increase in private spending. Or, only when the resources allocated to the government are substantially reduced, the resources allocated to the private sector will be substantially increased. This means that the government's spending cuts are the precondition for achieving the objective of lowering costs. Only on this basis can tax and fee cuts in the true sense be truly implemented.

Considering the purpose of cost cutting and the main task of supply-side structural reform, we can be sure that the shift from "borrowing money to reduce taxes and fees" to "borrowing money and spending less to reduce taxes and fees" is a big step forward towards real tax and fee cuts.

IV. **Spending less as the fundamental way**

The above discussion actually tells us that although the practice of "borrowing money and spending less to reduce taxes and fees" is better than that of "borrowing money to reduce taxes and fees", it is not the fundamental way to cut taxes and fees. What is more essential or more in line with the objective of cost cutting and the main task of supply-side structural reform is spending less—cutting government spending would make room for tax and fee cuts. While tax and fee cuts, we should cut government spending on the same scale. In this way government revenue and expenditure will be rebalanced. This kind of operation can be called "spending less to reduce tax and cut fees".

It is fair to say that this is the most thorough tax and fee cuts in the true sense. On the one hand, if the tax and fee revenue and government expenditure are reduced on the same scale at the same time, the current and future corporate tax and fee burden will be reduced accordingly. The reduction of such burden will not just stay in the short term so its sustainability can be ensured. On the other hand, the part of corporate tax and fee burden that can be reduced means a transfer of resource allocation power so that the change of resource allocation that is really beneficial to businesses will take place. More importantly, such tax and fee cuts will not bring about any fiscal or financial risks.

The only likely constraint is the room left for cutting government spending or the possibility of breaking through the barriers of vested interests to cut government spending. Practicing fiscal frugality has been agreed on at least in the government system. Since there are trillions of yuan in fiscal deposits and larger deposits of government agencies and organizations, there must be some situations where the actual spending needs are smaller than the expenditure listed in budget and thus the part can be offset by reducing expenditure in the budget of the next year. In addition, some government departments do spend money lavishly or for the sake of spending money. It is safe to say that a significant portion of the money in the cases listed above could be treated as the "base" for cutting government spending.

It is not impossible to reduce taxes and fees and cut government spending at the same time as long as we make up our minds and consider problems from the standpoint of the cause of the Party and the country.

Therefore, after making the shift from "borrowing money to reduce taxes and fees" to "borrowing money and spending less to reduce taxes and fees", we should and must promptly put the best choice of "spending less to reduce taxes and fees" on the agenda and thus make another necessary shift.

V. **Structural adjustment as the second-best choice**

In fact, there is another option for reducing taxes and fee, that is, to make structural adjustments to tax and fee revenue. While some taxes and fees are reduced, other taxes and fees may be increased. Or while the tax and fee burden of some payers is reduced, that of other payers may be increased. This will not change the total amount of tax and fee revenue and the scale of related government spending, or break the balance between government revenue and expenditure. This kind of operation can be called "structural tax and fee cuts".

It is fair to say that this is the second-best choice of tax and fee cuts operation. On the one hand, the total amount of tax and fee revenue and the scale of government spending are not affected, so the balance between government revenue and expenditure will not change. On the other hand, while tax and fee cuts is achieved, the structure of tax and fee revenue can be improved through structural adjustment, so that the two objectives of reducing the tax and fee burden of businesses and improving the tax and fee structure can be both achieved.

To adopt such an approach, we may need to answer a number of questions. What taxes and fees are to be reduced and what are to be increased? Into what category or group do the related taxpayers and fee payers? What obstacles need to be overcome to achieve such a structural adjustment? One of the important elements of this round of fiscal and tax reforms initiated at the Third Plenary Session of the 18th CPC Central Committee is to "gradually increase the proportion of direct taxes" on the premise of stabilizing tax burden. Moreover, an increase in the proportion of direct taxes means a decrease in the proportion of indirect taxes. It also means the increase of personal tax burden and the reduction of corporate tax burden, which is in line with the goal of improving the tax and fee structure and promoting social equity and justice. Undoubtedly, structural tax and fee cuts will not bring about a substantial reduction in the total amount of taxes and fees, but it is effective in reducing the tax burden of businesses and promoting the current round of fiscal and tax reforms.

In this sense, structural tax and fee cuts is a second-best choice after spending less to reduce taxes and fees.

At this point, we can draw a basic conclusion that the tax and fee cuts, based on the new normal of economic development and in the context of supply-side structural reform, cannot follow the old path of demand management. In this sense, it may be hard to give up the practice of borrowing money to reduce taxes and fees in the short term, but fundamentally it is by no means an appropriate option. Therefore, on the basis of borrowing money and spending less to reduce taxes and fees, we should actively create conditions and gradually make the shift to "spending less to reduce taxes and fees" and "structural tax and fee cuts", or a combination of the two. This should be the purpose of this round of tax and fee cuts.

5 Direct Tax Reform: A Discussion from the Perspective of Financial Risk Mitigation[4]

The direct tax reform discussed in this article specifically refers to the reform initiative proposed by the Third Plenary Session of the 18th CPC Central Committee. It features the levying of personal income tax system based on adjusted gross income and the introduction of real estate tax and is aimed at "gradually increasing the proportion of direct taxes", as one of the two components of this round of tax reform.

After the Third Plenary Session of the 18th CPC Central Committee, the discussion on direct tax reform has reached an unprecedented level in both depth and breadth. Although the understandings are mixed and views are divergent, no analysis of direct tax reform has been directly made from the perspective of financial risk mitigation.

However, it should be noted that the 2017 National Financial Work Conference raised the prevention and control of financial risks to unprecedented heights, and recognized the extreme importance of winning the tough battle of preventing and defusing major risks. It is undoubtedly very necessary for us to make an in-depth and systematic review of the relationship between direct tax reform and the prevention and defusing of financial risks. Based on that, we should identify, give early warning,

[4] This is a slightly revised version of an article first published in *Taxation Research*, No. 10, 2017.

detect and cope with such risks as early as possible just as President Xi Jinping has pointed out. In addition, we should be prepared for the worst-case scenario and strive for the best results.

I. Starting with two tax-related phenomena

Direct tax reform and financial risks seem to be at odds with each other at first glance, but if we look closer and deeper, we will find that in today's China they are absolutely a pair of highly related, contradictory phenomena that we must pay much attention to.

Let's start with two tax-related phenomena that are of concern to the general public.

First, tax and fee cuts. A closer look at the basic trajectory of tax and fee cuts so far shows that tax cuts as the majority of this round of tax and fee cuts are nearly all targeted at indirect taxes. In particular, the main approach is to replace BT with VAT. According to statistics, the scale of tax reduction by replacing BT with VAT was 573.6 billion in 2016, and reached about seven hundred billion yuan from May 2016 to April 2017. As the initiative enters the phase of tax rate simplification in July 2017, the scale of tax reduction will further increase. It should be noted that government spending has not been cut at the same time and the reduction in government revenue caused by tax and fee cuts has been apparently made up for by increasing deficit and issuing more government bonds. In other words, the source of funding to support tax and fee cuts, mainly through the replacement of BT with VAT, is the money borrowed by the government rather than the money saved by the government. What we are pursuing is essentially a path of borrowing money to reduce taxes and fees.

Second, tax reform. A close examination of the tax reform process so far shows that among the six taxes and one law involved in the reform (VAT, excise tax, resource tax, environmental protection tax, personal income tax, real estate tax and Law on the Administration of Tax Collection) efforts that have been initiated or are in progress are all targeted at indirect taxes. Specifically, the indirect tax reform featuring replacing BT with VAT is basically intended to cut taxes. In contrast, there is basically no progress in the direct tax reform mainly involving personal income tax and real estate tax and intended to increase taxes. It should be noted that the most important change in this round of tax reform compared with previous ones is to improve the structure of the tax system by reducing the proportion of indirect taxes and increasing the proportion of direct taxes on the premise of stabilizing the tax burden to promote fairness and justice in taxation. The direct result of the indirect and direct tax reforms is that the revenue from indirect taxes is reduced while that from direct taxes is not increased at the same time. The reduction in revenue brought about by this can only be made up by increasing deficit and issuing more government bonds. In other words, the funding used to support the indirect tax reform is the money borrowed by the government rather than the money from other sources. What we are taking is essentially a path that relies on borrowing money to advance tax reform.

Although these two phenomena have occurred on the two levels of policy arrangement and reform action respectively, their direct impacts are the same. They both rely on borrowing money to be implemented and promoted which will lead to deficit increase and additional issuance of government bonds. The deficit in the general public budget jumped to 2.18 trillion yuan in 2016 and then climbed to 2.38 trillion yuan in 2017, and the deficit-to-GDP ratio rose from 2.4% in 2015 to 3% in 2016 and 2017. At the same time, the issuance of local government special bonds listed in the budgets of government-managed funds jumped to four hundred billion yuan and eight hundred billion yuan respectively in 2016 and 2017.

The situation at the local government level is even more serious. A huge quantity of debts arose on financing platforms from 2008 to 2010 which still pose grave financial risks today. Putting that aside, in 2015, the control over the issuance of local government bonds was relaxed and the swap of matured bonds was allowed. The developments since then show that due to multiple factors such as the long-standing tradition of running local fiscal deficits not publicly, the huge demand for the swap of local debts, and the idea of boosting GDP growth, hidden fiscal deficits have been made public and various forms of local government debts, including special local bonds, swap bonds and industrial investment funds, have expanded rapidly, coupled with serious illegal borrowing and guarantee. The situation must be addressed carefully, or it may get too tricky to cope with.

II. **It is hard to sustain and involves risks**

The problem is that both tax and fee cuts supported by borrowing money and tax reform supported by borrowing money would be hard to sustain in the medium to long term.

The borrowed money will have to be repaid in the end, and the only choice that can be made is the way it is repaid. This applies not just to businesses and individuals, but also to the government. Ultimately the government will need to repay the money either with future tax and fee revenue or with newly issued bonds for debt swap.

Moreover, the interest expenses brought by the additional issuance of government bonds would be ultimately added to government expenditure. This added part is to be made up either by collecting more tax revenue or by issuing more government bonds.

The repayment of principal or payment of interest will eventually result in additional government spending. If the government expenditure in other areas cannot be reduced correspondingly or the tax and fee revenue from other sources cannot be increased correspondingly, it will result in the pressure of increasing deficit and issuing government bonds, or even a vicious circle in which government debt keeps growing. This has been proved time and again by stories in the history of countries around the world, including the European debt crisis and the United States fiscal cliff.

A more important problem is that both the monetary policy of quantitative easing and the traditional fiscal policy which focuses on increasing investment and expenditure in China are facing repeated challenges. To meet all macroeconomic policy objectives, tax and fee cuts has in fact evolved into the focus of macroeconomic regulation and main task of supply-side structural reform. In the general context of deepening reform across the board initiated at the Third Plenary Session of the 18th CPC Central Committee, fiscal and tax reforms, as the foundation and important pillar of governance, have always been regarded as a fundamental and key project. In particular, tax reform has been playing a leading role in this regard, making it a crucial part of this fundamental project.

Tax and fee reduction must be advanced as the focus of macroeconomic regulation and main task of supply-side structural reform. Tax reform must also be pushed forward as a key project to deepen reform across the board and a fundamental project of fiscal and tax reforms. If we fail to promptly give up the approach of borrowing money to support tax and fee cuts and tax reform, it will affect the implementation of tax and fee cuts and tax reform, the implementation of macroeconomic regulation and supply-side structural reform, and even the attainment of the objectives of deepening reform across the board and fiscal and tax reforms. Since financial security a strategic and fundamental issue that concerns national security, the steady and healthy development of the economy and the overall development of the Chinese economy and society, the incurred real and potential financial risks should never be underestimated. More importantly, since fiscal security is the last line of defense against all financial and social risks, we should indeed stay vigilant against the risks posed to long-term stability of the country.

III. **Structural adjustment is the soul**

Furthermore, fundamentally speaking, the current round of tax and fee cuts and tax reform are different from conventional ones in that they are focused on structural rather than total output problems. In other words, the main goal of this round of tax and fee cuts and tax reform is to improve the tax structure rather than adjust the total amount of taxes and fees. This round of tax and fee cuts and tax reform should focus on structural adjustment rather than quantity adjustment.

For the former, the focus of current macroeconomic policies is supply-side structural reform rather than demand management, and the current round of tax and fee cuts implemented in the context of supply-side structural reform is by no means indiscriminate but clearly targeted. Mainly corporate taxes and fees, rather than individual taxes and fees, are included in the scope of reduction. Under the current tax structure, most of the taxes and fees paid by businesses are indirect rather than direct taxes and fees. Therefore, this round of tax and fee cuts is mainly targeted at the indirect taxes and fees paid by businesses.

As far as the latter is concerned, the current round of tax reform centered on the overall goal of deepening reform across the board does have a focus, according to the arrangements made at the Third Plenary Session of the 18th CPC Central Committee. Although six taxes are included in the current round of tax reform, an examination of corporate and individual taxes or indirect and direct taxes shows that all corporate or indirect taxes are to be reduced while all individual or direct taxes are to be increased. Therefore, the tax reform is mainly to reduce the indirect taxes paid by businesses.

It is not difficult to find that the two have the same goal. The taxes or fees to be cut in the tax and fee cuts initiative and the taxes to be cut in the process of tax reform are both mainly indirect taxes and fees paid by businesses. Since they are targeted at indirect taxes and fees instead of all taxes and fees, it suggests that the purpose of this round of tax and fee cuts and that of this round of tax reform are both structural adjustment. This round of tax and fee cuts is a structural one and so is this round of tax reform. Structural adjustment is the key element that makes this round of tax and fee cuts and this round of tax reform very different from previous ones.

This is a very important conclusion. It tells us that the reduction of indirect taxes and fees paid by businesses is closely related to the increase of direct taxes and fees paid by individuals. Unless the scale of government spending is reduced simultaneously, reducing the indirect taxes and fees paid by businesses must be accompanied by increasing the direct taxes and fees paid by individuals. Such structural adjustment is the soul of this round of tax and fee cuts and tax reform.

In other words, this round of tax and fee cuts and tax reform must and can only follow the path of structural adjustment. Any deviation from it, especially the tax and fee cuts and tax reform supported by borrowing money, is against the original purpose of this round of tax and fee cuts and tax reform. It may also directly incur financial and other risks.

IV. Direct tax reform is an important milestone

Then how exactly should we do it?

The above discussion has clearly shown us that tax and fee cuts must be sustained, and tax reform must be advanced, but it is unsustainable and risky to do it by borrowing money. Thus, we have no choice but to cut government spending while continuing to reduce taxes and fees, or to launch direct tax reform while continuing to advance tax reform. Another option is to combine the two, i.e. while continuing to implement and promote tax and fee cuts and tax reform, we seek to cut government spending and launch direct tax reform.

The problem is complicated by the fact that the room left for cutting government spending is limited. Globally speaking, there are very few successful examples of cutting government spending. Therefore, while making great efforts to reduce the scale of government expenditure, we should concentrate our efforts on accelerating the launch of the proposed direct tax reform, which is a truly feasible option for us.

This means that the most important reason why we have embarked on the path of relying on borrowing money to support tax and fee cuts and tax reform is nothing more than the fact that direct tax reform has not been advanced in tandem. It is the absence of progress on direct tax reform, which focuses on personal income tax and real estate tax and is intended to increase taxes, that has posed a series of challenges to tax and fee cuts and tax reform so far and even made them hard to sustain and full of risks.

It also reminds us that only when we understand the current round of tax and fee cuts and tax reform from the perspective of structural adjustment can related actions be truly carried out. Only when the direct tax reform aimed at increasing taxes is substantially advanced, can the tax burden of businesses be truly reduced. In the meantime, the indirect tax reform mainly focused on replacing BT with VAT will not deviate from the path of cutting taxes and the tax reform's objective of improving the tax structure will be achieved.

Given that financial risk mitigation affects the cause of the Party and the country, tax and fee cuts is crucial to the success of supply-side structural reform, and it is imperative to carry out a direct tax reform aimed at gradually increasing the proportion of direct taxes and the current round of tax reform aimed at improving the tax structure, it is undoubtedly an appropriate choice for us to focus on accelerating the direct tax reform that focuses on personal income tax and real estate tax, and continue to implement and promote tax and fee cuts and tax reform so that no regional and systemic financial risks are posed.

At this point, we can draw a basic conclusion that in today's China we should consider the major plan of financial risk mitigation and ensuring the country's financial security with a broader and longer-term vision and that direct tax reform is a fundamental and supportive measure that must be implemented at a faster pace.

This means that we should not continue with the current tax and fee cuts and tax reform, supported by increasing deficit and issuing more government bonds. This also means that for the current round of tax reform, it is not only necessary for the reform to launch the reform of personal income tax system based on adjusted gross income and specific income types as soon as possible and to introduce real estate tax. It is necessary not only for reform and macroeconomic regulation, but also for improving the ability to mitigate financial risks and ensuring the country's financial security. Therefore, we should strive to create all possible conditions for the implementation of direct tax reform, which has already been included in the plans made by the Third Plenary Session of the 18th CPC Central Committee and is the central and most challenging part of the current round of tax reform. There are basically no other choices on this issue.

6 Improving the Local Tax System: A Tough Fight We Must Win[5]

In the report to the 19th CPC National Congress, President Xi Jinping said when addressing the reform of the taxation system, "We will deepen reform of the taxation system, and improve the local tax system." It shows clearly the focus of tax reform in the next stage. It is safe to say that from now on, the current round of tax reform, which was initiated at the Third Plenary Session of the 18th CPC Central Committee, will increasingly focus on local taxes and advance around the main task of building the local tax system. In other words, improving the local tax system is a tough battle to fight in this round of tax reform.

The basis for such a conclusion includes a number of factors that are both independent from and closely related to each other.

First, as socialism with Chinese characteristics enters a new era, the principal contradiction in Chinese society has changed to that between the people's ever-growing needs for a better life and unbalanced and inadequate development. Since this is a historic change that has an overall bearing on the cause of the Party and the

[5] This is a slightly revised version of an article first published in *China Tax News* on November 13, 2017.

country, a closer look at the current taxation in China shows that the two aspects of this new principal contradiction have both put forward new requirements for taxation.

The people's yearning for a better life is manifested not only in their material and cultural needs, but also in the growing needs for democracy, the rule of law, fairness, justice, security and the environment. This includes the demand for achieving fairness and justice in the distribution of tax burden and that for promoting social equity and justice through tax regulation. The rationale behind this is simple. As human society develops, people's aspiration for a better life grows stronger, making it more necessary to achieve fairness and justice in the distribution of tax burden and to promote social equity and justice through tax regulation.

Imbalanced and inadequate development is manifested not only in private goods and services provided by the market system, but also in public goods and services provided by the government system, and not only in goods and services, but also in institutional design including the design of the tax system. This includes the unbalanced structure of the tax system and the unbalanced distribution of tax burden.

The high proportion of revenue from turnover taxes and overly high proportion of revenue from corporate sources have been a weakness of China's current tax structure, which has brought about the most serious problem, namely undermining fairness and justice in the distribution of tax burden and hindering the effective regulation of income distribution and wealth through taxation. To better meet the people's growing needs for a better life, and in particular their growing needs for democracy, the rule of law, fairness, justice, security and the environment, and thus promote all-round human development and social progress, it is urgent to make a structural adjustment to the tax system by gradually increasing the proportion of direct taxes and reducing that of indirect taxes correspondingly. At the same time, we should gradually reduce the proportion of tax revenue from corporate sources and increase that of tax revenue from personal sources.

Second, unlike previous rounds of tax reform, the biggest change in the current round of tax reform launched at the Third Plenary Session of the 18th CPC Central Committee is to achieve fairness and justice in taxation by improving the tax structure—gradually increasing the proportion of direct taxes and reducing the proportion of indirect taxes on the premise of stabilizing tax burden. However, a close examination of the tax reform process so far shows that among the six taxes and one law involved in the reform (VAT, excise tax, resource tax, environmental protection tax, personal income tax, real estate tax and Law on the Administration of Tax Collection) efforts that have been initiated or are in progress are all targeted at indirect taxes. Specifically, the indirect tax reform featuring replacing BT with VAT is basically intended to cut taxes. In contrast, there is basically no progress in the direct tax reform mainly involving personal income tax and real estate tax and intended to increase taxes.

The direct result of the indirect and direct tax reforms is that the revenue from indirect taxes is reduced while that from direct taxes is not increased at the same time. The reduction in revenue brought about by this can only be made up by increasing deficit and issuing more government bonds. In other words, the funding used to support the indirect tax reform is the money borrowed by the government rather than the money from other sources. What we are taking is essentially a path that relies on borrowing money to advance tax reform. From all perspectives, this path is both unsustainable and risky. To reach the goal of this round of tax reform, we must return to the path of improving the tax structure—carrying out direct and indirect tax reforms at the same time. The gradual increase of direct taxes will offset the corresponding decrease of indirect taxes and the gradual increase of personal tax sources will offset the corresponding decrease of corporate tax sources.

Third, in the direct tax reform to better meet the people's needs for a better life or to improve the tax structure, the main types of direct taxes involved are personal income tax and real estate tax. Once these two types of taxes are connected with the revenue-sharing fiscal system, we may find that they can be included in the local tax system as the main types of taxes. Real estate tax, in particular, has always been as a local tax or a major local tax. In this sense, the stagnation of reform concerning personal income tax and real estate tax in the current round of tax reform can also be attributed to the absence of progress in local tax reform or the development of the local tax system.

Fourth, it should be noted that the fiscal relationship between central and local governments is one of the basic relations that need to be handled well in the modern governance system. Moreover, the adjustment of such a fiscal relationship has been quite slow in the current round of fiscal and tax reforms, thus hindering progress in such reforms. It is fair to say that a considerable part of the adjustment effort is to push forward local tax reform or the development of the local tax system so that a breakthrough will be made in the direct tax reform featuring personal income tax and real estate tax.

Now we can come to the conclusion that the direct tax reform featuring personal income tax and real estate tax should be initiated as soon as possible and that the tax reform with a focus on improving the local tax system should be promoted. It is a tough task to fulfill for pushing through this round of tax reform and for adapting to the historic change of principal contradiction in Chinese society and better meeting the people's needs for a better life. Well fulfilling this tough task is a practical and theoretical necessity for socialism with Chinese characteristics entering a new era.

7 What Kind of Tax and Fee Cuts Do We Really Need?[6]

In today's China, tax and fee cuts is undoubtedly a high-frequency word. It is a central topic in the discussions about the design of macroeconomic policies, the demands of entrepreneurs, and even the expectations of ordinary people. In other words, tax and fee cuts concerns countless Chinese people.

The problem is that the idea of tax and fee cuts must eventually be translated into action. To ensure policy implementation, we must come up with an action plan that is

[6] This article was published in *Economic Daily* on December 7, 2018, and slight changes were made when the book was published.

both practical and effective. Such an action plan must certainly be based on accurate and professional analysis. Then we would need to answer the five questions. Why should we cut taxes and fees? For whom should we cut taxes and fees? What kind of taxes and fees should be cut? What should be used to support tax and fee cuts? With what approach should we cut taxes and fees?

The more crucial question is that it is not difficult to answer the above questions in the context of traditional tax and fee cuts. Based on past experience and available theories, we can easily give a set of logically self-consistent answers. However, the relevant practices in the past were adopted when the Chinese economy was in a stage of high-speed growth. The theoretical system that supported the practices was closely related to the Keynesian theory of demand management and the economic reality in the stage of high-speed growth. Since we are discussing tax and fee cuts in the context of high-quality development rather than high-speed growth and the focus of macroeconomic policies in the shift to high-quality development is supply-side structural reform rather than demand management, the above questions should be analyzed from at least two dimensions and at least two sets of answers should be provided accordingly. We must carefully compare the two sets of answers offered from two different dimensions and then make a proper choice.

I. **Why cut taxes and fees: To boost demand or to reduce costs?**

Tax and fee cuts are certainly made to achieve certain objectives. Different objectives would mean different or even very different methods and actions.

Tax and fee reduction in the traditional sense is usually considered one of the expansionary measures of proactive fiscal policy and its main objective is to increase demand. To increase demand, tax and fee cuts would be aimed at the adjustment of total output and focused on the demand side. The basic logic of actions is that tax and fee cuts would increase the disposable income of businesses and individuals. The increase of businesses' disposable income helps to increase the demand for investment. The increase of personal disposable income helps to increase the demand for consumption. The increase of either demand for investment or demand for consumption would lead to the increase of total demand.

Tax and fee reduction in the stage of high-quality development is one of the measures taken for supply-side structural reform and its main objective is to lower costs. To lower costs, tax and fee cuts would be aimed at structural adjustment and focused on the supply side. The basic logic of actions is that tax and fee cuts would lower the costs in taxes and fees, one of the components of the prices of products and services, and thus reduce the costs of production and operation for businesses. The reduction of production and operation costs may help businesses to improve their supply structure or the quality of supply. The improvement in both cases would ultimately help advance the reforms for improving the quality, efficiency and impetus of economic development.

II. **Whose taxes and fees are to be cut: Who are the intended beneficiaries?**

Tax and fee cuts should certainly be implemented to taxpayers and fee payers. At present, taxpayers and fee payers in China include both businesses and individuals.

Should the cuts be random? Or should they be well-targeted? Different targets would mean different or even very different methods and actions.

Since the main objective of tax and fee cuts in the traditional sense is to increase demand, what specific demand is increased does not matter as long as total demand is eventually increased. It can be the demand for investment or consumption, or the demand for both. Therefore, no targets are specified for tax and fee cuts aimed at increasing demand, unless there are special considerations. In this case, there is often no need to distinguish between businesses and individuals. Taxes and fees can be cut for both businesses and individuals and more can be cut for both. In a word, tax and fee cuts are reduction in the total output, rather than structural reduction.

The main objective of tax and fee cuts, which is linked to supply-side structural reform when we move into a stage of high-quality development, is to lower costs and all actions are clearly targeted. It should be noted that the costs here refer to the costs of businesses, so tax and fee cuts are targeted at businesses rather than individuals. The taxes and fees to be cut are mainly those paid by businesses rather than those paid by individuals. The basic meaning of the expressions related to tax and fee cuts, such as business-related taxes and fees and cost reduction for the real economy, is to implement tax and fee cuts on businesses, especially the real economy. In a word, tax and fee cuts are structural reduction, rather than reduction in the total output.

III. **Which taxes and fees should be cut: direct or indirect taxes and fees?**

In China's current tax and fee system, there is a whole host of taxes and fees. In the end, cutting taxes and fees means cutting specific taxes and fees. Which tax or taxes should be cut? Which fee or fees should be cut? Different choices would mean different methods and actions.

With increasing demand as the main objective, tax and fee cuts in the traditional sense is relatively easy to be carried out. Guided by the policy of demand management, the government only needs to collect less taxes and fees. It does not matter whether they are direct or indirect taxes and fees as long as the purpose of increasing total demand can be achieved Therefore, for tax and fee cuts aimed at increasing demand, there is no need to choose the specific tax and fee types. Both direct and indirect taxes and fees can be reduced. Both direct and indirect taxes and fees can take up a larger share in the cuts. However, to directly affect the disposable income of businesses and individuals and thus rapidly increase total demand, in the past, most of the cut taxes and fees would be direct ones, especially those related to income.

It is more complicated to carry out tax and fee cuts aimed at cost cutting in the shift to high-quality development. Given the main task of supply-side structural reform, cost reduction should not only be implemented on the supply side and aimed at reducing the costs of businesses, but also focus on reducing their production and operation costs. Therefore, tax and fee cuts aimed at cost cutting is well-targeted and special attention is paid to the selection of specific tax and fee types. Since the purpose is to reduce the costs in production and operation, it is the taxes and fees incurred in production and operation that are to be cut. As far as China's current tax and fee system is concerned, it mainly refers to turnover taxes and fees represented by VAT. This means that the focus of tax and fee cuts in the stage of high-quality development aimed at cost cutting is to reduce indirect taxes and fees rather than direct ones.

IV. How to pay for tax and fee cuts: Increasing deficit or cutting spending?

Taxes and fees have always been collected as sources of revenue for the government. Therefore, the effort to cut taxes and fees comes with the question of how to make up for the decrease in revenue. Different approaches would mean very different actions.

In the context of demand management, tax and fee cuts with the main objective of increasing demand should and can only be made up by increasing deficit and issuing more government bonds, but not by cutting government spending. This is because the balanced budget multiplier theorem shows that when the government cuts taxes and fees and spending at the same time and on the same scale and the result is that total demand will also decrease on the same scale. This is tantamount to counteracting the effect of tax and fee cuts. Because of this, past practices of tax and fee cuts in China were mostly supported by increasing deficit and issuing more government bonds.

For tax and fee cuts in the context of supply-side structural reform with the main objective of lowering costs, the path we should and can only choose is to cut government spending rather than increasing deficit and issuing more government bonds. If the government cut taxes and fee on the one hand and increase deficit and issue government bonds on the other on the same scale, resource allocation will not change as a result—the resources that go to non-government sectors as a result of tax and fee cuts will return to the government sector along with the purchase of government bonds. Moreover, the debts borrowed by the government will eventually need to be repaid. Even if the principal of the debts can be extended indefinitely through the issuance of bonds for debt swap, the interest on the debts that must be paid on time will eventually be added to government spending and become an important factor that pushes up the future tax burden or future costs for businesses. A substantial increase in the future tax burden in exchange for the current decline in tax and fee costs is absolutely against the original purpose of cost reduction and supply-side structural reform. Because of this, tax and fee cuts aimed at cost cutting has been focused on cutting government spending in the interest of the people from the very beginning.

V. How to cut taxes and fees: Institutional reform or policy adjustment?

Tax and fee reduction must also be implemented with a certain approach. We can choose policy adjustment or institutional reform. They are based on different considerations and mean different actions.

Focusing on increasing demand, tax and fee cuts in the context of demand management is usually associated with cyclical fluctuations of the economy and implemented as a policy tool for counter-cyclical regulation. Since it is associated with cyclical fluctuations, tax and fee cuts would not be long-term but cyclical. As a policy tool for counter-cyclical regulation, tax and fee cuts will not be a sustained action, but a temporary one. Therefore, such tax and fee cuts are intended to achieve short-term balance. It is not a long-term solution, but an expedient. It is carried out often through policy adjustment. Once the economic situation changes or any adjustment of other purposes needs to be made, the tax and fee levels will often be adjusted accordingly or even return to their original levels.

Focusing on lowering costs, tax and fee cuts in the context of supply-side structural reform is usually associated with solving structural problems in the functioning of the economy, and implemented as a long-term strategy for sustained, healthy and steady economic development. Since it is connected with structural problems, tax and fee cuts would not be cyclical but long-term. As a long-term strategy to ensure sustained, healthy and steady economic development, tax and fee cuts will not be a temporary action, but a sustained and effective one. Therefore, such tax and fee cuts are intended to achieve long-term development. It is not an expedient, but a long-term solution. It is often carried out through reform actions targeted at the tax and fee system. Even if the structural problems are eased later on, or the economic development strategy changes and new adjustments to tax and fee levels are needed, a new round of actions based on institutional reform must be initiated to achieve the desired results.

VI. Stage of high-quality development: What is most needed is meaningful tax and fee cuts

The comparative analysis of tax and fee cuts from the above two dimensions is no more than to illustrate that there are differences between real and nominal reduction in taxes and fees. Since China is now in the shift to a stage of high-quality development, what we need most is real tax and fee cuts with cost reduction as the main objective, businesses as the key beneficiaries, turnover taxes and fees as the category to be cut, government spending as the source of financial resources, and institutional reform as the approach to implementation.

This conclusion is based on the fact that in the complex and volatile economic situation where external shocks are compounded by domestic structural problems, it is necessary for us to adjust total demand and the demand side and seek to increase domestic demand, such adjustments and efforts are secondary to structural and supply-side problems and are ultimately fine and proactive adjustments. The obvious changes in the external environment and the impact on external demand will not change the basic economic situation in the stage of high-quality development. It should not change the design of macroeconomic policies that focuses on supply-side structural reform. Moreover, we should not change the idea that innovation is the primary driving force, coordination is inherent, eco-friendliness is universal, opening up is the only way, and sharing is the fundamental purpose of economic development. Therefore, we should follow the guidance of the new development philosophy, carry out supply-side structural reform as the main task, continue addressing the main problems in a well-targeted way, and promote the implementation of a series of major strategic decisions on achieving high-quality development. This is the basic thinking and strategy that we should adhere to making choices on such issues as tax and fee cuts.

Chapter 7
Promoting High-Quality Economic Development

1 Introduction

The last chapter of the book, comprising five articles, is entitled "Promoting High-quality Economic Development".

A key factor in economic development is investment. In the context of China's current system, we should focus on investment listed in the central government budget. The scale, structure and change of investment not only have a profound impact on the Chinese economy, but also shows the direction of macroeconomic regulation. As the Chinese economy shifts from a stage of high-speed growth to a stage of high-quality development, the investment listed in the central government budget, designed in the stage of high-speed growth in response to the crisis, has shown deficiencies in many aspects. According to the requirements of high-quality development, it is undoubtedly necessary to make strategic adjustments in such aspects as specifying the areas of investment, returning to regular budget management, appropriately reducing the scale of investment, and actively preventing local debt risks. The article "Central Government Budgetary Investment Towards High-quality Development" is based on the Third-party Performance Evaluation Report on the Central Government's Investment in Capital Construction, a research project I led and entrusted by the Ministry of Finance in 2017.

Focusing on the real and main problems is essential to maintaining the focus of macroeconomic regulation in the process of promoting high-quality economic development. In the face of both short-term and long-term, external and internal, and cyclical and structural problems, we should not address just some of the problems or give the same weight to all the problems. We should strive to achieve the policy objectives of both strengthening counter-cyclical regulation and deepening supply-side structural reform, but the efforts on the two fronts should never be equal. Both total output control on the demand side and structural adjustment on the supply side must be based on the basic reality that the Chinese economy is entering a stage of high-quality development. Only on the basis of grasping the main theme of

P. Gao, *A Shift Toward High-Quality Development of China*,
Research Series on the Chinese Dream and China's Development Path,
https://doi.org/10.1007/978-981-99-8990-4_7

economic work in the stage of high-quality development can we fully understand these basic principles and thus avoid making detours in doing economic work. This article "Understanding Historical Patterns, and Grasping the Key Economic Tasks at Hand" offers a comprehensive explanation of the issue.

High-quality development and the efforts to promote it should not be understood in the general sense. Our understanding of the laws underlying high-quality development should be deepened on the basis of figuring out the logic in theory and practice. It should be noted that the shift to a stage of high-quality development and the entry into a new era of socialism with Chinese characteristics share a common foundation—the change of principal contradiction in Chinese society. It is undoubtedly an appropriate choice to define the features of China's current stage of economic development from the change of principal contradiction, and explain the necessity of shifting to a stage of high-quality development from the change of the economic development stage. As it is analyzed in the article "Deepening Our Understanding of Underlying Patterns of High-quality Economic Development", socialism with Chinese characteristics has entered a new era and the Chinese economy has entered a stage of high-quality development. The theoretical and practical logic behind the two are highly consistent. Promoting high-quality development is a path that conforms to the laws underlying economic development, and it is necessary for socialism with Chinese characteristics to enter a new era and for China's economic development to enter a new stage.

To promote high-quality economic development, we need to introduce practical and effective measures and plans. This depends largely on whether we can clearly define the priorities and key tasks for promoting high-quality economic development, on the basis of accurately and thoroughly understanding what high-quality economic development means. Based on such an understanding, I made explanations in five aspects in the article "Accelerating the Improvement of Institutions and Mechanisms that Facilitate High-quality Development". In response to the changes in development objectives, the efforts to promote high-quality economic development should focus on addressing the problem of unbalanced and inadequate development and meeting the people's ever-growing needs for a better life. In response to the changes in development philosophy, the efforts to promote high-quality development should focus on improving the quality and efficiency of economic development on the premise of fully implementing the new philosophy of pursuing innovative, coordinated, green, open and shared development. In response to the changes in main problems and main aspects of the problems in the functioning of the economy, the efforts to promote high-quality development should focus on improving the supply structure and the quality of supply. In response to the changes in the focus of macroeconomic policies, the efforts to promote high-quality development should focus on advancing supply-side structural reform as the main task. In response to the changes in the approach to macroeconomic regulation, the efforts to promote high-quality economic development should focus on promoting the reform of economic system and mechanisms.

Regarding the issue of continuing to practice and improve the basic socialist economic system and promoting high-quality economic development, the Fourth

Plenary Session of the 19th CPC Central Committee made three major decisions, namely fully applying the new development philosophy, advancing supply-side structural reform as the main task, and working faster to modernize the economy. In the institutional system for promoting high-quality economic development, development philosophy, focus of work, and economic system are not only important aspects, but also fundamental and supportive elements. They are essential to the creation of a basic institutional framework for facilitating high-quality economic development. At the invitation of the Theory Department of *People's Daily*, I wrote the article "Basic Institutional Framework for Facilitating High-quality Economic Development" as an outcome of my research on the guiding principles of the Fourth Plenary Session of the 19th CPC Central Committee. From fully applying the new development philosophy to advancing supply-side structural reform as the main task, working faster to modernize the economy, and ensuring the institutional support for promoting high-quality development, we can see a clear connection and consistent logic between them. This article can also be regarded as the conclusion of the whole book.

2 Central Government Budgetary Investment Towards High-Quality Development[1]

I. Largely an outcome of the financial crisis

In reality, the investment in the central government budget (also known as "central government investment in capital construction") refers to the central government funding for capital construction managed by the National Development and Reform Commission (NDRC). Although it has its origins in the capital construction investment appropriation in the period of planned economy and central government spending on capital construction in the general sense, it should be considered an outcome of the financial crisis to a large extent since it was introduced in response to the crisis.

In terms of scale, investment stayed within the range from twenty billion yuan to forty billion yuan before 1998. With the outbreak of the Asian financial crisis and the implementation of proactive fiscal policy, the figure rapidly increased to one hundred billion yuan in 1998. After that, it remained above one hundred billion yuan. In 2009, with the outbreak of the international financial crisis and the implementation of proactive fiscal policy again, it jumped up to 367.6 billion yuan and then started to grow year by year. By 2017, it had reached 507.6 billion yuan. For 2018, 537.6 billion yuan is planned to be allocated.

In terms of the management system, investment was incorporated into the framework of conventional central government budgeting together with other central government expenditures before 1998. In 1998, in response to the crisis, investment

[1] This is an abridged version of "Third-party Performance Evaluation Report on the Central Government's Investment in Capital Construction (2017)", a project commissioned by the Ministry of Finance.

began to be excluded in conventional budgeting and the Ministry of Finance put the funds under the management of NDRC which exercises the power of plan formulation and task assignment as well as the power of budgeting and funds management.

As far as the focus is concerned, the funds were mainly used for capital construction projects organized by the central government before 1998. Since 1998, investment has mainly focused on increasing domestic demand and, in particular, stimulating the investment demand of local governments and the private sector to maintain and stabilize growth.

II. **Multiple Signs of Maladaptiveness**

Facing the historic change in the Chinese economy from high-speed growth to high-quality development, the central government budgetary investment that was adopted in response to crisis is apparently no longer able to meet changes needs of the economy.

First, counter-cyclical operations have been replaced by pro-cyclical ones. The scale of investment in the central government budget, which is associated with crisis response, should have been adjusted in response to the cyclical changes in the economy and the principle of "keeping essential projects and canceling unnecessary ones" should be adopted. In fact, however, none of the projects established since the 12th Five-Year Plan have been canceled and investment has gone beyond the scope of capital construction to cover general expenditures, competitive areas, and areas of local fiscal powers. It is overlapped with other matters supported by central government funding, and its scale has become increasingly large.

Second, segmented management has become normalized. The segmented management approach, adopted in response to the crisis as a temporary measure, should have been replaced by conventional budget management again as the economy recovered. In fact, however, over the past 20 years since 1998, the approach has not only continued, but also become increasingly normalized with a growing size of segmented funds. In 2016, at the request of many sides, some central government projects involving a single investment of more than one hundred million yuan had been required to be reported the National People's Congress. It should be noted that such funds account for nearly one-fifth of the central government's expenditure. Excluding them from conventional budget management is a reality unacceptable for China, which has entered a new era and seeks to ensure every dimension of governance is law-based.

Third, it is one of the inducements to local debt risks. Segmented funds are excluded from conventional budget management. One of the prominent features of segmented management is that plan implementation is divorced from any financial constraint. This is mainly reflected in the special transfer payments made to local governments which account for four-fifths of central government budgetary investment. On the one hand, there is no constraint on the use of such funds and even no financial feasibility study would be carried out. On the other hand, for the consideration of leveraging local investment, local governments are required to provide a very high proportion of supporting funds. In the context of local governments' lack of funding and the urgent need for investment to drive economic growth, it is a common practice of local governments to act in violation of laws and regulations or borrow money in disguised forms. They would often blindly launch large projects with the help of financing platforms. This has become an important inducement to local debt risks, which should not be ignored.

Fourth, the assessment of investment performance is absent. Although the decision-making power for setting projects of investment in the central government budget lies with the central government, the organization and implementation of investment projects depend on local governments at all levels. Since such investment is excluded from conventional budget management and NDRC cannot take care of everything, the reality is that more attention is paid to the allocation rather than management of funds and the assessment of investment performance has not been put on the agenda. In fact, in recent years, the contribution of investment in the central government budget to economic growth has dropped from an all-time high of 0.15% to the current 0.02%, down 0.13 percentage point. Moreover, since the investment structure is yet to be improved, the key role of investment in helping improve the supply structure is not obvious.

III. **Strategic adjustments as a necessity**

Standing at the historical starting point of a new era and in light of China's realities, it is necessary to make strategic adjustments to the central government budgetary investment in the four aspects.

First, clearly define the role of investment. On the one hand, according to the requirements of the 19th CPC National Congress, the role of investment in the central government budget should be clearly defined as improving the supply structure, rather than driving economic growth. While making major adjustments to the ideas, thoughts and strategies about investment in the central government budget, we should screen all the existing investment projects and ensure that some are kept while some are canceled. In this way, investment will truly play a key role in improving the supply structure. On the other hand, on this basis, the project approval scope for investment in the central government budget should be limited to capital construction projects at the central level as well as cross-sector and cross-regional major national projects at the local level. Moreover, investment should be focused on not-for-profit projects, rather than for-profit projects. In terms of specific project arrangements, we should also pay attention to the coordination with other central government special funds and departmental budgets to avoid any conflicts.

Second, return to conventional budget management. Since China's economic development has entered a stage of high-quality development, it is natural to abandon the segmented management approach and return to conventional budget management. Therefore, based on the distinction between the dual roles of NDRC as the authority for managing overall investment in the central government budget and the specific body for managing the central government's special investment funds, the investment in the central government budget should be included in the conventional budget management procedures. Moreover, as required by the 19th CPC National Congress, comprehensive performance management should be implemented for such investment just like other fiscal expenditures. As a kind of special expenditure of the central government, the budgetary investment should not be excluded from normal budget management. Financial departments should work with NDRC to establish a dynamic supervision and performance assessment system for capital construction projects, and performance assessment results should be used to guide local investment activities.

Third, appropriately reduce the scale of investment. Since it is difficult to solve all problems related to investment in the central government budget and it will take a process to shift from focusing on investment's role in driving growth to focusing on improving the structure, in the context of clearly defining the role of investment, the focus of the current adjustment is to fundamentally change the practice of increasing investment and appropriately reduce the scale of investment.

To that end, we should transfer some project funds that overlap with other special funds of the central government to specific departments for management. In addition, the government should withdraw investment in fully competitive areas such as the service sector and in manufacturing and other industries that have been supported by market-oriented means such as funds, as well as PPP-based infrastructure projects in such areas as cultural tourism, industrial parks, economic development zones, and sewage and waste treatment. To curb local investment, improve the performance of capital construction investment and control debt risk, it is advisable to prepare a comprehensive budget for capital expenditure and debt as an appendix to the official budget report.

Fourth, actively guard against local debt risks. On the one hand, we should establish a system to demonstrate the financial affordability of local projects on the basis of clarifying the impact of central government budgetary investment transfer payments on implicit local debts. On the other hand, to cope with possible local debt risks, we should also improve the statistical system of government investment and debt, carry out an investigation of hidden debts, and devise the emergency response plan for local debt crisis.

3 Understanding Historical Patterns, and Grasping the Key Economic Tasks at Hand[2]

I. Blurred vision is the greatest challenge

The current Chinese economy undoubtedly faces many challenges. However, a careful examination of them shows that, unlike in the past, the top challenge is neither situation assessment nor policy design. Rather, it is blurred vision that may be brought about by the intricacies of situation assessment and policy design.

As far as situation assessment is concerned, the current economic situation is characterized by some worrying changes in a generally stable economic performance

[2] This is a slightly revised version of "Continuously Advancing Supply-Side Structural Reform", first published in *People's Daily* on April 25, 2019.

and a combination of short-term and long-term, external and internal, and cyclical and structural problems. All the problems come from two corresponding aspects rather than one, which is apparently the core of this assessment result. When short-term, external, and cyclical problems are mixed and interacted with long-term, internal, and structural ones, it is necessary to distinguish between them. Are there any main or secondary problems? If so, what are the main problems and what are secondary ones?

As far as policy design is concerned, in the face of problems from two aspects rather than one, it is our due choice to strengthen counter-cyclical regulation and deepen supply-side structural reform at the same time. It should be noted that counter-cyclical regulation is based on traditional macroeconomic theories represented by demand management and supply-side structural reform is a disruptive adjustment and directional change in response to demand management. When the macroeconomic policies of counter-cyclical regulation and supply-side structural reform are combined and interact with each other, it becomes necessary to make a distinction between them. Is there any difference between the two macroeconomic policies? If so, which one should be pursued as the main policy and which one as the auxiliary one?

If the above-mentioned problems and policies are indiscriminately mixed into one, it would easily lead to results in two aspects.

First, failing to identify the main problems correctly or even mistaking secondary problems for main problems, making it difficult to solve the prominent problems in the functioning of the economy in a targeted way.

Second, failing to identify the main policy correctly or even mistaking the auxiliary policy for the main policy, making it difficult to manage the direction, intensity and pace of macroeconomic regulation accurately and effectively.

II. Recognizing the true nature of the situation

Materialist dialectics tells us that the problems we face are always mixed. In the course of development involving various problems, there must be main problems, whose existence and evolution determine or affect that of other problems. Of the two aspects of each problem, there must be one main aspect whose nature determines or influences the nature of the other. Given the complicated problems, the macroeconomic policies we choose to implement are often mixed as well. In the policy system in which policies of multiple aspects coordinate with and support each other, there must be one policy whose implementation determines or affects that of other policies.

The problem is that both the main problems in the functioning of the economy or the main aspect of the problems, and the main macroeconomic policy should be identified based on the assessment of the bigger picture and the long-term trends.

A review of China's economic development since 2018 shows that there has been a shift from steady growth to worrying changes in a generally stable performance and a direct cause of the shift is the China–U.S. trade frictions. The trade frictions between China and the United States have occurred when the Chinese economy is shift from a stage of high-speed growth to a stage of high-quality development and China is taking the initiative to meet the requirements of high-quality development in all aspects to make a good start in this regard. From the perspective of the bigger picture and long-term trends, the occurrence of such frictions is nothing but an interlude on the path of pursuing high-quality development and thus a problem in the process of progress. This means that the external impact and economic downturn pressure caused by the China–U.S. trade frictions cannot be underestimated. Compared with structural and supply-side problems, however, the problems of total output and on the demand side are secondary after all. In other words, the former are what we are supposed to focus on while the latter are the obstacles that we have to overcome to accomplish the main task. Fundamentally speaking, the main problems in the functioning of the Chinese economy are still structural problems rather than total output problems and the main aspect of the problems remains on the supply side rather than the demand side.

Looking back at the trajectory of macroeconomic policies since 2018, we can also see that the idea of strengthening counter-cyclical regulation has been put forward against the backdrop of deepening supply-side structural reform as the main task and the direct cause is also China–U.S. trade frictions. Prior to that, although there were such expressions as moderately increasing total demand and continuously increasing domestic demand, they were based on the consideration of maintaining a stable economic performance. The focus was on paving the way for supply-side structural reform. The shift from moderately increasing total demand and continuously increasing domestic demand to strengthening counter-cyclical regulation reflects the pressure of policy adjustment brought about by obvious changes in the external environment. From the perspective of the bigger picture and long-term trends, however, stabilizing total demand by strengthening demand stimulus does not change the strategic intention of maintaining macroeconomic indicators within a proper range. Serving the main task of advancing supply-side structural reform is still the fundamental purpose. This means that strengthening counter-cyclical regulation is still a supporting measure or policy, compared with deepening supply-side structural reform. The nature of the latter as the focus of macroeconomic policies has not changed, and that of the former as an auxiliary policy has not changed either. In other words, the latter is the core objective that we are supposed to pursue at the stage of high-quality development, while the former is subordinate to the core objective. Fundamentally speaking, the focus of China's macroeconomic policies is still supply-side structural reform rather than demand management.

III. **The gist of maintaining strategic focus**

On the basis of identifying the main problems and the main aspect of the problems, we should seek to address them by defining the key tasks that have an overall bearing on the cause of the country. Seizing the focus in the combination of various macroeconomic policies to achieve policy coordination is not only a basic skill for doing a good job in carrying out economic work and also an underlying law whose understanding has been deepened based on many years of economic practices.

Given the worrying changes in a generally stable economic performance, the fundamental reason for our repeated emphasis on maintaining strategic focus is that the profound changes in the external environment and the possible impact on external demand will not change China's basic economic situation at the stage of high-quality development. It is based on the understanding that the main problems and main aspect of the problems in the economy remain unchanged and the focus of macroeconomic policies remains unchanged that we have always had the confidence to maintain strategic focus.

In this sense, the gist of maintaining strategic focus is to focus on the supply-side structural problems and supply-side structural reform while identifying or distinguishing between main and secondary problems and policies and thus precisely and effectively define the main theme of economic work at present.

First, in the face of both main and secondary problems, we should certainly not address just some of them or have no idea of any priorities. We should not adopt strong stimulus policies that will harm long-term development to achieve short-term balance and withstand the economic downward pressure, or be too focused on long-term development and structural adjustment while responding slowly to short-term fluctuations and the economic downturn pressure, thus making economic indicators fall out of a proper range. Moreover, we should not get lost amid the trade frictions between China and the United States, leaving behind the pursuit of high-quality economic development as the theme of the times, or pay less attention to long-term, internal and structural problems due to the prominent short-term, external and cyclical problems. Therefore, it is the focus of and a challenge in the economic work of the current stage to address supply-side structural problems, properly handle the relationship between total output and structure and immediate and long-term interests, and strengthen policy coordination.

Second, in terms of strengthening counter-cyclical regulation and deepening supply-side structural reform, we should certainly seek to reach both objectives, but the efforts made on the two fronts should not be equal. To maintain the good momentum of economic development and deepen supply-side structural reform, it is necessary to launch a series of measures aimed at stabilizing total demand in response to short-term shocks, but such adjustments should not be too drastic. Slow response may not be good, but overreaction and radical regulation would also be detrimental. In the final analysis, counter-cyclical regulation should be pushed forward around the main task of supply-side structural reform; they are by no means parallel. We should not change our commitment to further deepening supply-side structural reform when running into difficulties, or change course and adopt the practice of introducing mass stimulus again because of local and immediate problems. We should not replace the pursuit of quality with that of speed, jump from the supply side to the demand side, and concentrate on total output problems while leaving structural problems behind once the economy is under downward pressure. Therefore, the focus of economic work at present is to integrate measures for stabilizing total demand into the main task of supply-side structural reform and skillfully align them with structural adjustment.

Third, both the regulation of total demand and supply-side structural adjustment should be based on the basic reality that the Chinese economy has shifted to a stage of high-quality development. High-quality development is not empty talk, but involves a set of substantial factors. Each era has its defining theme and each stage of development has its particular mission. We should not look at today's economic situation with views from the stage of high-speed growth, or carry out today's economic work by replicating the old practices adopted in the stage of high-speed growth. The new development philosophy, supply-side structural reform, change of growth model and other major strategic decisions in response to the characteristics of the high-quality development stage are of fundamental significance for us to define development ideas, formulate economic policies and implement macroeconomic regulation at present and in the period ahead. Therefore, under the guidance of Xi Jinping Thought on Socialist Economy with Chinese Characteristics for a New Era, we should consider it the core and soul of economic work at present to blaze a path of doing economic work that is commensurate with the stage of high-quality development.

An important purpose of maintaining strategic focus is to stabilize expectations by maintaining a stable macroeconomic environment, and prevent frequent and excessive policy adjustments from causing panic and producing a negative impact on the economy. In this sense, while maintaining the overall continuity and stability of macroeconomic policies, we should make timely, proactive and fine adjustments, work towards established objectives at a proper pace, and strive to do our job well, translating pressure into a driving force to accelerate high-quality economic development. This is also a strategic choice that conforms to the laws underlying high-quality economic development.

4 Deepening Our Understanding of Underlying Patterns of High-Quality Economic Development[3]

High-quality development, a frequently discussed topic in China's economic circle, has taken on significance on many fronts. However, it was first proposed as a defining concept of the new stage of China's economic development. High-quality development and the efforts to promote it should not be understood in the general sense. We should address the issue from the source and seek to deepen the understanding of the laws underlying high-quality development on the basis of figuring out the logic on theoretical and practical levels.

As President Xi Jinping pointed out, "At present, the basic feature of China's economic development is to shift from a stage of high-speed growth to a stage of high-quality development."[4] Only by linking high-quality development with China's current stage of economic development and explaining it from the perspective of conforming to the laws underlying economic development can we possibly further promote the initiative to promote high-quality economic development.

---

[3] This is a slightly revised version of an article first published in *People's Daily* on August 20, 2019.

[4] "Xi Jinping's Speech at the Meeting with Prominent Figures Without Party Affiliation Convened by the CPC Central Committee on December 6, 2017", China News Service, December 18, 2017.

I. The change of principal contradiction in Chinese society reveals the characteristics of china's current stage of economic development

High-quality development has been placed in such an important place. Its significance is so great that it is directly related to the entry of socialism with Chinese characteristics into a new era. Each era has a defining theme and each stage of development has its mission. A basic sign of socialism with Chinese characteristics entering a new era is the change of principal contradiction in Chinese society.

Materialist dialectics tells us that in the course of development involving various problems, there must be main problems, whose existence and evolution determine or affect that of other problems. Of the two aspects of each problem, there must be one main aspect whose nature determines or influences the nature of the other. On the basis of identifying the main problems and the main aspect of the problems, we can make overall plans for advancing the cause of the country as a whole and solve them by fulfilling key tasks. To promote the cause of the Party and the country, we must figure out the principal contradiction in Chinese society.

The historic change of principal contradiction in Chinese society from "the contradiction between the people's ever-growing material and cultural needs and backward social production" to "the contradiction between the people's ever-growing needs for a better life and unbalanced and inadequate development" not only marks the entry of socialism with Chinese characteristics into a new era, but also has a wide and profound impact on the overall development framework. The needs of the people in the new era have not only been upgraded on the material and cultural levels, but also been extended beyond the scope of material and cultural products to democracy, the rule of law, fairness, justice, security, and the environment. Moreover, in the new era, the main factor that restricts the satisfaction of the people's needs has shifted from production capacity to unbalanced and inadequate development and the latter covers nearly all fields and all aspects concerning all-round human development and social progress.

The people's ever-growing material and cultural needs have evolved into the needs for a better life and unbalanced and inadequate development has replaced backward social production as the main constraint on the endeavor to meet the people's needs for a better life. This has identified the fundamental priorities China faces today while the principal contradiction in Chinese society is clearly defined.

Therefore, it is very important to accurately understand the two key concepts, i.e. "a better life" and "unbalanced and inadequate development". Although both the needs for a better life and material and cultural needs are about improving the lives of common people, the latter is based on the reality of material shortage and focuses on availability and quantity while the former is against the background of building a moderately prosperous society and focuses on quality. The two are apparently addressed not in the same stage of development. By the same token, although both unbalanced and inadequate development and backward social production are major constraints on the endeavor to meet the needs of the people, the latter focuses on the issues of availability and quantity and the effort to address it focuses on the size and speed of the economy while the former focuses on the issue of quality and the effort to address it focus on the quality and efficiency of the economy. The two are also apparently addressed not in the same stage of development.

Therefore, the major changes in the principal contradiction from material and cultural needs to the needs of a better life and from backward social production to unbalanced and inadequate development in fact reveal the characteristics of China's current stage of economic development, and also constitute the logical starting point of China's pursuit of high-quality economic development.

II. The change in the stage of economic development reveals the necessity of shifting to high-quality development

Different stages of economic development are intended to solve different problems and pursue different goals. The above-mentioned changes regarding the stage of China's economic development not only reveal the inevitability of shifting to high-quality development, but also pose new requirements for economic work in the new era.

In the past, given the contradiction between the people's ever-growing material and cultural needs and backward social production and the reality that the main aspect of the contradiction lies in backward social production, economic work would naturally focus on the size and growth rate of GDP. Great efforts would be made to increase the size and growth rate of the economy to solve the shortage in supply. In this stage, it would be definitely a choice that conforms to the laws underlying development to focus on the issues of availability and quantity.

In the new era, given the contradiction between the people's ever-growing needs for a better life and unbalanced and inadequate development and the reality that the main aspect of the contradiction lies in unbalanced and inadequate development, the focus of economic work would naturally be shifted from quantity and growth rate to quality and efficiency and from the supply of material and cultural products to the supply of almost all products including material, cultural, institutional and policy products. In this stage, it is also a choice that conforms to the laws underlying development to focus on the issues of quality and efficiency.

This means that with the change of principal contradiction in Chinese society, the stage of economic development is also changing. China's economic development has entered a new era along with socialism with Chinese characteristics. In the new era, quality and efficiency have become the priority of economic development, rather than the size and growth rate of GDP, which is a fact we must accept.

In fact, since the 18th CPC National Congress, we have been deepening our understanding of China's economic development in the current stage. The important conclusion that the economy is now in a slowing growth phase, a painful structural adjustment phase, and a phase of absorbing the adverse effects of previous stimulus policies and the recognition of the new development trends as the new normal of economic development both suggest that a series of new changes have taken place in the environment, conditions, tasks and requirements of China's economic development. The growth rate should be shifted from high speed to medium to high speed and the growth model should be shifted from being focused on scale and speed to being focused on quality and efficiency. The adjustment of the economic structure should be shifted from focusing on increasing quantity and capacity to adjusting the stock and improving the increment. The driving force of development should be shifted from the input of resources and low-cost labor to innovation. All these changes are inevitable when the Chinese economy reaches a certain stage of development, a more advanced stage marked by complete functions, more balanced structures, and better division of labor.

Against such an important background, the 19th CPC National Congress drew an important conclusion that the Chinese economy had shifted from a stage of high-speed growth to a stage of high-quality development, to fundamentally change the traditional model of launching projects to boost development and focus on improving the quality and efficiency of development to break all bottlenecks in China's economic development.

III. **Making good and steady progress in pursuing high-quality development**

In fact, this tell us that the change of principal contradiction in Chinese society and the change in the stage of economic development are like two sides of a coin, both of which constitute the basic symbol of socialism with Chinese characteristics entering a new era. The former corresponds to the cause of the Party and the country and is a major political conclusion while the latter corresponds to economic development and is a major economic conclusion. The two share the same economic foundation. High-quality development undoubtedly captures the key factor of principal contradiction in the new era. Pursuing high-quality development in response to the change of principal contradiction and addressing the problem of unbalanced and inadequate development as the focus of our economic work to better meet the people's ever-growing needs for a better life is not only a path we must take to solve the major problems facing China's development in the new era, but also an inevitable outcome of the entry of socialism with Chinese characteristics into a new era.

In a word, the entry of socialism with Chinese characteristics into a new era and the Chinese economy's shift to a stage of high-quality development are connected and highly consistent in the logic on theoretical and practical levels. High-quality development is the theme of economic work in the new era, and promoting high-quality development is the mission of economic work in the new era.

Furthermore, for China at present and in the period ahead, the fundamental purpose of defining development ideas, formulating economic policies and implementing macroeconomic regulation is to promote high-quality development.

It should be pointed out that in a country with a large economy and population, promoting high-quality development is not an easy task that can be accomplished overnight. Understanding that promoting high-quality development is a path that conforms to the laws underlying economic development and a necessity for the entry of socialism with Chinese characteristics into a new era and the entry of China's economic development into a new stage, we would not be easily affected by short-term changes and fall back to the old path when running into difficulties. As long as we focus on the long-term trends of the Chinese economy and the laws of history, we will have greater confidence and stay committed to the path of high-quality economic development.

5 Accelerating the Improvement of Institutions and Mechanisms that Facilitate High-Quality Development[5]

"We should continue to practice and improve China's basic socialist economic system and promote high-quality economic development." This is a strategic decision made by the Fourth Plenary Session of the 19th CPC Central Committee on economic work. It can be concluded that, on the premise of continuing to practice and improve China's basic socialist economic system, promoting high-quality economic development is not only the general guideline for the new stage of China's economic development, but also a key task of China's economic work in the new era.

The question is how to promote high-quality economic development by following the general guideline and accomplishing the key task.

High-quality economic development is a concept that involves a range of substantial factors and promoting high-quality economic development is also a task that requires a high level of expertise. One thing is crystal clear. To promote high-quality economic development, we need practical and effective measures and solutions. All this depends largely on whether we can fully and accurately understand the basic implications of high-quality economic development and build the systems and mechanisms for promoting high-quality economic development as soon as possible. Specifically, the most important is to clarify the focuses and key tasks in pursuing high-quality economic development. This is the top priority.

I. **Adapting to changes in development objectives: focusing on addressing unbalanced and inadequate development and meeting the people's growing needs for a better life**

Development objectives concern the purpose of economic work. In other words, the aim of economic work directly determines the direction of economic development.

Different from the stage of high-speed growth when the differences are mainly in material and cultural needs such as food and clothing, the stage of high-quality development is marked by greatly improved material conditions and the expanded scope and changed structure of people's needs. What people want are not just food and clothing, but better education, more stable jobs, more satisfactory incomes, more reliable social security, healthcare services of higher quality, more comfortable living conditions, and a more beautiful living environment. They also want their children to grow up better, have better jobs and live better lives. More importantly, as people shift from quantitative growth to the pursuit of higher quality, more and more people are looking beyond material and cultural needs to the needs for a better life that involves all aspects including material, cultural and ethical, social, institutional and ecological progress.

---

[5] This is a slightly revised version of an article first published in *Economic Daily* on December 3, 2019.

In response to the changes in development objectives, economic work in the stage of high-quality development should take addressing unbalanced and inadequate development and meeting the people's ever-growing needs for a better life as the focus and key task.

First, the supply of material and cultural products should be upgraded, and efforts should be made to increase and improve the supply of policy and institutional products represented by democracy, the rule of law, fairness, justice, security and the environment to meet the people's needs for a better life at a higher level and in a wider range.

Second, we should not only make the market play a decisive role in resource allocation, but also give better play to the role of the government, and assign the responsibility in addressing unbalanced and inadequate development to the market and the government at the same time.

Third, we should not only focus on the needs for a better life and unbalanced and inadequate development, but also address the people's greatest, most immediate and most practical concerns while continuing to promote economic development and better achieve all-round development in all undertakings so that people have a stronger, more direct and more tangible sense of fulfillment, happiness and security.

Fourth, we should not only ensure the people's right to subsistence and development, but also pay attention to their right to express and exercise their will on the basis of survival and development.

In this sense, high-quality development is development that can better meet the people's ever-growing needs for a better life. To promote high-quality economic development, we must strive to address the main constraint of unbalanced and inadequate development on the endeavor to meet the people's ever-growing needs for a better life and thus become increasingly closer to this goal.

II. **Adapting to changes in development philosophy: for using on improving the quality and efficiency of economic development**

As the fundamental factor that concerns the bigger picture and long-term interests, development philosophy is a crystallization of development ideas, especially those about the direction and focus of development. The right development philosophy directly determines the success of development.

Unlike in the stage of high-speed growth when GDP growth rate is the only focus, in the stage of high-quality development, the focus on GDP growth rate has given way to that on quality and efficiency. To put quality first means to strictly control quality in all fields and aspects of economic activities and to improve the quality of micro-products and services as well as the quality of macroeconomic growth, thus laying a solid foundation for high-quality development. To put efficiency first means to focus on the efficient allocation of factors of production in economic activities and promote the flow of factors to high-quality and efficient areas, thus maximizing efficiency in all aspects.

Furthermore, to improve the quality and efficiency of economic development, we should pursue innovative, coordinated, green, open and shared development. Innovation should be the primary driving force for development, coordination an inherent feature of sustainable and healthy development, greenness a necessary condition for sustainable development and an important manifestation of the people's pursuit of a better life, opening-up the only path to prosperity and development for the country, and sharing the fundamental purpose of economic development.

In response to the changes in development philosophy, economic work in the stage of high-quality development should be done on the premise of fully applying the new philosophy of pursuing innovative, coordinated, green, open and shared development and should take improving the quality and efficiency of economic development as the focus and key task.

First, the new development philosophy should be used to constantly correct the understandings and behaviors that are improper or even against the new development philosophy. The purpose is to truly embrace innovation, focus on coordination, advocate greenness, foster openness and promote sharing.

Second, we should not only introduce quality and efficiency indicators, but also put them first. We should shift the focus from GDP growth rate to quality and efficiency, making quality and efficiency the central factors in the whole economic evaluation system.

Third, we should gather pace in developing the indicator, policy, standard, statistical, and performance evaluation systems that are conducive to promoting high-quality development and make them the basic components of the economic work framework, creating a sound institutional environment for the pursuit of high-quality development.

In this sense, high-quality development is development that embodies the new development philosophy. To promote high-quality economic development, we must keep advancing the reforms for improving the quality, efficiency and impetus of economic development and accelerate the modernization of the economic system, thus achieving higher-quality, more efficient, more equitable and more sustainable development.

III. Adapting to changes in the main sources of tension in the economy and their contributing factors: focusing on optimizing the structure and improving the quality of supply

Structure and total output and supply and demand are the basic aspects of the market economy, like unity of opposites. However, in different stages of development, the prominence of problems is different and their role in economic activities is also different. The main problems and the main aspect of the problems are also different. It is not only a basic principle of materialist dialectics but also a basic skill for doing a good job in economic work to focus on the main problems and their main aspect and address them with targeted measures.

In the stage of high-speed growth, the main problem is material shortage and the economic output can only be increase by focusing on solving the problem of total demand. At the stage of high-quality development, the outstanding problem facing China's economic development is not material shortage but overcapacity, or not insufficient demand but changed demand with unchanged supply of products. The changes in the economic situation are not or are not mainly caused by cyclical and short-term factors, but increasingly by the combination of cyclical changes and new trends as well as short-term and long-term changes. "There are cyclical factors, but more structural and institutional factors." Therefore, fundamentally speaking, the main problems in the functioning of the Chinese economy are structural problems rather than total output problems, and the main aspect of the problems is on the supply side rather than the demand side. The root cause is the unsmooth flow of economic activities caused by major structural imbalances. Solving the problems that the supply system does not adapt to the changes in the demand structure and the flow of economic activities is not smooth is the most important factor in the stage of high-quality development.

In response to the main problems and their main aspect in the functioning of the economy, economic work in the stage of high-quality development should take improving the supply structure and the quality of supply as the focus and key task.

First, while paying attention to short-term economic fluctuations, we should introduce long-term structural factors. The effort to iron out short-term fluctuations on the demand side should be skillfully combined with that to solve long-term structural problems on the supply side.

Second, while focusing on the balance between total supply and demand, we should seek to improve the supply structure. The effort to address the imbalance between supply and demand should be closely linked with that to address a series of major structural imbalances such as those in industrial structure and regional development.

Third, we should focus on improving the supply-side structure, start with production, improve the quality and efficiency of the supply system, increase effective and medium- to high-end supply, and enhance the adaptability of the supply-side structure to changes in demand.

In this sense, high-quality development is development that focuses on improving the supply structure and the quality of supply. To promote high-quality economic development, we must focus on structural and supply-side problems and make a leap from low-level to high-level supply–demand balance.

IV. Adapting to changes in the central task of macroeconomic policies: focusing on advancing supply-side structural reform

In the face of complex problems, we would need to choose multiple macroeconomic policies. In the system of policies that are coordinated and support each other, there must be one main policy whose implementation determines or influences that of other policies. Supply-side structural reform is such a policy.

This is determined by the characteristics of the stage of high-quality development. Unlike in the stage of high-speed growth marked by demand management policy featuring counter-cyclical regulation, in the stage of high-quality development, it may be necessary to make corresponding adjustments on the demand side but the main problems in the economy have changed from total output problems to structural problems and the main aspect of the problems has changed from the demand side to the supply side. Since the priority has changed to structural adjustment on the supply side, the focus of macroeconomic policies should be naturally shifted from the demand side to the supply side and more efforts should be made on the supply side. The main task should be naturally expanded from the striking a balance between total supply and demand to achieving structural balance in supply and demand, and pay more attention to structural adjustment and the vitality of economic growth. This determines that supply-side structural reform is bound to replace demand management and become the focus of macroeconomic policies. At this time, even if counter-cyclical regulation is necessary, its purpose is to pave the way for supply-side structural reform, which is ultimately an auxiliary measure. In contrast to the supply-side structural reform that focuses on improving the supply structure and the quality of supply, demand management is not a parallel policy. In other words, demand management in the context of high-quality development plays a supporting role, while supply-side structural reform plays a leading role.

In response to the changes in the focus of macroeconomic policies, economic work in the stage of high-quality development should also take advancing supply-side structural reform as the focus and key task. We should not only stay committed to the main task of supply-side structural reform, but also further deepen supply-side structural reform in line with the policy of consolidating the gains in the five priority tasks, strengthening the dynamism of micro entities, upgrading industrial chains, and ensuring unimpeded flows in the economy.

First, we should consolidate the gains in cutting overcapacity, reducing excess inventory, deleveraging, reducing costs, and strengthening areas of weakness by accelerating the removal of excess capacity in more industries with overcapacity problem, lowering the costs of doing business in all sectors, and stepping up efforts to strengthen areas of weakness in infrastructure and other fields.

Second, we should strengthen the dynamism of micro entities by giving full play to the initiative of businesses and entrepreneurs, establishing fair, open and transparent market rules and a law-based business environment, promoting positive incentives and survival of the fittest, and developing more high-quality businesses.

Third, we should upgrade industrial chains by paying attention to the use of technological innovation and economies of scale to build new competitive edges and developing new industrial clusters.

Fourth, we should ensure unimpeded flows in the economy by accelerating the development of a unified, open, competitive and orderly modern market system, improving the financial system's capacity to serve the real economy, and fostering virtuous interactions between domestic market and producers, economic growth and employment increase, and finance and the real economy.

In this sense, high-quality development is development centered on supply-side structural reform. To promote high-quality economic development, we should focus on supply-side structural reform so that supply can better meet the people's ever-growing, upgrading and personalized material, cultural and ecological needs and the purpose of socialist production will be achieved.

V. In response to the change in macroeconomic regulation: promoting institutional reform as the focus and key task

Macroeconomic regulation in the market economy system has always been carried out through two means, i.e. policy adjustment and reform action.

It is an important condition for ensuring proper and effective macroeconomic regulation to use the two means in light of different objectives and circumstances.

Unlike in the stage of high-speed growth when policy adjustments are made in response to cyclical fluctuations and supply–demand imbalances, in the stage of high-quality development, facing the supply-side structural problems mainly caused by institutional obstacles, it may be necessary to achieve short-term balance through counter-cyclical regulation, but institutional obstacles can only be removed through institutional reform. Compared with long-term problems represented by structural imbalances, short-term ones such as economic downturn and insufficient demand are less important and we must go beyond policy operations and take reform actions on the institutional level. The core of supply-side structural reform is to identify supply-side structural imbalances and improve the supply structure and the capacity and quality of supply through reform.

This actually reminds us that, as the main task of economic work for high-quality development, supply-side structural reform is still within the scope of macroeconomic policies, but it should be by no means limited to the policy level. Institutional reform should also be included and even more importantly, reform should be the driving force. We should skillfully combine policy adjustments with reform actions, stabilize demand by means of supply-side structural reform, adopt more reform methods, and make more use of market-oriented and law-based approaches. This is the path we must take to implement macroeconomic regulation in the stage of high-quality development.

In response to the change in macroeconomic regulation, economic work in the stage of high-quality development should also take promoting institutional reform as the focus and key task.

First, we should look at the progress in building an economic system featuring an effective market mechanism, dynamism of micro entities and adequate macroeconomic regulation and ensure that the market plays a decisive role in resource allocation and the government better plays its role.

Second, we should look at the progress in practicing and improving the socialist economic system and ensure that the public and non-public sectors of the economy reinforce each other.

Third, we should look at the progress in building a law-based and enabling international business environment and ensure that administration is streamlined, power is delegated to lower levels, services are improved, and a unified, open, competitive and orderly modern market system is put in place.

Fourth, we should look at the progress in promoting reforms for improving the quality, efficiency and impetus of economic development and modernizing the economic system and ensure that higher-quality, more efficient, more equitable and more sustainable development is achieved.

The list goes on.

In this sense, high-quality development is development that mainly relies on reform actions to implement macroeconomic regulation. To promote high-quality economic development, we must pave the way for supply-side structural reform by pushing forward various basic reforms and ensure sustained and healthy economic development and overall social stability.

Many more can be added to the list, but the focuses and key tasks in the pursuit of high-quality economic development listed above are surely the most important. They are interconnected and interdependent.

In a word, high-quality development must be understood thoroughly and accurately. We should be pragmatic and effective in defining the focuses and key tasks of economic work in the stage of high-quality development. The creation of systems and mechanisms for promoting high-quality economic development should conform to the trends of the times and the laws of history. Only by meeting the requirements of high-quality development and building systems and mechanisms for promoting it can we avoid wrong decisions or undesired results and make good and steady progress in pursuing high-quality economic development.

6 Basic Institutional Framework for Facilitating High-Quality Economic Development[6]

The Fourth Plenary Session of the 19th CPC Central Committee connected "practicing and improving the basic socialist economic system" with "promoting high-quality economic development" for the first time. It also made three major decisions on promoting high-quality economic development, namely "fully applying the new development philosophy, pursuing supply-side structural reform as the main task, and working faster to modernize the economy". It should be noted that this is planning for high-quality economic development in the context of practicing and improving socialism with Chinese characteristics so the development of institutions is undoubtedly a main theme. It is fair to say that the above-mentioned three decisions epitomize the institutional arrangements for promoting high-quality economic development.

Promoting high-quality economic development requires a whole system of institutions. Specifically, those in the important fields and key aspects play a fundamental and supportive role, and constitute the framework of the whole system. It should be noted that the above-mentioned three points are institutional arrangements made from the three aspects of development philosophy, focus of work, and economic system respectively. In the system of institutions that promote high-quality economic development, development philosophy, focus of work, and economic system are not only in important fields and key aspects, but also play a fundamental and supportive role.

[6] This is a slightly revised version of "Understanding High-Quality Economic Development in Depth" first published in *People's Daily* on May 7, 2020.

In other words, we have initially set up a basic institutional framework for facilitating high-quality economic development.

The 19th CPC National Congress reached a major conclusion that the Chinese economy has shifted from a stage of high-speed growth to a stage of high-quality development. The Central Economic Work Conference held later defined the promotion of high-quality development as "the fundamental requirement for defining development ideas, formulating economic policies, and implementing macroeconomic regulation at present and in the period ahead". The Fourth Plenary Session of the 19th CPC Central Committee initially set up a basic institutional framework for facilitating high-quality economic development. The basic trajectory of efforts to promote high-quality economic development so far shows that the focus of promoting high-quality economic development has entered the stage of institutional building.

I. **Applying the new development philosophy on a broad scale**

Thinking precedes action. The philosophy of pursuing innovative, coordinated, green, open and shared development officially put forward at the Fifth Plenary Session of the 18th CPC Central Committee in October 2015 is crystallization of development ideas, especially those about the direction and focus of development. It is surely a key component of the system of institutions for promoting high-quality economic development.

The new development philosophy is based on the reality that the Chinese economy has shifted to a stage of high-quality development. It is also aimed at solving the prominent problems in China's development.

Since the 18th CPC National Congress, we have been deepening our understanding of China's economic development in the current stage. The important conclusion on three overlapping phases, the recognition of new development trends changes as the new normal of economic development, and the conclusion that the Chinese economy has shifted from a stage of high-speed growth to a stage of high-quality development based on the historical change in the principal contradiction in the Chinese society all show that a series of new changes have taken place in the environment, conditions, tasks and requirements of China's economic development. The growth rate should be shifted from high speed to medium to high speed and the growth model should be shifted from being focused on scale and speed to being focused on quality and efficiency. The adjustment of the economic structure should be shifted from focusing on increasing quantity and capacity to adjusting the stock and improving the increment. The driving force of development should be shifted from the input of resources and low-cost labor to innovation. All these changes are inevitable when the Chinese economy reaches a certain stage of development, a more advanced stage marked by complete functions, more balanced structures, and better division of labor.

As the development stage changes, the development philosophy must certainly change. In the stage of high-speed growth, in the face of material shortage, the focus is on the issues of availability and quantity, so the size and growth rate of GDP are naturally the core objectives. GDP is the only thing that matters. When China shifts to a stage of high-quality development, we need to focus on the issue of quality to build a moderately prosperous society. In addition to the size and growth rate of GDP, we should at least add the quality and efficiency of GDP to the list of core objectives. On this basis, we should put the quality and efficiency of GDP before the size and growth rate of GDP, and adhere to the principle of putting quality and efficiency first.

Since we want to improve the quality and efficiency of economic development, we must give prominence to the new development philosophy and pursue innovative, coordinated, green, open and shared development in the stage of high-quality development. To sum up, we should ensure that innovation is the primary driving force for development, coordination is an inherent feature of sustainable and healthy development, greenness is a necessary condition for sustainable development and an important embodiment of people's pursuit for a better life, opening up is the only path to prosperity and development, and sharing is the fundamental purpose of economic development.

Furthermore, the new development philosophy is a whole and the requirements involve many dimensions, rather than just the economic dimension, or a single indicator of GDP growth. Efforts in all aspects should be mobilized to form a synergy. We should not perform tasks selectively based on our preferences, or take on only some tasks without handling the rest.

This means that high-quality economic development is, above all, development that embodies the new development philosophy. To promote high-quality economic development, we must apply the new development philosophy and concentrate our attention on solving the problem of unbalanced and inadequate development. We must not return to the old path of simply focusing on GDP, or the practice of pursuing development at the cost of the environment, let alone the model of extensive growth.

To truly apply the new development philosophy, we must embed it into the institutional framework for promoting high-quality economic development as a fundamental and supportive factor that concerns the bigger picture and long-term interests. For China in the shift to high-quality development, this is institutional guarantee for advancing the reforms for improving the quality, efficiency and impetus of economic development and for achieving higher-quality, more efficient, more equitable and more sustainable development.

II. Pursuing supply-side structural reform as the main task

The main task in the Chinese context is the main factor that plays a leading role in the pursuit of development. In the context of promoting high-quality economic development, supply-side structural reform officially proposed at the 11th meeting of the Central Leading Group for Financial and Economic Affairs in November 2015 is a main factor that plays a leading role in economic work. In the system of institutions that promote high-quality economic development, supply-side structural reform is undoubtedly a key component.

Similarly, supply-side structural reform was proposed on the basis of a comprehensive analysis of the characteristics of the Chinese economy in the current stage. It is also aimed at solving the prominent problems and their main aspect in the economy in the stage of high-quality development.

Structure and total output and supply and demand are the basic aspects of the market economy, like unity of opposites. However, in different stages of development, the prominence of problems is different and their role in economic activities is also different. The main problems and the main aspect of the problems are also different. In the stage of high-speed growth, in the face of material shortage, we should focus on the issues of availability and quantity and seek to increase the economic output by addressing total demand problems. In the shift to a stage of high-quality development, material shortage is replaced by the need to build a moderately prosperous society, and the issues of availability and quantity are replaced by the issue of quality. The main problems are no longer total output problems, but structural problems, and the main aspect of the problems is no longer the demand side, but the supply side.

Since the main problems and their main aspect have changed, the main task of economic work must certainly be changed accordingly. The change means a shift from the demand side to the supply side, from the focus on total demand to the supply structure, from short-term balance to economic growth, and from policy adjustments to reform actions. In other words, in the shift from a stage of high-speed growth to a stage of high-quality development, the focus of economic work has become structural adjustment on the supply side mainly through reform actions. Therefore, supply-side structural reform is bound to replace demand management and become the main task of economic work.

Furthermore, supply-side structural reform is, in essence, a disruptive adjustment and directional change of demand management. In this context, even if it is necessary to implement demand management represented by counter-cyclical regulation, its purpose is to pave the way for supply-side structural reform, which is ultimately an auxiliary measure. In contrast to supply-side structural reform that focuses on improving the supply structure and the quality of supply, demand management is not a parallel policy. Fundamentally speaking, demand management plays a supporting role, while supply-side structural reform plays a leading role.

This means that high-quality economic development features supply-side structural reform as the main task. To promote high-quality economic development, we must focus on this main task and ensure that supply better meets the people's ever-growing, upgrading and personalized material, cultural and ecological needs to achieve the purpose of socialist production.

To truly implement supply-side structural reform, we should embed it into the institutional framework that promotes high-quality economic development as a fundamental and supportive factor that plays a leading role in the pursuit of development. In other words, only when supply-side structural reform runs through the whole process of economic development can we provide a solid and reliable institutional guarantee for high-quality economic development.

III. **Working Faster to Modernize the Economy**

A strong country must have a strong economic system. Both the new development philosophy and the main task of supply-side structural reform should be finally implemented through and reflected in the effort to develop the economic system. Modernizing the economy which was proposed by the 19th CPC National Congress is a strategic goal of China's development and an inevitable requirement of the laws underlying economic development. In the system of institutions for promoting high-quality economic development, modernizing the economy is apparently a key component.

Modernizing the economy has been put forward on the basis of a profound analysis of the shortcomings and weaknesses in China's economic system. It is also intended to solve the prominent problems in the stage of high-quality development.

The new stage of development needs the support of a new economic system. As the Chinese economy shifts from a stage of high-speed growth to a stage of high-quality development, the economic system has become increasingly unsuitable for the new stage of development. We should not only shift from low-end to medium- and high-end industries, but also shift from traditional growth drivers to new ones such as entrepreneurship and innovation, network economy, digital economy and sharing economy. In addition, as reform has entered a crucial period, the Chinese economy is now in a critical period of changing the growth model, improving the economic structure and transforming the growth drivers. Only by applying the new development philosophy, pursuing supply-side structural reform as the main task, and transforming the existing economic system can we push China's economic development to a new stage.

The effort to modernize the economy in the context of high-quality development is composed of social and economic activities in all fields and on all levels. The system covers a wide range of factors. It is necessary to build an industrial system featuring innovation-led and coordinated development as well as a unified, open, competitive and orderly market system. It is necessary to establish an efficient and fair income distribution system as well as an urban–rural and regional development system featuring local advantages and coordination. It is necessary to build a resource-saving and environment-friendly green development system as well as a diversified, balanced, safe and efficient system for all-round opening up as well as an economic system that gives full play to the role of the market and better play to the role of the government. Therefore, to modernize the economic system, on the one hand, the new development philosophy should be fully applied; on the other hand, it should be based on supply-side structural reform and be promoted through innovation in systems and mechanisms.

Furthermore, the real economy is not only the foundation of a country's economy, but also the fundamental source of wealth and an important pillar of national prosperity. The focus of the effort to modernize the economic system must certainly be placed on the real economy. Great efforts should be made to accelerate the development of advanced manufacturing, helping make China competitive in manufacturing. The Internet, big data and artificial intelligence should be deeply integrated with the real economy. Moreover, finance, as the lifeline of the real economy, should also improve efficiency in serving the real economy in an all-round way.

This means that high-quality economic development is development achieved based on a modern economic system. To promote high-quality economic development, we must fully consolidate the basic project of modernizing the economic system, and focus our attention on guiding the effort to modernize the economic system with the new development philosophy and promoting the change of growth model, the improvement of the economic structure and the transformation of growth drivers through supply-side structural reform.

To truly modernize the economy, it is necessary to embed it into the system of institutions for promoting high-quality economic development as a fundamental and supporting factor that concerns the strategic objectives and priorities and consider it a key component of the system. In other words, using the power of institutions to accelerate the pace in modernizing the economy is not only a fundamental requirement for providing institutional guarantee for promoting high-quality economic development, but also the only choice for making good and steady progress in the pursuit of high-quality economic development.

Fully applying the new development philosophy, pursuing supply-side structural reform as the main task and working faster to modernize economy are in essence interconnected and have a highly consistent logic. Creating a basic institutional framework for facilitating high-quality economic development with them as the key components is bound to have a significant and far-reaching impact on institutional building for promoting high-quality economic development and then translating institutional advantages into effective governance in the process of promote high-quality economic development.

References

Fang Fuqian. "Searching for the Theoretical Source of Supply-Side Structural Reform," *Social Sciences in China*, 2017 (7), p.50.

Xi Jinping. "Speech at the Symposium on Work Concerning Philosophy and Social Sciences", Xinhua News Agency, May 17, 2016.

Xi Jinping. "Speech at the Second Plenary Session of the Fifth Plenary Session of the 18th Central Committee of the Communist Party of China (Excerpt)" (October 29, 2015), in *Excerpts from Xi Jinping's Expositions on Building a Moderately Prosperous Society in All Respects*, compiled by the Literature Research Office of the CPC Central Committee, Central Party Literature Publishing House, 2016. pp.38–42.

Xi Jinping. "Speech at the End of Inspection in Qinghai Province" (August 24, 2016), in *Excerpts from Xi Jinping's Expositions on Socialist Economic Development*, compiled by the Literature Research Office of the CPC Central Committee, Central Party Literature Publishing House, 2017, p.107.

Xi Jinping. "Speech at the Central Economic Work Conference" (December 15, 2012), in *Excerpts from Xi Jinping's Expositions on Socialist Economic Development*, compiled by the Literature Research Office of the CPC Central Committee. Central Party Literature Publishing House, 2017. p.315.

Xi Jinping. "Speech at the Central Economic Work Conference" (December 10, 2013), in *Excerpts from Xi Jinping's Expositions on Socialist Economic Development*, compiled by the Literature Research Office of the CPC Central Committee, Central Party Literature Publishing House, 2017. p.73.

Xi Jinping. "Economic Work Must Adapt to the New Normal of Economic Development" (December 9, 2014), in *Excerpts from Xi Jinping's Expositions on Socialist Economic Development*, compiled by the Literature Research Office of the CPC Central Committee, Central Party Literature Publishing House, 2017. pp.74–79.

Xi Jinping. "Speech during the Survey in Chongqing" (January 4-6, 2016), in *Excerpts from Xi Jinping's Expositions on Socialist Economic Development*, compiled by the Literature Research Office of the CPC Central Committee, Central Party Literature Publishing House, 2017. p.33.

Xi Jinping. "Speech at the Seminar on the Study and Implementation of the Guiding Principles of the Fifth Plenary Session of the 18th CPC Central Committee by Major Provincial and Ministerial Leaders (January 18, 2016), in *Excerpts from Xi Jinping's Expositions on Socialist Economic Development*, compiled by the Literature Research Office of the CPC Central Committee, Central Party Literature Publishing House, 2017. pp.98–101.

Xi Jinping. "Speech at the Central Economic Work Conference" (December 14, 2016), in *Excerpts from Xi Jinping's Expositions on Socialist Economic Development*, compiled by the Literature

P. Gao, *A Shift Toward High-Quality Development of China*,
Research Series on the Chinese Dream and China's Development Path,
https://doi.org/10.1007/978-981-99-8990-4

Research Office of the CPC Central Committee, Central Party Literature Publishing House, 2017. pp.111–113.

Xi Jinping. "Speech at the Central Economic Work Conference" (December 14, 2016), in *Excerpts from Xi Jinping's Expositions on Socialist Economic Development*, compiled by the Literature Research Office of the CPC Central Committee, Central Party Literature Publishing House, 2017. p.115.

Xi Jinping. "Speech at the 13th Meeting of the Central Leading Group on Financial and Economic Affairs" (May 16, 2016), in *Excerpts from Xi Jinping's Expositions on Socialist Economic Development*, compiled by the Literature Research Office of the CPC Central Committee, Central Party Literature Publishing House, 2017. p.105.

Xi Jinping. "Speech at the End of Inspection in Qinghai Province" (August 24, 2016), in *Excerpts from Xi Jinping's Expositions on Socialist Economic Development*, compiled by the Literature Research Office of the CPC Central Committee, Central Party Literature Publishing House, 2017. pp.107–108.

Xi Jinping. "Speech at the 13th Meeting of the Central Leading Group on Financial and Economic Affairs" (May 16, 2016), in *Excerpts from Xi Jinping's Expositions on Socialist Economic Development*, compiled by the Literature Research Office of the CPC Central Committee, Central Party Literature Publishing House, 2017. p.106.

Xi Jinping. "Speech at the Central Economic Work Conference" (December 14, 2016), in *Excerpts from Xi Jinping's Expositions on Socialist Economic Development*, compiled by the Literature Research Office of the CPC Central Committee, Central Party Literature Publishing House, 2017. p.113.

Xi Jinping. "Speech at the Central Economic Work Conference" (December 14, 2016), in *Excerpts from Xi Jinping's Expositions on Socialist Economic Development*, compiled by the Literature Research Office of the CPC Central Committee, Central Party Literature Publishing House, 2017. p.112.

Xi Jinping. "Secure a Decisive Victory in Building a Moderately Prosperous Society in All Respects and Strive for the Great Success of Socialism with Chinese Characteristics for a New Era–Delivered at the 19th National Congress of the Communist Party of China", People's Publishing House, 2017. pp.21–35.

Xi Jinping. "Speech at the 38th Collective Study of the Political Bureau of the 18th CPC Central Committee" (January 22, 2017), in *Excerpts from Xi Jinping's Expositions on Socialist Economic Development*, compiled by the Literature Research Office of the CPC Central Committee. Central Party Literature Publishing House, 2017. p119.

Xi Jinping. "Secure a Decisive Victory in Building a Moderately Prosperous Society in All Respects and Strive for the Great Success of Socialism with Chinese Characteristics for a New Era–Delivered at the 19th National Congress of the Communist Party of China", People's Publishing House, 2017. pp.11–12.

Xi Jinping. "Speech at the Central Economic Work Conference" (December 14, 2016), in *Excerpts from Xi Jinping's Expositions on Socialist Economic Development*, compiled by the Literature Research Office of the CPC Central Committee, Central Party Literature Publishing House, 2017. p.21.

MIX
Papier aus verantwortungsvollen Quellen
Paper from responsible sources
FSC® C105338

If you have any concerns about our products,
you can contact us on
ProductSafety@springernature.com

In case Publisher is established outside the EU,
the EU authorized representative is:
Springer Nature Customer Service Center GmbH
Europaplatz 3, 69115 Heidelberg, Germany

Printed by Libri Plureos GmbH
in Hamburg, Germany